GENTRY AND COMMON FOLK

GENTRY AND COMMON FOLK

Political Culture on a Virginia Frontier 1740–1789

ALBERT H. TILLSON, JR.

THE UNIVERSITY PRESS OF KENTUCKY

Copyright © 1991 by The University Press of Kentucky

Scholarly publisher for the Commonwealth,
serving Bellarmine College, Berea College, Centre
College of Kentucky, Eastern Kentucky University,
The Filson Club, Georgetown College, Kentucky
Historical Society, Kentucky State University,
Morehead State University, Murray State University,
Northern Kentucky University, Transylvania University,
University of Kentucky, University of Louisville,
and Western Kentucky University.

Editorial and Sales Offices: Lexington, Kentucky 40508-4008

Library of Congress Cataloging-in-Publication Data

Tillson, Albert H., 1948-
    Gentry and common folk : political culture on a Virginia frontier,
1740-1789 / Albert H. Tillson, Jr.
        p.   cm.
    Includes bibliographical references and index.
    ISBN 0-8131-1749-6
    1. Virginia—Politics and government—Colonial period, ca.
1600–1775   2. Political culture—Virginia—History—18th century.
3. Social classes—Virginia—History—18th century.   4. Virginia
—History—Revolution, 1775–1783—Social aspects.   5. United States
—History—Revolution, 1775–1783—Social aspects.   I. Title.
F229.T58   1991
973.2—dc20   91-8181

For Babs and my parents

Contents

List of Map, Tables, and Figure   viii

Acknowledgments   ix

Introduction   1

1. Land, People, Economy, and Government   5

2. The Political Culture of the Colonial Elite   20

3. The Militia and Popular Localism   45

4. The Roots of Backcountry Order   64

5. Toward the Republic   78

6. The Tory Challenge   101

7. Finishing the Revolution   117

8. John Stuart's History of the Greenbrier Valley   138

Conclusion   159

Notes   163

Index   223

Map, Tables, and Figure

MAP

The Upper Valley of Virginia   6

TABLES

1. Analysis of the Augusta County Quitrent Roll, 1760-1762   13
2. Analysis of Upper Valley Land Tax Records, 1787   14
3. Landownership among Montgomery County Justices of the
Peace and Tories, 1777–1781   200

FIGURE

1. Structural Summary of the "Memoir of Indian Wars"   157

Acknowledgments

A large number of people have helped me to complete this book. At the University of Texas, Philip White, Howard Miller, Barnes Lathrop, and Anthony Orum read and commented on earlier drafts. Richard Beeman, Michael Bellesiles, Emory Evans, Warren Hofstra, Turk McCleskey, and Gregory Nobles kindly provided me with preliminary copies of their own work on backcountry topics. The staffs of various archival centers, particularly the Virginia Historical Society, the Virginia State Library, the Library of Congress Manuscript Division, the McCormick Library of Washington and Lee University, and the Mormon Genealogical Center in Tampa, Florida, have been extremely helpful, as have the interlibrary loan offices of the University of Texas, Pan American University, and the University of Tampa. At the University of Tampa, Martin Denoff and Stephen Magriby patiently helped me enter and analyze much of the data in chapter 1. The *Virginia Magazine of History and Biography* and the *Journal of Southern History* have allowed me to use portions of this book which initially appeared in their pages, and these sections have profited tremendously from the attention of the editors and outside referees of those journals. At the University Press of Kentucky the outside readers made many helpful suggestions regarding the style and content of the manuscript. The University of Texas, the Colonial Dames of America, and the University of Tampa Faculty Development Fund helped finance my research. My parents have encouraged and supported me on countless occasions. Finally, although my wife, Babs Uzenoff, works in the world of modern epidemiology, she has graciously shared in and enriched much of mine.

Introduction

Two issues dominate much of the historiography of eighteenth-century Virginia and carry substantial implications for the emerging scholarship on the southern backcountry. First, historians have differed in analyzing the characteristics and delineating the limits of the deferential political culture that sanctioned the power of Virginia's leading men. Second, they have debated the extent to which the American Revolution challenged and altered that deferential culture. This study explores both these issues in the development of the upper, or southern, Valley of Virginia.

Historians of eighteenth-century Virginia have long emphasized the role of deferential and hierarchical values in maintaining that society's political order. According to this interpretation, ordinary Virginians expressed their own humility and acknowledged the superiority of their leaders in a wide variety of political and social interactions. Virginia leaders encouraged respect for their status by conspicuous displays of wealth and by affirmations of their willingness to sacrifice personal well-being for the good of the entire polity. The reciprocal nature of the culture further strengthened its hold on Virginia: ordinary Virginians were expected to defer to the superiority of their leaders, and those leaders in turn frequently acknowledged the particular merits of the "simple folk."[1]

In recent years several scholars have suggested that this deferential culture was declining in the prerevolutionary period. Rhys Isaac asserted that the rise of evangelical religion, with its emphasis on austerity and egalitarianism, challenged the conspicuous consumption and hierarchical values that underlay the established order. Dale Benson noted that the expanding activities of Scottish tobacco factors reduced the economic power of the leading planters. In his analysis of Lunenburg County, Richard Beeman suggested that the culture of deference failed to develop in much of the backcountry because regional leaders lacked the wealth and prestige required to overawe their neighbors and compel respect for their status.[2] According to James Titus, the lack of popular support for prosecution of the Seven Year's War indicated the weakness of deferential values and the precarious authority of provincial leaders.[3]

Although the Revolution itself has received less attention than the late colonial period, scholars have debated the effect of the war and the succeeding years on the Old Dominion. Jack P. Greene and others have argued that the revolutionary era produced no substantial erosion of popular respect for the elite or the values that sanctioned its authority. Indeed, some scholars have suggested that the revolutionary crisis reinvigorated the gentry and reduced existing frictions within the Virginia population.[4] Nevertheless, the war effort clearly placed major strains on popular support for political authority. Even during the first year of the Revolution, the war-induced shortage of salt led to unrest and some violence.[5] John David McBride and other scholars have emphasized the popular resentment aroused by wartime conscription, taxation, and currency depreciation.[6]

Some historians have suggested that the Revolution not only strained but transformed Virginia's political culture. According to Rhys Isaac, the Revolution produced a new republican order, based on the contractually limited delegation of power to government by individual citizens. This republicanism, together with the continued growth of evangelical religion, undercut deferential standards, which relied on both an all-encompassing social hierarchy sanctioned by time-honored custom and a widespread use of conspicuous consumption to demonstrate status. In *Chesapeake Politics, 1781-1800*, Norman K. Risjord asserted that the economic strains of the war and postwar years combined with existing sectional antagonisms to produce the beginnings of issue-oriented partisan politics in Virginia, Maryland, and North Carolina.[7] Moreover, in an examination of several postrevolutionary elections, Risjord found limited but suggestive evidence of movement from deferential toward issue-oriented voting among lower-class Virginians.[8]

Both the controversy surrounding deferential culture and the debate over the nature of the Revolution have influenced recent scholarship on the southern backcountry, the frontier area stretching southward across the western portions of Pennsylvania, Maryland, Virginia, the Carolinas, and Georgia. Richard Beeman and others have suggested that the strength or weakness of ties between local backcountry leaders and provincial authorities explains much of the variation in the social and political order in different portions of the region.[9] Some scholars have examined the role of class antagonisms and other internal divisions in shaping the development of backcountry societies.[10] Students of the backcountry have also extensively examined the impact of the Revolution on the social and political order of the southern frontier. According to some analysts, patriot authorities won over the common people by their responsiveness to local needs, their relative moderation in maintaining authority and order, and their willingness partially to democratize state governments.[11] Other scholars have asserted that the war did little to change the nature of government and that the patriots won largely through repression rather than persuasion.[12]

This book addresses these issues in Virginia and backcountry historiography. The chapters on the colonial period assert that although regional leaders did espouse the deferential culture of eastern Virginia, much of the upper valley population rejected these political attitudes. Their dissent became especially strong in the militia and other defense activities. Moreover, the nature of this rejection indicates the beginnings of an alternative popular political culture based on the economic realities of small-scale agriculture, the preference for less hierarchical, more consensual styles of leadership, and an attachment primarily to local neighborhoods rather than to county, colony, or empire.

Despite the strength of popular dissent from the political values of the elite, however, the upper valley experienced less disorder than many other portions of the backcountry. In part this relative tranquillity may be attributed to the emergence of an elite that developed close ties to provincial authorities. Yet the willingness of that elite to compromise with popular dissidents also played a vital role. Indeed, many of the subsidiary leaders in direct contact with local neighborhoods and militia companies learned to act as intermediaries between their superiors and popular groups.

The chapters on the revolutionary era analyze the way the events and the ideology of America's war for independence interacted to transform this backcountry region's political culture. By creating tremendous demands for manpower and economic support, the war effort led to greater discontent than ever before and forced regional leaders to make substantial concessions to popular sentiment. Moreover, the republican ideology sanctioned by the Revolution not only justified these concessions but also legitimated the mobilization of popular support for challenges to established leaders and institutions. Chapter 8 uses the technique of structuralist analysis to examine the way one local leader's historical narrative of the revolutionary era reflected his awareness of the change from deferential to republican political values.

The importance of culture for this study requires a definition of the term at the outset. In its most conventional sense, a culture is the body of values, beliefs, assumptions, and expectations shared by a group of people. Obviously a group's most abstract religious and political principles are part of its culture. Yet a culture can include elements much more closely related to the material environment. As various scholars have suggested, a people's expectations and customs regarding such things as entertainment, the use of food, the conduct of work, and the nature of warfare are important parts of the culture.[13] A culture may also include a people's perception of continuing patterns in all areas of life as well as in customary methods for confronting material and social reality.

Ultimately, a dialectical relationship ties human cultures to their social and material environments. As Bernard Bailyn, Gordon Wood, and other historians of the American Revolution have compellingly demonstrated, people's cultural values and expectations can influence their perceptions of the "real" world and, more important, can lead them to transform that world.[14] Thus human cultures can alter their social and material environments. Conversely, the real world can shape culture by demonstrating the appropriateness or inadequacy of particular values, ideals, or assumptions. This study argues for just such a dialectical relationship between the "ideal" world of cultural values and the "real" world of events and material forces in the upper valley throughout the late eighteenth century.

CHAPTER ONE

Land, People, Economy, and Government

Diverse circumstances combined to make the upper Valley of Virginia distinct from the rest of the colony and yet to connect it closely to the center of the province. The region stretches south and west from approximately the present northern border of Augusta County for some two hundred miles to the North Carolina line. It is bounded on the east by the Blue Ridge Mountains and on the west by the main body of the Appalachians. In the eighteenth century, geography and population set the area apart from eastern Virginia and to some degree from the lower valley to the north. Moreover, the upper valley developed an economy very different from that of the east. Nevertheless, political conditions led the region's leaders substantially to recreate both the governmental institutions and the political culture of eastern Virginia.

The Blue Ridge Mountains begin as a single ridge in northern Virginia and divide into a series of ridges below the James River. Throughout the eighteenth century, these mountains created a major barrier along the eastern edge of the entire Valley of Virginia. Adequate transportation routes through the Blue Ridge were particularly scarce in the southern or upper portion of the valley.[1] Despite attempts to improve the navigability of the James River as it passed through the mountains, neither this nor any other water routes provided satisfactory transportation to the east. Several widely separated roads crossed the Blue Ridge by the end of the colonial period. Yet land travel to the east also remained slow and difficult.

To some degree, geography also distinguished the upper valley from the area to the north. The latter region, called the lower valley because of its lesser elevation, was drained by the Shenandoah and

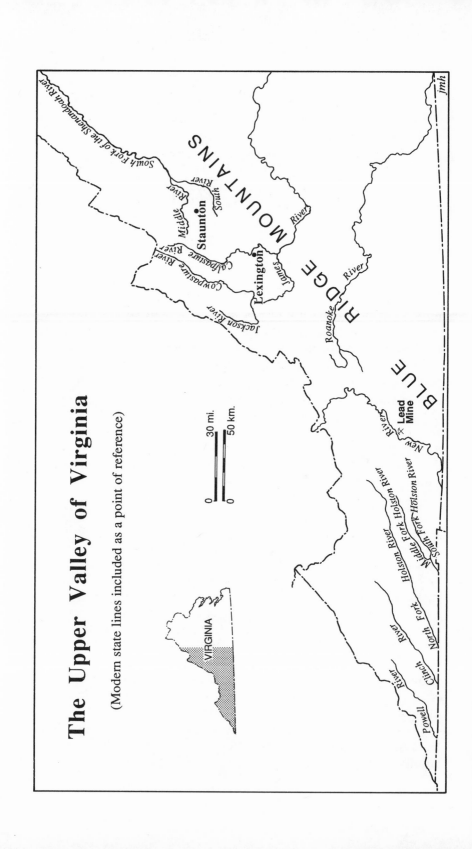

The Upper Valley of Virginia

(Modern state lines included as a point of reference)

its tributaries, which were part of the Potomac River system. Although the northern edge of the upper valley fell within the Shenandoah watershed, most of the region lay outside this area. The James River and its tributaries drained a substantial area south of the Shenandoah. South of that lay the Roanoke River, which flowed southeastward into North Carolina. The areas farther south and west drained into the tributaries of the Mississippi and Ohio rivers. Among the major streams on what eighteenth-century settlers called the "western waters" were the New River, which flowed northwest from North Carolina across the valley into present-day West Virginia, and the Holston, Clinch, and Powell rivers at the southwestern end of the valley.

Not only the river systems but also the nature of the land differentiated the upper from the lower valley. The lower valley included large continuous areas of nonmountainous land. In contrast, most of the area to the south consisted of small valleys separated by areas of nonarable mountain land. Thus, though no major barriers impeded north-south transportation in the lower valley, a series of ridges separated the major watersheds of the upper valley.

Unlike the seventeenth-century settlers of eastern Virginia, who immediately confronted the powerful Powhatan Confederation, the first European inhabitants of the valley encountered no substantial Indian population. Archaeological excavations and local traditions suggest that the region had not always been so empty. Well into the colonial era, Indian communities maintained largely agricultural economies and palisaded villages in various parts of western Virginia.[2] By the early eighteenth century, however, these Indian inhabitants were gone. Disease and other environmental factors may have reduced their numbers, but the pressure exerted by the Iroquois Confederacy to the north was probably more decisive. The "southern wars" of the Iroquois apparently began in the 1670s, when the Susquehanna Indians drew them into an alliance against a number of rival groups who had become tributaries of the Virginia government. By the early eighteenth century, Iroquois parties were attacking the Cherokees on both sides of the Appalachians as well as the Catawbas and other groups located farther to the east. When a major portion of the Tuscarora tribe migrated from North Carolina to Iroquois areas in Pennsylvania and New York after 1712, they probably encouraged further attacks on their former neighbors. The movement of Shawnees and other Iroquois allies into Ohio in the second quarter of the eighteenth century further exacerbated the situation because distance reduced the ability of English authorities to keep these western groups at peace. For their part, the Cherokees, Catawbas, and other southern tribes launched attacks against their enemies to the north.[3]

Consequently, the upper valley's first European settlers moved into an apparently empty but nevertheless dangerous environment. The "southern" and especially the "northern" Indians traveled through the region on their way to war. One major Iroquois route ran southward up the valley before crossing the Blue Ridge near present-day Roanoke, and war parties of the Shawnees and other Ohio Indians regularly used the New River valley. Throughout the colonial and revolutionary periods, these circumstances, together with the continued westward thrust of white settlement, would lead to intermittent clashes with the Cherokees, Shawnees, and other Indians.

As European occupation of the upper valley progressed, the region's population and the pattern of settlement further distinguished it from areas to the east and north. Many settlers, including some leaders, were eastern Virginians of English ethnicity. Nevertheless, the entire Valley of Virginia was settled predominantly from the north and predominantly by non-English people. Scotch-Irish, Germans, and other groups migrated southward from Pennsylvania into the western parts of Maryland, Virginia, the Carolinas, and Georgia, creating a multiethnic backcountry society that differed sharply from the English-dominated areas to the east. The Scotch-Irish were the dominant group in most of the upper valley, in contrast to the strong German presence in the lower valley.[4]

Settlement began as early as the 1730s. Such men as William Beverley from eastern Virginia and Benjamin Borden, Sr., from New Jersey acquired large land grants and encouraged settlers from the middle colonies to move into the region. Among the major leaders who came by this route were John Lewis, who arrived in the Staunton area by 1740, and Robert Breckinridge, who settled there at about the same time. In addition to the immigrants from the north, many settlers entered the upper valley from eastern Virginia. Some were native Virginians. Others, like James Patton and his nephew William Preston, sailed from Ulster to the Chesapeake and then traveled across Virginia to the upper valley. Following their arrival in 1738, both Patton and Preston would play major roles in the political development of the region.

By 1749 the upper valley had an adult white male population of 1,423, and by 1755 it had grown to 2,273.[5] Although many settlers fled the region during the Seven Years' War, the combined population of slaves and adult white males reached some 4,800 persons by 1773.[6] During the mid-1780s the inhabitants included approximately 8,800 slaves and adult white males, and the federal census of 1790 indicated a total of 46,811 white and black men, women, and children.[7]

As the population grew, Virginia gradually created new counties in the region. When Augusta County was established in 1745, it encompassed the entire upper valley. Fifteen years later, the southern part of the region was made into Botetourt County. In 1772 Fincastle County was created on the "western waters," and in 1776 it was divided into Montgomery and Washington counties, which centered on the New and Holston watersheds respectively.[8] Then in 1778 Rockbridge County was formed from adjoining portions of Augusta and Botetourt counties.

In contrast with the tobacco-driven economy of eastern Virginia, the upper valley was characterized by small-scale, largely subsistence agriculture. Throughout the late colonial and revolutionary eras, most landowners held from one to five hundred acres, and relatively little of the land was cleared for cultivation. According to Robert Mitchell, settlers throughout the Shenandoah and James watersheds typically cleared less than 10 percent of their acreage in the mid-eighteenth century. By 1800 from 20 to 25 percent of the average farm was available for cultivation.[9] Moreover, because Mitchell's estimates include the more developed lower valley and exclude the remote "western waters" they presumably overstate upper valley cultivation.

In view of the poor quality of roads in the early years of settlement and the consequent difficulty in reaching markets, this failure to maximize production quickly is understandable. In 1753 a group of Moravian travelers reported that bad roads began immediately south of Staunton and continued from there to the Roanoke River. The hilly sections were so steep and slippery that the men helped the horses by pushing their wagon up the hills, and several times they had to unload much of their baggage. Going down the hills was equally difficult and often dangerous. On one occasion they "attached a pretty large tree to the wagon, locked both wheels, while the brethren held fast to the tree. But the wagon went down so fast that most of the brethren turned somersault, however, without injury to anyone." By the end of the day they were exhausted but had traveled only sixteen miles. A few days later they reached a place where the road became so narrow that they had to use their axes to get through. As one of the men recorded, "We had to make a new way or else improve the old." Not surprisingly, these and other Moravian travelers reported difficulty in buying bread for themselves or feed for their horses: in many areas, little surplus was available for sale.[10]

In several parts of the upper valley, early settlers supported themselves chiefly by hunting rather than farming. Thus though Moravian missionaries found little bread available along the upper branches of the James River in 1749, they reported that every house in the area had a supply of bear meat and that the people lived "like savages."[11] Farther down the river a local leader charged four hunters with vagrancy and setting fire to the woods in 1746.[12] German Sabbatarians who moved from Pennsylvania to the New River valley in the late 1740s found themselves "in the midst of a pack of nothing but raggamuffins, the dregs of human society who spend their time in murdering wild beasts."[13] Several of these New River hunters appeared at the Augusta County Court in February 1747 in a dispute over the alleged theft of forty-three deerskins, and one of them, John Connoly, was charged with a number of other offenses during these years.[14]

By the end of the colonial period, the region's economy had become more commercialized and more complex. As early as the 1750s, many settlers expanded their economic involvements beyond subsistence agriculture by practicing crafts, operating taverns, or obtaining credit for the purchase of land.[15] Many settlers had begun to raise cattle for markets outside the region. In 1758 two Augusta men drove a herd to Pennsylvania, and a Staunton merchant, William Crow, regularly delivered large herds to Winchester, Philadelphia, eastern Virginia, and other markets. Grain production also increased substantially. By 1740 a gristmill was operating at Staunton. Thirty-five years later, there were thirteen within a five-mile radius of that place. The demand for military supplies during the Seven Years' War and the Revolution encouraged still greater production and sale of wheat and other food products.[16]

Textile production also played a growing role in the upper valley economy. In Ulster the Scotch-Irish had grown flax and woven it into linen, and they quickly began these practices in America. Most upper valley linen, however, was probably made for local consumption. More important, after the early 1760s, many upper valley settlers began growing hemp for export to eastern Virginia, encouraged by British bounties. Production reached 121,700 pounds in Botetourt County in 1769 and averaged 100,000 pounds annually in Augusta during the early 1770s. Military needs during the Revolution led to continued high levels of production until prices declined in the postwar years. This commercialization of the region's agriculture led to a growing importation of indentured servants in the late colonial period.[17]

These economic changes also encouraged both urbanization and the development of a merchant class. In 1753 Staunton, the Augusta County seat, held only about twenty houses.[18] Forty years later, it contained nearly two hundred, as well as eight inns, three of which were reported to be quite large. By that time, the towns of Lexington and Fincastle contained one hundred and sixty houses respectively.[19] Especially in Staunton, a class of merchants began to emerge. By the early 1760s George and Sampson Mathews were involved in a diverse array of commercial activities. They operated a store and an ordinary, bought and sold town lots and tracts of land in the surrounding countryside, and imported slaves and servants for local sale.[20] At least five other merchants worked in Staunton in the 1760s. These men developed connections with counterparts in such eastern Virginia centers as Fredericksburg and Richmond, and they supplied not only individual consumers throughout the upper valley but also a substantial number of rural stores and ordinaries that sold to travelers and local residents.[21]

Despite these changes, small-scale agricultural production for local consumption remained a mainstay of the upper valley economy well into the postrevolutionary era. Wheat cultivation may have expanded during the late colonial period and especially during the Revolution in response to the demand for military supplies. Nevertheless, as late as 1789, the counties of Augusta, Rockbridge, and Rockingham had only one "merchant" or "manufacturing" mill capable of producing large quantities of flour for export to the east.[22] Not surprisingly, when the state established thirty centers for flour inspection in 1787, none were located west of the Blue Ridge.[23] Even after 1800 transportation costs severely limited exports. Thus state authorities estimated that such expenses absorbed three-fourths of Virginia's expenditures in the War of 1812, and in 1820 the Board of Public Works blamed high freight costs for the absence of settlers on much of the rich agricultural, timber, and mineral lands around the headwaters of the James River.[24] Presumably transportation costs also discouraged settlers from clearing much of their land and may have discouraged investments in slave labor as well. According to the federal census of 1790, slaves made up from 6.3 to 14.4 percent of the total populations of the upper valley counties, while comparable percentages for the counties immediately across the Blue Ridge to the east fell between 15.7 and 44.4 percent.[25]

Throughout the late colonial and revolutionary eras, the upper valley population shared unequally in the region's economic resources, especially in the distribution of land. In the early 1760s, when Augusta County encompassed the entire upper valley, approximately 70 percent of the landowners listed on the quitrent roll owned less than the average or mean amount of land. Even among the wealthier settlers, there was substantial inequality: landowners at the ninetieth percentile of the population owned over one-third more land than those at the eightieth percentile level.[26] Table 1 lists the means, medians, and percentiles of means for landholding according to the quitrent roll, as well as the amounts of land owned by settlers at each decile level of registered landholders. The numbers in parentheses represent calculations based on the assumption that all entries bearing the same first and last names were the same individual; those before the parenthesis reflect an assumption that each entry represented a different individual.[27] A quarter-century later, the region's land taxes revealed essentially the same picture. In 1787 over 70 percent of the landholders again owned less than the mean acreage, and the difference between the eightieth and ninetieth percentiles was even greater than in the 1760s. Table 2 summarizes the land tax data using the same format and assumptions as Table 1.[28]

In addition to this inequality among the landholders, a substantial portion of the population may have been landless. The entries on the Augusta quitrent roll represent little more than half of the adult white male population, and at least one scholar has concluded that landholders may have been a substantially smaller proportion of the population for much of the colonial period. It is possible that many of the remaining settlers rented land or worked for wages.[29]

Table 1. Analysis of the Augusta County Quitrent Roll, 1760-1762

Cumulative Percentile of Population	Acreage
10	121.2 (142.400)
20	185.0 (200.000)
30	200.0 (225.000)
40	244.0 (282.600)
50	287.5 (336.000)
60	328.0 (400.000)
70	396.4 (500.000)
80	446.8 (647.600)
90	618.5 (950.000)
Mean acreage	398.999 (532.641)
Median acreage	287.500 (336.000)
Percentile of mean	70 (73)
N of cases	1,112 (833)

Although it is impossible to be certain about their exact numbers, it seems more likely that many nonlandholders simply "squatted" on land without acquiring legal ownership or had their land surveyed but did not complete the process of acquiring formal title. In both cases, these people avoided having to pay for the land or the taxes on it. These benefits, however, involved considerable insecurity: squatters could be ejected from the land, losing all the labor invested in clearing fields, building cabins, and making other improvements. Nevertheless, scattered references in upper valley correspondence suggest widespread use of these practices, and an economic analysis of southside Virginia, the region east of the Blue Ridge, concluded that they were common there as well.[30]

The upper valley's richer and poorer inhabitants apparently differed substantially in other aspects of their material lives. Although an analysis of estate inventories can reveal much about this subject, the problems of using the inventories must be acknowledged. Presumably the deceased individuals who left wills and whose estates were inventoried were among the older and wealthier members of their society. If nothing else, increasing age tended to bring increasing wealth through a process of accumulation. Some historians have attempted to correct for these distortions by comparing the age and economic profiles of decedents to those of their entire societies, but the absence of adequate age and wealth

Table 2. Analysis of Upper Valley Land Tax Records, 1787

Cumulative Percentile of Population	Acreage
10	82.800 (90.000)
20	100.000 (110.000)
30	150.000 (152.000)
40	199.000 (200.000)
50	210.000 (240.000)
60	270.000 (300.000)
70	331.000 (400.000)
80	400.000 (510.200)
90	600.000 (800.000)
Mean acreage	367.444 (456.509)
Median acreage	210.000 (240.000)
Percentile of mean	73 (77)
N of cases	4,277 (3,443)

profiles for the upper valley renders such corrections impractical.[31] Moreover, Virginia inventories listed neither the land owned nor the debts owed by the estate, and Virginia law allowed any debt-free testator to direct that his estate not be inventoried.[32] Although many inventories specified a total value of the estate, not all did so. Even for those that did, the assessments may be very misleading because land and the estate's debts were excluded from the calculations and the value of money vacillated greatly during the revolutionary years. Finally, perusal of upper valley inventories makes it clear that individual assessors varied widely in their reporting practices. For example, many inventories included long lists of personal clothing, but many others mentioned none, even in cases in which the decedent was an obviously wealthy and prestigious man. It may well be that in communities so new and so geographically dispersed as the upper valley counties, it was particularly difficult for public authorities to impose standardization upon assessors.

Nevertheless, an analysis of inventories can be helpful if their limitations are recognized. Because of the exclusion of landed property and of debts owed, the inventories can illuminate material possessions and conditions of life but not overall economic status. More important, given the uncertain relationship between the individuals whose estates were inventoried and their entire society, the analysis must be seen as indicating only a part of the total variation

in material conditions: some individuals may have had more substantial material possessions than those who were inventoried, and
almost certainly many had less. Finally, given the varied reporting
practices of different assessors, attention must focus on the types of
property that seem to be most consistently reported. The analysis
that follows is based on an examination of 418 inventories from three
upper valley counties. They include all Botetourt County inventories from 1770 to 1789 (108), all Washington County inventories from
1777 to 1789 (111), and all Augusta County inventories for 1746-47
(12), 1754-56 (52), 1764-66 (52), 1774-76 (48), and 1784-86 (35). Thus
the sample encompasses all Botetourt and Washington inventories
for the period covered by this study and a representative selection
from Augusta. It also includes inventories from throughout the late
colonial and revolutionary years and from frontier as well as more
developed areas.[33] For much of the analysis, the estates are divided
into those that owned no slaves or servants (325), those that owned
just one (48), and those that owned more than one (45). In the
absence of information about total wealth of the decedents, this
seems the best way to separate groups of relatively prosperous and
relatively poor individuals. As do the problems noted above, this
last procedure encourages an underestimation of the material dep-
rivations of the region's humbler inhabitants by lumping them
together with some who were relatively wealthy but did not own
slaves or servants.

The analysis makes clear that there were substantial differences
in the material comforts of life for the upper valley's richer and
poorer settlers. Slaveless and servantless individuals owned very
little furniture: only 14.5 percent of the 325 inventories included two
or more chairs.[34] In contrast, two or more chairs appeared in 29.2
percent of the estates with one slave or servant and 46.7 percent of
those with more than one. Feather beds appeared in 33.3 percent of
the multiple-servant inventories, 12.5 percent of the one-servant
inventories, and 11.1 percent of the servantless inventories. Not
surprisingly, silver or gold appeared in 33.3 percent of the multiple-
servant inventories but only in 10.4 percent of those with one
servant and 6.5% of those with none. Kitchen furnishings also
varied by economic class: sustantial quantities of pewter and china
were nearly twice as common in multiple-servant as in servantless
inventories, and spices, spice mortars, and pepper boxes were
nearly three times as common in the former category.[35] Although
rarest among servantless inventories (26.5 percent), candles,

lamps, and lanterns were far from common among those with one servant (31.3 percent) and those with more than one (33.3 percent). Apparently many homes were illuminated only by fireplaces, pine knot torches, and similar devices.[36] Books, however, were surprisingly common among all categories of inventories: four or more were owned by 33.2 percent of the servantless households, 35.4 percent of the one-servant households, and 55.6 percent of the multiple-servant ones. These last figures, however, may by distorted by the relative rarity of inventories for poorer and illiterate settlers.

Poorer settlers also appear to have had much less involvement in commercial exchanges beyond their farms and communities. Thus wagons and carts appear in 57.8 percent of multiple-servant inventories and 39.6 percent of one-servant inventories, but only 16.3 percent of servantless inventories.[37] In contrast, an analysis of Hardy County, a cattle-raising area in present-day West Virginia, found that virtually every farmer owned a wagon in the 1780s.[38] Wealthier estates were also much more likely to possess weights and measures, again indicating more frequent involvement in commercial exchange. Such items were listed in 55.6 percent of multiple-servant inventories and 41.7 percent of one-servant inventories but in only 27.1 percent of servantless inventories. Although the differences were less substantial, servantless estates were less likely to include cash or debts owed to them by other persons.[39] It may be revealing that multiple-servant inventories averaged 32.9 horses and cattle, one-servant inventories 18.6, and servantless inventories only 13.2.

Nevertheless, common folk produced not only for their own subsistence but also to some degree for local exchange. As early as 1749 Moravian travelers encountered a shoemaker and tanner living in the Roanoke River Valley. In such a remote area the man presumably did much of his business for other local settlers and did not live by this craft alone.[40] Similarly, the many gristmills that appeared in the early period of settlement produced flour mainly for local consumption,[41] probably exchanging the services of the miller for a portion of the farmer's flour. Wealthier farmers often hired the labor of poorer neighbors in exchange for credit toward rent, a share of the crop, or other considerations.[42] Local exchanges of goods and labor must have been especially common in the production of textiles, for 46.8 percent of the servantless estates owned spinning wheels, but only 14.2 percent owned looms, and only 12.0 percent had both looms and wheels. Thus although many families could spin linen, wool, or other fiber into thread, a substantal majority of them had to turn to someone else to convert that thread into cloth that could be used for personal apparel and other purposes. Such interdependence was apparently less common among wealthier families: 18.8 percent of one-servant inventories and 35.6 percent of multiple-servant inventories listed both wheels and looms.[43] A similar local interdependence appeared in the small Scotch-Irish community of Opequon in the lower valley near Winchester. Wheels were more common than looms, and many spinners may have relied on neighbors for a supply of flax fiber. Furthermore, a network of small local debts in estate inventories suggests extensive exchanges among the settlers.[44]

Particularly when the limitations and probable distortions of the inventory data are considered, it becomes clear that many common folk lived economic lives that were far humbler and substantially less cosmopolitan and commercialized than those of their society's leaders. Ultimately these economic contrasts would contribute to social and political frictions.

Whatever the upper valley's economic differences from eastern Virginia, local government closely followed eastern models. In 1745 the governor appointed a group of men to serve as members of the Augusta County Court. As in the east, the court not only dispensed justice but also collected taxes, maintained public roads, and administered other aspects of county government. Although the governor reappointed the justices annually, these officials quickly established their de facto independence, serving long terms and routinely naming the men the governor appointed to fill vacancies on the court. The Augusta justices' independence also resembled the political practice of eastern Virginia. As additional counties were created in the upper valley, their courts operated in much the same way.

Two other political institutions were also imported from eastern Virginia. The vestry administered the affairs of the Anglican church and provided poor relief, and the county militia served as the basis for local defense. Both these institutions will be discussed in more detail in later chapters.

Because so much land remained unclaimed throughout the colonial period, the county surveyor was more powerful in the upper valley than in long-settled areas to the east. Surveyors for all

Virginia counties were nominated by the College of William and Mary and appointed by the governor. Once in place, they played a critical and lucrative role in the distribution of unclaimed land. Individuals wishing to purchase such land registered it with the surveyor or an authorized assistant. Eventually these officials would survey the desired tract, issue a plat, and record the transaction.[45] The surveyors exercised some control over the initial registration of land, and they could choose when, where, and for whom they would survey. Therefore, they often were able to reserve the best land for their friends or even for themselves. This prerogative, in addition to the substantial fees they collected, made the county surveyorship a much desired and powerful position in the upper valley and other frontier areas.[46]

Eastern Virginia provided a political culture that regional leaders could imitate to enhance their power. A small circle of elite families dominated most Virginia counties in the eighteenth century, deriving power not only from their control of governmental institutions but also from their ability to command the deference of the common people. Ordinary Virginians acknowledged the political and social superiority of the gentry in many areas of life. These attitudes were visible in the proceedings of county courts and vestries as citizens expressed their humility and their dependence upon the worthy justices and vestrymen. The physical layout of many Anglican churches reinforced the standards of deference. The leading families occupied pews that were centrally placed and slightly elevated, and other churchgoers often waited for the members of the elite before entering or leaving the church on the day of services. In exchange for the respect accorded to them, leaders were expected to defer to more humble citizens by providing refreshments at elections and other public occasions and by sacrificing their own immediate interests while ruling for the benefit of the entire community. These values permeated even the language of eastern Virginia, for it consistently distinguished between leaders and common people as "gentle" and "simple" folk, thereby reinforcing the assumption that the two groups should possess different rights and responsibilities.

The established patterns of eastern Virginia life also afforded an array of techniques by which leaders might demonstrate and enhance their status. Most obviously, they could display their wealth in such socially sanctioned forms as big houses, elaborate furnishings, and fine clothing. Whenever possible, members of the eastern gentry located their houses so that they dominated the surrounding landscape. According to one observer, Robert Carter's home in Westmoreland County was visible from six miles away. Successful self-assertion in social intercourse could also enhance status. In eighteenth-century Virginia, far more than in other societies, dancing and other approved modes of social interaction became forms of competitive conviviality in which persons struggled to attain individual prestige even as they expressed their solidarity with their community and culture. Rhys Isaac's analysis of behavior at a dance expresses this tone of competitive conviviality very well:

Even in the most convivial activities, a palpable element of contest was subtly incorporated. The company formed a circle, observing and informally adjudicating their performances in the center. A kind of challenge and response was rendered explicit (and extended to include females) in the "cutting out" ritual [one couple replacing another in the center]—which would certainly have been controlled by the judgment of the onlookers. Even the pitting of the fiddler against dancers in a test of endurance carried intimations of contest.[47]

Although competitive conviviality and self-expression permeated much of eastern Virginia life, the culture required recognized leaders to exercise self-restraint in their political and social lives. Justices and other public officials were to conduct themselves with dignity and moderation, checking their own excesses and controlling the misguided behavior of the common folk. Military leaders especially were to control their men. Although civil leaders and militia officers might provide refreshments for their subordinates, they were not to engage in the same extremes of drunkenness and frivolity as the common people. Few leaders were so despised by their peers as were those members of the elite who lost self-control and surrendered to excessive drinking, gambling, or financial misbehavior.[48]

Despite the geographic, economic, and demographic factors that differentiated their region from eastern Virginia, upper valley leaders worked to replicate both the political institutions of the east and the deferential culture that supported them. As the following chapters will show, they enjoyed only partial success.

CHAPTER TWO

The Political Culture
of the Colonial Elite

Throughout the colonial period a small elite group dominated upper valley politics. These men shared the major social characteristics of the eastern Virginia gentry. Moreover, ties with the east were an important source of political and economic power and were one reason why upper valley leaders adopted the hierarchical and deferential values of eastern Virginia. Ultimately neither the upper valley's Scotch-Irish and Presbyterian character nor the unstable conditions of frontier life substantially weakened their acceptance of eastern political values. Nevertheless, the differing degrees of that acceptance apparently contributed to factional divisions among the region's leaders.

Despite the frontier conditions of the upper valley in the late eighteenth century, the composition of the local leadership class closely resembled its eastern model. With few exceptions, regional leaders were significantly wealthier than other settlers, and many owned substantial fortunes. As in eastern Virginia, kinship and other social relationships tied together the most prominent members of the elite. In addition, years of common service in the county courts and other institutions of local government helped unify this group.

By the standards of their society, most upper valley leaders were very wealthy men. In the Augusta quitrent roll of 1760-62, the median acreage for all settlers was between 280 and 340 acres. The medians for Augusta justices of the peace in 1749, 1765, and 1773 were 554, 450, and 355 acres respectively, if it is assumed that each individual owned only the single largest tract listed under his name. In Botetourt the corresponding median for 1770 was 418 acres.[1] Since many of these men clearly owned more than a single tract of land, assuming that each owned the single largest tract rather than one of the other tracts listed under his name substantially understates their actual wealth.[2] Although the median acreages for Augusta justices declined through the colonial period, this probably reflected the appointments in later years of men who had been relatively young when the quitrent roll was compiled and therefore owned less land than they would when they reached the courts.[3]

In any case, the most prominent members of the gentry were especially prosperous. According to the Augusta quitrent roll, the county's eight burgesses of the colonial period possessed an average of 3,787 acres. Although James Patton's 25,264 acres artificially inflated this figure, the median landholding was 995 acres, and the average with Patton's land excluded was 1,015 acres. Moreover, Israel Christian, the smallest landholder among the burgesses, operated several stores in the region and traded extensively with eastern Virginia merchants, valley settlers, and Indian groups to the west. Although he owned only 550 acres in 1762, Christian eventually acquired over 3,300 acres which he owned singly or in partnership with various relatives.[4]

Kinship also unified upper valley leaders. The connections of William Preston illustrate its role in the acquisition and distribution of wealth and power. As a child Preston came to the valley from Ireland with the families of his father and his uncle James Patton. Patton became a major land speculator, and he held the offices of burgess, justice of the peace, county lieutenant, and sheriff in Augusta. After becoming Patton's protégé, Preston rose to the positions of burgess, sheriff, and justice of the peace in Augusta County, and he later became the county surveyor and a justice of the peace in Botetourt, Fincastle, and Montgomery counties. One of Preston's sisters married the prominent Presbyterian clergyman John Brown, and two others married Robert Breckinridge and John Howard, both of whom served as justices of the peace in the upper valley. The Breckinridge family played a particularly prominent role in regional politics for several decades. Francis Smith, the brother of Preston's wife, moved to the valley after Preston obtained for him the contract to build an Anglican church. Once established there, he became a justice of the peace, deputy surveyor, and deputy sheriff in Botetourt County. At one point, when he had fallen out of Preston's good graces, Smith acknowledged the totality of his dependence upon his kinsman: "I shall always be ready to make a fair Settlement with you & . . . I shall with cheerfulness give up as much as will satisfy you if it is to be had[.] And as the chief part I am now in Possession of was gathered through your Prudent Direction I suppose after you are paid off I may with Propriety Repeat part of the Church ceremony & say Naked came I into the world & Naked I will go out."[5] Preston's marriage also tied him to Edward Johnson, a Scots merchant near Richmond with whom he associated in the sale of indentured servants, the purchasing of hemp, and other enterprises.

Another network of kinship and marriage connected valley leaders Israel Christian, William Christian, William Fleming, William Bowyer, and Stephen Trigg. These men served on the county courts and in other important public offices throughout the colonial period. Similarly, John Lewis and his sons Andrew, Charles, and Thomas were related to the McClanahan and Madison families. In addition to serving as justices of the peace, Andrew Lewis held various important military positions, Charles Lewis was elected an Augusta burgess, Thomas Lewis served as Augusta surveyor throughout the colonial period, and John Madison served for a time as Augusta burgess and as clerk of the Augusta County Court. Various members of the McClanahan family served as justices of the peace, vestrymen, and sheriffs in Augusta County during the late colonial and revolutionary years. Moreover, despite some friction between them, there were ties of kinship between the Lewis and the Patton-Preston groups.

Kinship connections proved particularly strong at the uppermost levels of power. Of the eight Augusta burgesses in the colonial period, five were tied to the Lewis, Christian, or Patton-Preston clans, and another was related to the land magnate Benjamin Borden and several other local leaders. In Fincastle County, three of the four colonial burgesses were related to Israel Christian. Two of Botetourt's three burgesses, William Preston and Andrew Lewis, belonged to powerful families, and the third had married the widow of Benjamin Borden, Jr. The Lewis and Patton-Preston clans also monopolized the lucrative position of county surveyor: Thomas Lewis held the Augusta surveyorship throughout the colonial period, William Preston held the Botetourt position until 1772 when he became Fincastle surveyor, and Thomas Lewis's nephew succeeded Preston in Botetourt.[6]

Other social connections beyond those of kinship were also important for members of the upper valley gentry. When Botetourt County was created in 1769, William Preston won the surveyorship largely through the efforts of his kinsman Thomas Lewis, but also with the help of John Madison, the Augusta County clerk.[7] Preston himself provided political and economic assistance to such friends as David Robinson. Robinson served as an officer in Preston's ranger company during the Seven Years' War, and the two men visited each other socially. Robinson often wrote humorous and convivial letters to Preston, teasing him about his dancing lessons, courtship, and marriage.[8] In 1757 Preston recommended Robinson for a militia commission, and in 1770 he served as security for Robinson's brother in the payment of a substantial debt.[9] Robinson also developed social connections with William Fleming, who apparently recommended him for at least one political position.[10] Other upper valley leaders frequently sought appointments for their friends. During the preparation of the Point Pleasant expedition in 1774, for example, several leaders collaborated in raising a company for James Robertson, who had difficulty in recruiting because he was on active duty in a remote part of the valley and probably because of his autocratic style of leadership. Afterward Robertson thanked "all my good friends, for assisting me in Geting my Compy made up as I though it was neerely impossible to do it."[11]

Continuity of membership on the county courts also encouraged cohesion among the gentry. Such continuity was admittedly modest within the total membership of the courts, particularly in the early years, for in 1765 only nine of the thirty-seven Augusta justices had been on the court fourteen years earlier.[12] In 1773, however, fourteen of the twenty-eight justices had been on the court in 1765, and in the newly created Botetourt County, thirteen of the thirty justices listed in 1770 had been Augusta justices in 1765.[13] In Fincastle County in 1773, ten of seventeen justices had been Botetourt justices three years earlier.[14]

Continuity of service was stronger still among the more senior justices and among those who attended most frequently, groups that presumably exerted a disproportionate influence. In 1772 all fourteen Augusta justices of the quorum, the most senior members, had been on the court in 1765, as had thirteen of their fifteen Botetourt counterparts.[15] In Fincastle County in 1773, all nine justices of the quorum had been on the Botetourt court in 1770.[16] Moreover, six of the seven Botetourt justices who attended most frequently in 1770 and four of the nine Augusta justices who attended most frequently in 1773 had been on the court in 1765.[17]

24   GENTRY AND COMMON FOLK

Even in Augusta County's less stable early years, continuity was
stronger among the justices of the quorum than among the others:
in 1763 nine of the nineteen justices of the quorum had been on the
court in 1751, as had three of the five most frequent attenders.[18]
   Thus the group that dominated public life in the colonial upper
valley shared many attributes of the eastern Virginia elite. Virtually
all leaders were significantly wealthier than their neighbors. Especially in its upper levels, the gentry was unified by ties of kinship
and other social relationships. Finally, the shared experience of
service in local government provided an important basis for cohesion.

   Throughout the colonial period, upper valley leaders looked to the
eastern Virginia elite for appointments, land grants, and other
political favors. As the region developed closer economic relations
with the east, commercial ties became important. Upper valley
leaders also provided a variety of economic and political services to
their eastern counterparts.
   From the beginning of settlement in the upper valley, the local
gentry sought help from prominent eastern Virginians in obtaining
important appointments. John Lewis, for example, became the
agent of land magnate William Beverley through the ties of an
eastern kinsman to Beverley and other major Rappahanock valley
leaders.[19] James Patton, Lewis's major rival, became acquainted
with Beverley even before his immigration from Ulster: as a ship
captain, Patton collaborated with the eastern leader in bringing Irish
settlers to Beverley's valley lands. When Beverley became absentee
commander of the Augusta militia, Patton was named to the post
immediately under him, giving him effective command of the
county's defense activities.
   Eastern contacts were particularly important when valley leaders competed for desirable offices. In 1767, for example, Israel
Christian began agitating for the division of Augusta County in the
hope of gaining the lucrative surveyorship in the new county for his
son. Many other regional leaders disliked Christian, and opposition
to his efforts developed quickly.[20] William Preston, the other major
candidate for the surveyorship, mobilized his friends and contacts
in the upper valley and eastern Virginia to influence the masters of
the College of William and Mary, who were to make the appointment.[21] In February 1768 he obtained a promise from Edmund
Pendleton, a burgess and influential Williamsburg attorney, to write

in his behalf to John Blair, a member of the college's Board of Visitors and its representative in the provincial assembly.[22] Another Williamsburg acquaintance, Richard Starke, also promised to write to Blair, and in 1769 Augusta surveyor Thomas Lewis visited each of the college masters and obtained promises of support for Preston. Lewis also contacted the prominent Albemarle land speculator Dr. Thomas Walker on Preston's behalf, and he urged Preston to continue efforts to influence college president James Horrocks "by means of Mr. Everard."[23] Significantly, at least one of Preston's friends predicted that Christian's unpopularity with eastern leaders would defeat him. John Madison wrote Preston in March 1767: "The Stupid Performance handed about by Captain Christian, I mean his petition for a [county] Division, gave me no uneasiness Especially as I made no Doubt he would back it himself which, if I am not Mistaken in that Gentlemans Popularity below [i.e., in eastern Virginia] would have been the worst complement he Could possibly have paid it"[24] In the end Preston received the appointment.

Since Virginia law specified that land grants of more than four hundred acres acres had to be made by the Governor's Council, connections with the councillors and other influential eastern Virginians proved important for valley leaders seeking large land acquisitions.[25] Thus in obtaining a one-hundred-thousand-acre grant on the New and Clinch rivers, James Patton, John Preston, John Buchanan, and other valley leaders took on as a partner Benjamin Waller, a Williamsburg attorney who served as clerk of the Governor's Council. Among the other eastern Virginia partners were William Waller, Benjamin's brother and a Spotsylvania County burgess; Zachary Lewis, a wealthy Spotsylvania lawyer; and Robert Green, a former Orange County burgess.[26] When seeking another one-hundred-thousand-acre grant, Patton promised to give four-fifths of the land to Governor Robert Dinwiddie, council member Richard Corbin, and their friends.[27] In 1745 another group of upper valley leaders including John Lewis, Charles Lewis, and the Augusta burgess John Wilson joined such eastern Virginians as Edmund Pendleton, William Beverley, and House speaker John Robinson, Sr., in a company that received a hundred-thousand-acre grant on the Greenbrier River.[28]

In some cases, litigation over landownership tied the upper valley gentry to prominent eastern Virginians. Local leaders such as William Preston often dealt with Edmund Pendleton and other Williamsburg attorneys in the resolution of these conflicts.[29] At least one land dispute led to more extensive development and manipulation of eastern ties.[30] Under Virginia law, if a person began but did not complete the process of obtaining title to a tract of land, another individual could gain possession of that land by filing a caveat or petition with the General Court in Williamsburg. Especially in the upper valley, many landholders did not complete the complex process of obtaining title because of the expense and the subsequent necessity to pay quitrents on fully titled land. Nevertheless, relatively few challenges were filed against these incomplete titles until a group led by John Madison, Jr., the son of the Augusta County clerk, began a systematic effort in 1769. The group obtained a list of all incomplete land titles in Augusta County from the auditor's clerk in Williamsburg, and they hired Thomas Jefferson to handle the litigation. Ultimately they filed more than four hundred caveats and petitions.

Although the Madison group developed ties to Jefferson and various Williamsburg officials, their antagonists, who included William Preston, Andrew Lewis, Israel Christian, and other upper valley leaders, outdid them. Preston somehow received early word of the caveats against his property and prevailed upon an official in Williamsburg to complete the process of obtaining title for four tracts, possibly back dating the titles. Then, in 1770, a bill was introduced in the House of Burgesses to require the parties filing these caveats and petitions to post substantial security fees against the possibility that they might lose the case and be required to pay court costs. The burgesses referred the bill to a special committee consisting of Edmund Pendleton, Thomas Walker, John Blair, and Thomas Jefferson. Pendleton, who had drafted the bill, was a longtime associate of Preston's and represented him and other valley leaders in some of this litigation.[31] Walker was heavily involved in land speculation with Preston, Lewis, and other upper valley leaders, and Blair was the influential leader whom Pendleton had asked to support Preston for the Botetourt surveyorship two years earlier. After the bill's passage, the General Court dismissed most of the Madison group's litigation for failure to post security and ordered the plaintiffs to pay court costs to the defendants. The court apparently never invoked the new law against anyone else. Thus, for both the Madison group and their antagonists, connections in Williamsburg and eastern Virginia had played a crucial role in this controversy.

As the upper valley's trade with eastern Virginia grew, commercial ties with that region became more important for local leaders. Because most early settlers emigrated from the north, trade with Pennsylvania and the middle colonies remained significant throughout the colonial period.[32] The economic activity generated by the Seven Years' War and the development of hemp cultivation, however, made contacts in eastern Virginia increasingly important.[33] Many upper valley leaders obtained credit from merchants in eastern Virginia.[34] Some members of the valley elite developed more complex economic connections with the east: Felix Gilbert, an Augusta merchant and justice of the peace, developed a strong enough relationship with Albemarle land speculator Dr. Thomas Walker that he felt free to borrow a substantial amount of Walker's money from a Fredericksburg merchant without obtaining Walker's permission in advance.[35] Similarly, William Preston entered various enterprises with a Richmond merchant, his brother-in-law Edward Johnson. Preston collected debts due to Johnson from valley settlers, recommended him to persons making purchases in the east, and tried to smooth Johnson's relations with disgruntled customers. At one point Johnson asked Preston's help in minimizing the inroads of a new competitor in Preston's area.[36] During the last few years before the Revolution, Preston and Johnson collaborated in the extensive importation of indentured servants for sale in the upper valley.[37]

The upper valley gentry performed a variety of favors and services for prominent eastern Virginians. William Preston, for example, handled the sale of land owner by Edmund Pendleton, negotiating with settlers who had squatted on parts of the land, collecting partial payments, and dealing with other problems.[38] When it appeared that some of this land might be in North Carolina, Pendleton requested that Preston secure token rents from squatters to strengthen his claims of ownership. Other eastern leaders sought assistance and advice from Preston in their land transactions. William Byrd asked him to make sure that his ownership of Fincastle County's courthouse site and another valley tract was secure, and Nicholas Davies asked whether he thought it was worthwhile to survey and obtain titles for tracts in various parts of the region. In 1769 Amherst County burgess William Cabell requested that Preston appoint John Floyd as a surveying assistant, and John Aylett, a Bedford County leader, asked for Preston's help in opening a legal practice in Botetourt County. Thomas Lewis and William Preston contracted to collect money due to various Williamsburg attorneys, and other eastern Virginians asked Preston to handle their upper valley debts.[39]

Thus a complex network of relationships connected the upper valley elite to eastern Virginia. Regional leaders derived much of their political power from ties with provincial authorities. Moreover, both land speculation and commerce encouraged the development of economic associations with the eastern elite.

In part because of these ties to eastern Virginia, upper valley leaders adopted much of that region's deferential culture. In many aspects of their social and political lives, they showed a concern with status, authority, and the means of sustaining them that closely resembled the attitudes of their eastern contemporaries. The county courts proved a particularly important arena for the affirmation of deferential values, and the upper valley gentry further sought to impose these values on the rest of their society.

Like their eastern Virginia counterparts, upper valley leaders constantly strove to maintain and enhance their status. Thus Reverend John Craig became embroiled for a time in the rivalry between John Lewis and James Patton over "which of them should be highest in commission & power." The competition grew so bitter that Craig found it impossible to befriend one of the men without antagonizing the other. Another colonial leader, Andrew Lewis, showed similar concerns. According to one contemporary, Lewis had "a distant & reserved deportment which rendered his presence more awful than engaging."[40]

The upper valley gentry's preoccupation with status was reflected in the deference accorded them by subordinates and inferiors who recognized this as a prerequisite to winning their favor. Thus in apologizing for violating the instructions of Fincastle surveyor Willian Preston, deputy surveyor Fancis Smith stressed his humility and dependence upon Preston. Persons applying to the Augusta vestry for financial support characteristically emphasized their own humility and helplessness and the worthiness, wisdom, and stature of the vestrymen. Most petitioners did not request specific amounts of support, and though Hugh Green asserted that five shillings a week was "Little Enough for his Trouble" in caring for an impoverished woman, he added that he was "Willing to Humbly Accept what your Worships thinks Proper."[41]

As in eastern Virginia, prominent men in the upper valley sought to enhance their stature by acquiring prestigious forms of property. As early as 1747, Robert Bratton, a wealthy Augusta landowner and business associate of William Preston, owned such expensive items of clothing as a silk gown and several pairs of silver buckles. Adam Breckinridge, the brother of an early Augusta sheriff and justice of the peace, took so much pride in his clothing that when he abruptly fled from Augusta, he instructed his brother to keep his clothes and let no one else wear them but himself. When Gabriel Jones, a prominent valley attorney and Augusta burgess, advertised the flight of his slave Bacchus in 1774, he noted that the fugitive had taken "two white Ruffa Drill Coats, one turned up with blue, the other quite plain and new, with white figured Metal Buttons, blue Plush Breeches, a fine Cloth Pompadour Waistcoat, two or three thin or Summer Jackets, sundry Pairs of white Thread Stockings, five or six white shirts, two of them pretty fine, neat Shoes, Silver buckles, a fine Hat cut and cocked in the Macaroni Figure, a double-milled Drab Great Coat, and sundry other Wearing Apparel."[42]

Houses and their furnishings provided upper valley leaders with a particularly important means of overawing their neighbors. Even in eastern Virginia, glass windows and brick chimneys were relatively rare in the prerevolutionary period, and conditions in the upper valley were still more primitive.[43] As late as 1784, a list of buildings in and around the town of Fincastle revealed that twenty-one of the fifty-nine dwellings were temporary cabins which lacked any sort of chimney. Another twenty-seven were more substantial log cabins, and only eleven were made of sawn lumber or brick.[44] Yet as early as 1748 the Augusta vestry provided for the construction of a home for their minister which was to include such features as two brick or stone chimneys and a number of glass windows.[45] In an age when most Virginians owned at best a few books, such upper valley leaders as William Preston, William Fleming, John Madison, Andrew Lewis, and Thomas Lewis arranged to have personal libraries purchased for them in London. The libraries included the classics, ancient history, English poetry, religious writings, polemics, and other categories. When he died in 1783, Preston owned 273 volumes.[46] As was documented in chapter 1, furniture, silver and gold, and substantial kitchen furnishings were far more prevalent in the homes of the elite than in those of common folk.

Although the effects of conspicuous consumption in enhancing status were seldom directly visible, at least one explicit indication of such results has survived. Reverend Samuel Houston recollected that his father's acquisition of glass windows for their cabin substantially improved the family's standing in their upper valley neighborhood.[47]

In the upper valley, as in eastern Virginia, social visiting and conviviality served to strengthen ties among members of the elite and to demonstrate their wealth and stature through conspicuous idleness. Kin and friends were widely dispersed in an expanding frontier society, and extended visits proved particularly important in maintaining social ties. In his correspondence with his brother-in-law William Preston, Reverend John Brown frequently expressed disappointment when plans for visits went awry. Such leaders as Thomas Lewis, David Robinson, Robert Breckinridge, and William Preston made trips to visit with each other or paused on their way to other places to visit for a few days with relatives and friends.[48]

In a variety of settings, the upper valley gentry esteemed the skillful display of conviviality, jocularity, and other forms of competitive self-expression that enhanced status in eastern Virginia. William Preston took dancing lessons and received a good-natured teasing from David Robinson, which implied that such skills were well within the parameters of social convention. In 1773 Stephen Trigg asked his sister-in-law if she intended to spend part of the summer at "the Springs," a customary social practice for the eighteenth-century Virginia elite. At one point David Robinson flippantly reported to William Fleming that "some sage Christians" in his area were attributing Indian attacks near Staunton to "the reigning Vices of the Place," his jocular tone indicating how fully many upper valley leaders accepted these "reigning Vices." As the tone of Robinson's letter suggests, the gentry also prized virtuosity in humorous expression: Robinson's correspondence with Fleming and Preston often took such a tone, and in 1760 John Madison teased Preston about his surreptitious courtships on a journey to eastern Virginia.[49]

Throughout the colonial period, county court meetings served as a gathering point for elite socialization in much the same way they did in eastern Virginia. As early as 1746, two ordinaries operated at the Augusta courthouse, suggesting that court days attracted a significant crowd.[50] The next year another man who had a license to operate an ordinary at his home was charged with improperly selling liquor at court.[51] Within a year of its creation, Botetourt County had authorized two ordinaries to operate at its courthouse.[52] In their correspondence, such upper valley leaders as

William Preston, Robert Breckinridge, William Christian, David Robinson, and Arthur and William Campbell spoke of meeting at court for business, socializing, or political discussions.[53] Some men attended or were assumed to attend with such regularity that mail was directed to them there.[54]

As in eastern Virginia, the county courts provided an important arena for the affirmation of authority, hierarchy, and deference. The Augusta justices worked to uphold their institutional dignity, repeatedly punishing offenders for cursing, disturbing, or otherwise showing disrespect to the court. The Botetourt court was little different: offenders were fined, imprisoned, or placed in the stocks. Some of the offenses receiving the courts' attention were minor: in 1762 three soldiers were imprisoned for marching into the Augusta court with their hats on, and three other men received fines for disturbing the court "by Playing at Ball."[55] Another challenge to the courts' dignity was more direct: in 1762 James Hutcheson was fined for "pissing in the Court House whilst the court was setting."[56]

Upper valley courts upheld not only their collective authority and dignity but also that of individual justices and local officials. On several occasions the courts dealt with persons who disturbed or assaulted county officials.[57] Verbal as well as physical abuse gained the attention of the courts: several justices initiated complaints against men who cursed and insulted them.[58] In 1748 the Augusta Court proceeded against a man who had criticized the senior justice James Patton by calling him "a Sorry fellow & not worthy to wipe his Shoes."[59] The courts also attempted to protect individuals prominent outside the boundaries of purely political life. In 1747 the Augusta court ordered that John Graham be arrested for his threats and abuse to the Anglican minister John Hindman.[60] The courts repeatedly punished indentured servants who ran away, unjustly complained, or otherwise failed to respect the authority of their masters and the laws governing their status.[61]

Significantly, the courts often pardoned or dealt leniently with offenders who expressed penitence and renewed deference to the authority of the justices and other local leaders. In 1748, for example, the Augusta court pardoned James Perkins after he apologized for the use of "opprobrious language." The next year Valentine Sevier and William Shurley apologized for their misbehavior and were discharged after paying fees. In apologizing for offensive statements about the prominent attorney Gabriel Jones, one offender "declared that he Could not remember that he had said the words in the Declaration mentioned but that if he did he was in Liquor, for that he knew no harm of the Plaintiff [Jones] and that he was sorry for saying the same." The court required the man to pay Jones's court costs and dismissed him.[62] Even James Hutcheson, who had been charged with urinating in the courthouse, was excused from paying fines after he "Acknowledged his fault & begged the pardon of the Court." In such cases the justices' chief objective was not to punish transgressions but to compel recognition and acceptance of their dignity and authority.[63]

The courts regularly proceeded against elite as well as less prominent offenders. As the rulers of a deferential society, the justices sought to enforce not only the prestige but also the responsibility of those in prominent positions. Accordingly, individuals who refused to serve as justices of the peace were called before the court to explain the reasons for their refusal.[64] Justices and other officials who failed to perform their duties properly were fined or reprimanded. Thus Augusta justice Samuel Gay was forced to apologize for unjustly threatening to have Andrew Campbell whipped and placed in the stocks.[65] The Augusta court also summoned justice Erwin Patterson to answer charges of contempt for refusing to give up a stolen mare he had recovered.[66] The courts often proceeded against justices who did not complete or return their tithable lists, and they punished lawyers who neglected their duties or were disorderly during trials.[67] In 1746 the Augusta court passed an order "that any attorney Interupting another at this Barr or speaking where he is not Imploy'd forfeit five shillings."[68] Although the courts repeatedly punished unruly indentured servants, they also took measures against masters who physically abused servants, refused to pay their freedom dues, or otherwise failed to respect their rights. After receiving several complaints from his servants, the Augusta court even ordered Valentine Sevier not to "correct" them without first obtaining an order from a justice of the peace.[69]

As in eastern Virginia, upper valley courts punished swearing, vagrancy, and other moral offenses as a means of asserting their authority over the rest of their society. In Lunenburg County, a backcountry region east of the upper valley, the courts' failure to prosecute such crimes apparently reduced their prestige and their influence on the citizenry.[70] In contrast, the upper valley courts regularly proceeded against such offenses as vagrancy, illegal hunting of deer, adultery, bastardy, drunkenness, gambling, and swearing.[71] They also inquired into the domestic life of upper valley families, examining in 1773, for example, a complaint against Edward Beard that he was failing to raise his two sons "in a Christian like manner."[72] On several occasions, the courts charged settlers with breach of the Sabbath and disturbing religious services.[73]

Through appointments to various minor offices, justices both asserted their authority over their fellow citizens and incorporated them into the hierarchy of authority in their deferential culture. Every year the courts appointed upper valley citizens to serve on both grand and petit juries. The grand juries, which indicted persons for moral transgressions, failure to perform official duties, and other offenses, were particularly important. Men who refused to serve on the juries or who left before completing their duty were summoned into court. After hearing their explanation or apology, the court might fine them, acquit them, or excuse them from part or all of the penalty.[74]

The justices sought in other ways, to extend their authority beyond the courts to include all sections of their counties. In addition to their role in the courts, individual justices of the peace exerted power in their immediate communities, dealing with minor crimes, receiving and advertising stray livestock, and performing other local functions.[75] At frequent intervals they compiled lists of inhabitants in their neighborhoods who were subject to taxation.[76] When the courts established new roads, they often required local justices to appoint the citizens who would clear and maintain them.[77]

The courts also attempted to maintain a network of constables, with one in each neighborhood throughout their counties.[78] Thus on two occasions in 1748, the Augusta court ordered that indentured servants be returned to their masters by being conveyed "from Constable to Constable."[79] As settlement extended up the valley, the courts appointed constables and road overseers in new frontier areas. In April 1746, for example, the Augusta court appointed several constables in the Roanoke valley, an outlying area that would be largely abandoned in the face of Indian attacks a decade later.[80] The same year, the court appointed road overseers still farther south, in the New River watershed.[81] In 1750 it appointed a constable on the Greenbrier River, an area in which settlement had only recently begun and which would remain a frontier until the Revolutionary War.[82] Once these officials were appointed, the courts continued to scrutinize their conduct, frequently proceeding against those who neglected their responsibilities.[83]

Although the upper valley gentry differed from their eastern Virginia counterparts in two important respects, neither fundamentally weakened their loyalty to the east's political values. The upper valley elite's predominantly Scotch-Irish and Presbyterian character distinguished it from the Anglican and English elite of eastern Virginia. Especially during the chaotic period of early settlement, upper valley leaders also departed from the restrained standards of behavior espoused in the east. Nevertheless, neither of these deviations from eastern standards seriously challenged the culture of deference.

The most obvious difference between the leaders of eastern Virginia and those of the upper valley was the prevalence of Scotch-Irish Presbyterians among the latter group. One modern scholar has estimated that the Scotch-Irish constituted two-thirds of the population of present-day Augusta and Rockbridge counties, the most thickly settled portion of the upper valley for much of the colonial period.[84] The Scotch-Irish also predominated within the gentry.[85] At least five of Augusta County's eight burgesses were Presbyterians, and even the supposedly Anglican vestry board contained many of them.[86]

These Scotch-Irish leaders remained conscious of their ethnic origins. For example, James Thompson, a justice of the peace and a grandson of valley land magnate James Patton, named his house Kilmacrenan in honor of the area from which Patton had come to America.[87] The prestigious Lewis family retained so much property in Ulster that one family member made a return visit to settle an estate.[88] William Preston, an Augusta burgess and later surveyor of Botetourt and Fincastle counties, maintained a correspondence with several Ulster relatives. The tone of these letters was rather formal, dealing chiefly with the health and welfare of family members, and the correspondents apparently wrote no more than once a year.[89] Nevertheless, the ties of kinship remained strong enough that in 1774 Preston found surveying work for a newly arrived Irish kinsman. Three years later, Preston helped this relative obtain the lucrative surveyorship of Washington County over the strenuous objections of that county's court.[90] Similarly, Preston's brother-in-law, Reverend John Brown, found a job for an Irish relative when informed of his arrival.[91]

Most upper valley leaders were Presbyterian, and several played an active role in that church's affairs. Augusta justices of the peace James Patton and John Christian served on the first commission of the Tinkling Spring church. Alexander Breckinridge, whose father and brothers were leaders in regional politics, also served on this first commission.[92] At one point William Preston directed to the Synod of Philadelphia and New York a set of recommendations designed to reduce the scarcity of Presbyterian ministers in the region. Preston also joined in several efforts to persuade individual ministers to accept positions in his community.[93]

In some respects upper valley Presbyterianism undercut the deferential values the gentry sought to impose. The Tinkling Spring congregation, for example, apparently tried to restrict the authority of its lay officials. A resolution in 1741 appointing five commissioners described them as "trusty & well-beloved friends." Yet it also required that all five commissioners be notified of any meetings at which assessments might be made and that church members be given a month's written notice before payments were due. The resolution further specified that the commissioners should be accountable not only to the minister but also to a larger portion of the membership, the session.[94] This desire to restrict authority may have reflected the personal friction between two local leaders, James Patton and John Lewis, both of whom belonged to the Tinkling Spring church.[95] In 1770, however, fifteen years after Patton's death, the session found it necessary to pass resolutions stipulating that a majority of the sessions and of the heads of families was required to conduct congregational business. These resolutions also declared that any smaller number of people would be considered "disorderly & tending to breake the peace & unity of the same & shall not be binding."[96] Thus both internal friction and efforts to limit the authority of leaders remained significant parts of congregational life.

Presbyteriansim, however, generally supported rather than undermined the deferential values of the elite. Given the emphasis on ministerial authority in the church's dogma and institutional structures, this is hardly surprising.[97] Thus in asking Reverend Charles Cummings to become their minister, two Holston River congregations promised him "that we will receive the word of God from your mouth, attend on your ministry, instructions, and reproofs in public & private, & submit to the discipline which Christ has appointed in his church administered by You while regulated by the word of

God & agreeable to our confession of Faith & Directory."[98] Church officials worried about the status of lay leaders as well as ministers, as was evident in a poem recorded in the Tinkling Spring Commissioners Book:

> when I am tried in scandal's court
> stand high in honour welth and witt
> all others who inferior sitt
> conceive themselves in conscience bound
> to joyne and drag me to the ground.[99]

Upper valley Presbyterian churches sought not only to maintain the stature of their ministers and lay leaders but also to enforce order and the acceptance of authority among their members. Individual churches tried to prevent Presbyterians within their established boundaries from joining other congregations.[100] In addition, they settled disruptive disputes between their members, dealing with such issues as false accusations, questionable business practices, and sexual transgressions.[101]

The upper valley gentry apparently felt little discontinuity between the system of authority in the Presbyterian church and that of the secular government. In 1746, for example, the Tinkling Spring commissioners appeared before two Augusta justices of the peace and received judgments against various church members who had not paid their allotted share of expenses. This action in itself would not be significant, but in several of the cases the justices moved beyond the immediately relevant contractual obligations of church members to a consideration of the rights and responsibilities governing the church's internal relationships. They ordered that James Armstrong, William Knox, and Andrew Cowin pay their share of building costs, *unless* within twelve months they could get orders of presbytery or synod releasing them from membership in the church. When Andrew Cowin testified that Reverend Craig had not visited him, examined him, or done "his Deuty as a Pastrel minister to him," the justices excused Cowin from payment of his church dues and ordered Craig to reimburse the commissioners for that amount.[102]

Regional leaders evidently felt a measure of continuity even between the Presbyterian and Anglican orders. Despite several efforts to remove them, many prominent Presbyterians served on the ostensibly Anglican vestry board in Augusta County throughout the colonial period.[103] Admittedly the Augusta vestry resisted the full establishment of Anglican institutions for some time. When they accepted Reverend John Hindman as their minister in 1747, for example, they extracted several promises: he would not insist on the purchase of a glebe (or ministerial residence) for at least two years, he would hold services in the courthouse and private homes *"Instead of a Church,"* and he would not urge the governor to order a change in these conditions.[104] Hindman died less than two years later, and the vestry did not replace him for another three years. In the late 1750s the vestry twice refused to appropriate funds for the construction of a church.[105] Much of this resistance, however, reflected fiscal conservatism rather than hostility to the Anglican church. In imposing conditions on Hindman in 1747, the vestry had required that he not insist on the purchase of a glebe for two years "until the Parish be more able to Bear such Charges." Moreover, later that year the vestrymen allowed John Smith and several other men to build a "chapel of ease," "Provided that it doth not affect the Parish now or later nor exempt them from their proportion of the parish levy."[106]

Whatever the reason for these delays, the largely Presbyterian vestry did eventually develop the full institutional structure of Virginia's Anglican church in Augusta County. By 1755 a glebe was completed, and in 1760 the vestry authorized the construction of a church in Staunton "in a fashionable & Workmanlike manner." The construction contract called for a gallery with two windows in the west end of the church and "a Pulpit Reading Desk & Clerks seat to be built . . . with a Canopy over the pulpit & pilaster neatly voluted"[107] In 1766, when the Presbyterian church at Tinkling Spring ordered the construction of a pulpit, the contract specified that it be built "in the same mode etc of the Church pulpit in town."[108] The pulpit in town belonged to the Anglican church, which had been completed three years earlier.[109] That the Tinkling Spring leaders simply referred to it as "the church . . . in town" and that they copied its internal furnishings suggest that they felt some measure of continuity and common identity between their community's Presbyterian and Anglican institutions.

Although upper valley Presbyterianism generally strengthened eastern values, the aggressive social and economic conduct of the region's early leaders directly challenged the eastern emphasis on self-restraint as a quality of leadership in a deferential culture. The activities of James Patton, a major leader of the 1740s and 1750s, demonstrated the possibilities for such conduct in a new and disorganized society. For much of this time, the struggle for power and prestige between Patton and John Lewis entangled their minister, Reverend John Craig. Apparently Craig considered the two men typical of the congregational leadership, whom he described as "proud, self-interested, contentious, and ungovernable." According to Craig, he was unable to resolve the differences between Lewis and Patton or even to maintain good relations with both at the same time: "They both had good interest with the people of their own party; and one of them always by turns a bitter enemy to me, which was very harmful both to my peace and interests[.] They by turns narrowly watched every step of my conduct—marred my support to the utmost of their power, used their interest with the people to drive me from the place or starve me out for want of support." In his efforts to discredit Craig, Patton even ordered a constable to carry him off at the end of church services in full view of the congregation.[110]

Patton showed an equal lack of restraint in his land speculation activities. At one point he pressed the Augusta County surveyor into making his son-in-law John Buchanan a deputy surveyor without going through the legally required process of applying to the masters of the College of William and Mary. Patton then had to conceal the illegality of the appointment or the extensive surveys Buchanan had made for him might have been jeopardized.[111] One upper valley settler even accused Patton of stealing the survey plats for 1,035 acres from him so as to obtain ownership of the land in his own name, and in 1746 the Augusta court ordered that Patton be indicted for improperly removing a document submitted as evidence in pending litigation.[112]

Benjamin Borden, Sr., a major land speculator and an Augusta justice of the peace, also developed a reputation for unethical practices. In 1748 the Augusta County Court found him guilty of falsifying quitrent records.[113] Another instance of sharp practices apparently surfaced the next year when six settlers asked the Augusta court to alter their deeds to show that they had paid purchase money to Borden.[114] In 1751 James Bell claimed that he and seventeen other men had made entries for land with Borden but had received no deeds.[115] After the senior Borden's death, his son wanted to sell the family's entire grant to someone who would take responsibility for the quitrents, and after the son's death in 1753, ownership of much of the Bordens' land remained in litigation for the rest of the century.[116]

Erwin Patterson, a merchant, Indian trader, and Augusta justice of the peace, was accused of various crimes and unethical practices. In 1753, for example, he was accused of having a visiting Cherokee leader beaten, a charge he denied. Possibly in connection with this incident and with their competition in the Indian trade, Patterson alleged that another settler, Samuel Stalnaker, had overcharged the Cherokees for corn. Patterson's claims upset the local settlers, who had much more respect for Stalnaker than for Patterson. The accusations also alarmed James Patton, who apparently believed Stalnaker's denial and feared the results of discontent among the frontier settlers.[117]

Perhaps the most extreme instance of unrestrained competition among the early gentry occurred in the Augusta election riot of 1755.[118] Although the surviving documents present an unclear picture, the riot resulted either from the repressive measures used by Augusta sheriff James Lockhart in administering the election or from the disruptive conduct of Richard Woods, David Cloyd, and Joseph Lapsley. All four were men of prominence in the region. In addition to serving as Augusta sheriff and justice of the peace, Lockhart was appointed a vestryman and churchwarden, and his son Patrick was later prominent in upper valley politics. Woods and Lapsley were both Augusta justices, and Woods later became a justice and sheriff in Botetourt County. According to the Augusta quitrent roll of 1760-62, Cloyd owned 1,060 acres, which placed him among the region's most wealthy men.[119]

All four men blamed the riot on the aggressive and improper behavior of their peers. As Woods, Cloyd, and Lapsley told it, the riot resulted from Sheriff Lockhart's autocratic misconduct of the election. Lockhart refused to let several people vote after finding out which candidates they supported. Perhaps worse, he left the courthouse several times during the day, which brought the voting to a halt. At one point he tried to keep Lapsley from voting by throwing him against a bench.

In his defense, Lockhart charged that Lapsley, Woods, and Cloyd had exceeded the bounds of proper conduct. While standing outside the courthouse, Lapsley loudly offered to wager that Mr. Preston and Mr. Alexander would win the election. Woods noisily urged support for Alexander and also offered to wager. When informed that the voting was going against his desires, Cloyd urged the crowd to use force to stop the election. Inside the courthouse, Lapsley pushed Sheriff Lockhart against a table, and Lapsley and

Cloyd refused to leave after voting. Shortly thereafter, Woods knocked out the candles in the courthouse, and the riot began. Lockhart was thrown onto a table, which broke under him, and Lapsley called out, "Lads, stand by me. I'll pay the fine, cost what it will. You know that I am able."[120]

Although personal conduct at this election obviously violated eastern Virginia's standards of political order, at least one aspect of the riot seems consistent with the eastern culture. In addition to shoving Sheriff Lockhart, Joseph Lapsley's alleged transgressions included noisily offering to make wagers in behalf of his candidates and calling out during the riot that he would pay whatever fines were assessed. This conduct can be seen as a more extravagant version of the eastern elite's custom of competitive self-assertion, using the traditional media of gambling and (by offering to pay all fines) conspicuous expenditure. In the context of a new society, with its opportunities for rapid acquisition of wealth and prestige and its lack of long-established authority, such uncurbed self-expression and self-assertion are not surprising. The sense of personal restraint, order, and respect for established authority which inhibited such conduct in the east was slower to develop among the upper valley gentry. As the region increased its stability and its intercourse with eastern Virginia, the assimilation of values became more balanced and complete.

The nature of internal frictions within the upper valley elite should be considered. Not surprisingly, these tensions often resulted from the competition for power in a frontier society. Economic as well as purely political interests frequently played a decisive role. Proposals for creation of new counties naturally proved a focal point for conflict, and ties of kinship shaped alignments in many of these struggles. Finally, some evidence suggests that particularly in several controversies surrounding Israel Christian, differing degrees of approval for the culture of eastern Virginia may have influenced divisions among the gentry.

Throughout the colonial period upper valley leaders quarreled over positions of power and prestige. The struggle between James Patton and John Lewis over "which of them should be highest in commission and power" divided the Tinkling Spring church during the early years of settlement.[121] After Patton's death in 1755, Lewis's son Andrew and Patton's protégé John Buchanan fought for years over their respective statuses as field officers in the Augusta County militia. In August 1755 Governor Dinwiddie refused Buchanan's request to charge Lewis with contempt and disobedience.[122] The next year Buchanan had an audience with the governor in which he received explicit approval of his position as second in command under county lieutenant Lewis and commander in chief in Lewis's absence.[123] In 1763 William Fleming apparently revived the conflict in a letter to Governor Francis Fauquier. By this time Buchanan was the county lieutenant, and Fleming blamed the inadequacy of Augusta's defenses on the unfitness of all the militia officers. In particular he alleged that Buchanan lived in a remote part of the county and failed to take full control of militia activities. According to Fleming, if the anticipated Indian attacks were to be defeated, "an Active County Lieutenant" was needed, and he specifically recommended Andrew Lewis.[124]

Another bitter dispute developed in 1770 over the position of sheriff in the new county of Botetourt. Although the governor appointed Richard Woods when the county was first created, the Botetourt court quickly recommended that Israel Christian replace him. In arguing for his own appointment, Christian charged that Woods was negligent in his duties as sheriff and justice of the peace. He further argued that since Woods had already served as Augusta sheriff, it was unfair to other Botetourt justices to let him serve again before they had a turn. Also serving on the Botetourt court was William Preston, who had unseated Christian as an Augusta burgess in 1765, defeated Christian's early attempts to create the new county, and gained the county surveyorship over Christian's son. Predictably, Preston opposed the court's recommendation of Christian, and four other justices joined Preston's opposition. Christian appealed to provincial authorities and ultimately received the appointment.[125]

Competition for commissions as officers on active military duty also divided the gentry. In 1764 several officers charged Andrew Lewis with improper conduct when he dismissed them from active duty.[126] When the Point Pleasant expedition was organized in 1774, many leaders who failed to receive commissions were resentful. Arthur Campbell, for example, made several efforts to gain an appointment for the expedition, but William Preston finally ordered him to supervise local defense in the Holston region.[127]

The desire for economic as well as political gains led to conflicts among upper valley leaders. The selection of a courthouse site normally increased the value of surrounding land, and this decision caused a controversy in Botetourt County in 1770. A committee of Botetourt justices recommended that the courthouse be placed on land donated by Israel Christian. Since Christian held other land in the immediate vicinity, including a mill site, he stood to profit from his donation. John Bowyer, the only committee member to dissent from this decision, had feuded with Christian several times in Augusta County. Bowyer may also have wanted to locate the courthouse on a tract he owned in the same area.[128] Moreover, the Botetourt court records for 1770 contain repeated orders for the county surveyor to lay out prison bounds, town lots, and other areas at the courthouse site.[129] William Preston, the county surveyor and Christian's chief rival, may have been trying to delay or prevent the establishment of the courthouse on that land. Perhaps significantly, the House of Burgesses, in which Preston served, did not finally validate the selection of the courthouse site until after Preston's replacement as Botetourt burgess two years later.[130]

Because county divisions not only created new offices for aspiring leaders but also reduced the jurisdiction and fees of incumbent officeholders, attempts to promote such divisions led to strong conflicts among the gentry, as occurred in the struggle to create Botetourt County in the late 1760s. For several years both sides petitioned the provincial government, lobbied prominent eastern leaders, and maneuvered in the legislature.[131] During these years proposals for new counties in the James River watershed and in northern Augusta County also created controversy.[132] Following the organization of Fincastle County in 1772, another group petitioned for a new county on the Holston River in 1774, arguing that the distance between them and the Fincastle courthouse was too great.[133] As early as 1748 Augusta County clerk John Madison jokingly charged John McFaran with agitating for a new county when McFaran alleged that the tithable list from his area was too small.[134] Although no scheme was afoot, Madison's joke, with its insinuation that the proponents of proposals to divide the county improperly inflated population counts, was clearly understood by those present. Thus even at this early date, upper valley leaders recognized the likelihood of such proposals, their questionable propriety, and their potential for creating conflict.

The efforts of John Madison, Jr., and his associates to caveat large quantities of land in Augusta brought them into conflict with William Preston, Andrew Lewis, and other valley leaders. Suspicion persisted between the antagonists for years afterward. In 1774

Thomas Lewis warned Preston not to make entries for land surveyed by an unsupervised apprentice because this violated Virginia law. Lewis noted in his letter that "John Madison makes himself very busy on Such Occasions."[135] Caveating schemes led to several other conflicts. Caveating by the Christians led to friction with William Preston in 1770, and in 1767 Preston, Thomas Lewis, and other leaders presented a petition to the Governor's Council to counter a large-scale use of caveats by a combination of individuals whose identity and numbers were uncertain.[136]

Because ties of kinship served as bonds of cohesion among the gentry, factional alignments dividing local leaders often reflected such relationships. The kinship connections of William Preston and Israel Christian shaped the Botetourt court's vote to recommend Christian for county sheriff in 1770. Preston and two of his relatives accounted for three of the five votes against the recommendation of Christian, and three of Christian's relatives were among his supporters on the court (although his brother-in-law Francis Smith did not join his dissenting kinsmen on this vote). Earlier that year the committee of Botetourt justices appointed to select a courthouse site had also divided along lines of kinship: Israel Christian and his sons-in-law William Fleming and Stephen Trigg had supported locating the courthouse on a tract owned by Christian. The one dissenter had been John Bowyer.[137] Apparently some outside observers saw valley politics as a clash of competing clans: during the struggle over the Botetourt surveyorship, Richard Starke of Williamsburg assured William Preston that he would not be supplanted by "anyone descended from the loins of Israel Christian."[138]

Although most quarrels arose from competition for wealth and power, some evidence suggests that the varying measures of acceptance of eastern Virginia culture also influenced controversies among the upper valley gentry. This was particularly visible in a series of conflicts involving Israel Christian. In November 1767, for example, the largely Presbyterian vestry of Augusta County was asked to sign a declaration of conformance to the doctrines of the Anglican church. Except for Christian, all the members complied. A majority of the vestrymen than objected to Christian's signing the proceedings of the meeting. Two years later, when Robert Breckinridge also refused to sign the endorsement of Anglican doctrine, both he and Christian were removed from the vestry.[139]

The antagonism toward Christian seemingly arose in part from his opposition to gambling and other modes of competitive conviviality central to traditional Virginia culture. John Bowyer and Christian clashed several times over gambling. In August 1762 Christian charged that Bowyer had obstructed his efforts to suppress gaming, and less than six months later Christian and Archibald Alexander charged Bowyer himself with gambling.[140] As noted earlier, in relating reports of Indian attacks near Staunton, David Robinson quipped that "some sage Christians . . . impute this [the attacks] to the reigning vices of the Place." Robinson's sarcastic tone, along with the similar exploitation of the connotations of Christian's surname in other correspondence of the period, suggests a criticism of Christian's antagonism to the "reigning vices" of Staunton.[141]

Christian's apparent unpopularity in eastern Virginia also may have resulted from his lack of sympathy with the region's values. During the campaign to create Botetourt County in the late 1760s, John Madison suggested to William Preston that Christian's personal promotion of the proposal in eastern Virginia was "the Worst Complement he Could possibly have paid it," "if I am not much Mistaken in that Gentleman's Popularity below" (i.e., in eastern or lower Virginia).[142] Significantly, Christian's ties to the east were largely with Patrick Henry, who was often at odds with the predominant provincial leaders and had strong affinities with the evangelical movement which challenged their political and social values. Christian's son William became involved in land speculation with Henry, studied law with him, and eventually married his sister.[143]

For most of the colonial period, however, the differences in cultural orientation between the Christians and their antagonists were relatively minor. Like Preston and his friends, the Christians participated in the deferential culture that developed in the county courts. They shared a concern with status and authority, and they supported most of the conventional means for sustaining them. Their families engaged in extensive social visits and other forms of competitive conviviality. The greatest challenge to the dominance of eastern values came not from internal divisions among the upper valley gentry but rather from the rejection of those values by large portions of the nonelite population.

CHAPTER THREE

The Militia
and Popular Localism

The upper valley gentry espoused the values of eastern Virginia in defense activities as well as in civil government. As in the county courts, militia leaders showed a tremendous concern with the maintenance of status and authority, demanding deference from subordinates and according it to their superiors. In addition, the elite consistently supported offensive expeditions that ranged far beyond the frontiers, conciliation of potential Indian allies, and other methods of imperial expansion in preference to the localized defense of upper valley communities. These defense priorities reflected upper valley leaders' cosmopolitan orientation, as well as their desire for prestigious and remunerative military duty and their interest in opening up new lands for speculation. Yet many common settlers did not share these attitudes and priorities. Their dissent was particularly evident in widespread defiance of elite-sanctioned values in the militia and other defense efforts. Moreover, an underlying network of popular interests and values can be discerned, which provided a unifying rationale for these acts of defiance and constituted the rudiments of a less deferential, more localistic, popular political culture.

For much of the upper valley population, the county court was a less significant arena of public life than the obligations of militia. In these activities, the values of the gentry frequently met with popular defiance. Indiscipline, desertion, refusal to perform military duty, and violence toward friendly Indians offended the elite's concern with order and authority. These offenses also contradicted the elite's commitment to provincial rather than local priorities and its concern with territorial expansion in the struggle with the French.

Despite the importance of county court meetings for the elite, most settlers had little contact with this element of government. Many of the justices attended only sporadically. Of the twenty-three Augusta County justices who attended at least one session in 1749, only one came to more than half the sessions, and only eight came to more than one-fourth of them. In 1762 two of the twenty-two justices attending were present at more than half of the sessions, and ten came more than one-fourth of the time. In 1773 two of the thirty-two attending justices came more than half the time, and thirteen came to more than one-fourth of the sessions. Botetourt County justices did slightly better: in 1770 seven of twenty-seven attending justices came to a majority of their court's sessions, and ten were present at more than one-fourth.[1]

If the justices attended only irregularly, it is hardly surprising that many common settlers seldom came to court. Thus in 1774 William Preston reported that "not one Man perhaps in ten [in the Holston River region that was petitioning for a separate county] have business in court once in two or three years."[2] As late as 1782, William Christian suggested that in the southern part of the upper valley, adequate popular support for a proposal to the legislature could not be obtained through public meetings at court days, even at the time of legislative elections, because so few people attended.[3] It is suggestive that in 1768, three men appointed by the Augusta vestry board to procession the landholdings in a portion of that county were uncertain to whom they should address their report and thus began it with the words: "To the Worshipfull court of Augusta county or to the vestry."[4] Apparently even some minor officials failed to understand the basic functions of county government.

For most settlers the militia and other defense activities served as centers of interaction with their government and fellow citizens. In militia companies and other settings, varying models of political relationships could be sanctioned and challenged. Moreover, because the actions taken there frequently had an immediate impact on local settlers, they especially influenced the political and social attitudes of common people in the upper valley. Significantly, in rejecting the idea of soliciting popular support for the legislative proposal at county courts in 1782, William Christian suggested that the petition's supporters work instead through the militia companies.

The institutional structure of the upper valley militia was similar to that of eastern Virginia. As in the east, a county lieutenant supervised the militia in each county, assisted by several other field officers with the ranks of colonel, lieutenant colonel, and major. These men, who were normally among the most prominent leaders of their area, appointed the company captains and lesser officers and made most of the decisions relating to the defense of their counties. The militiamen themselves, who included the entire able-bodied male population, were organized for training purposes into companies, each commanded by a captain and several lesser officers and each encompassing a particular geographic area. Each company mustered several times a year in its own neighborhood, and a general muster of the entire county was held annually.[5]

Although much of the eastern Virginia militia's combat duty took place outside their training companies and their home counties, circumstances in the upper valley gave this service a more local focus. On some occasions upper valley settlers were recruited or conscripted for extended duty under special officers from outside their companies. In many cases, however, these officers came from the same part of the county. When the Point Pleasant expedition was organized in 1774, for example, various captains and subaltern officers on the Holston and Clinch rivers began their recruiting efforts with the men of their own and neighboring companies.[6] Moreover, field officers subordinate to the county lieutenant frequently supervised frontier defense in the portion of their county in which they lived.[7] Thus when men were mobilized for defensive purposes, they often served in areas not far from their own homes under officers who had at least some knowledge of their communities.[8] Men ordered to perform active service on the frontier often traveled to their posts with groups from their training companies and local neighborhoods. Such groups often retained a collective identity throughout their tours of duty, threatening in some cases to desert together unless allowed to return home.[9] Most important of all, the nature of Indian warfare and frontier defense meant that much of the militia's defense activities took place within the training companies. Many company captains supervised preparation of forts, ordered out scouts to warn of Indian raids, and mobilized their men to defend against those attacks.[10]

Throughout the colonial period, upper valley militia leaders complained of disciplinary problems. In 1774 William Doack told William Preston that he could not remain at the head of Clinch River because in his command, "everyone doeth according to freedom of

48   GENTRY AND COMMON FOLK

his own will." Arthur Campbell reported that another party failed
to complete its mission, drew provisions improperly, and then
refused to search for Indians after signs of their presence were
found. William Preston warned a subordinate serving on the lower
New River to prevent his men from needlessly firing their guns
while on patrol because that "detestable practice . . . not only
wastes ammunition which is very scarce but gives the enemy notice
where you are, so that they will either take the advantage of your
imprudence and surprise you, or pass by and ravage the country."
Preston's language here and in similar instructions to a small scout-
ing party strongly implied that, despite his opposition, this "detestable practice" was widespread. In 1756 Andrew Lewis complained
that many of the men on duty were permitted "to stroll about the
country." A year earlier, Governor Dinwiddie had responded to
reports of indiscipline by ordering Colonel James Buchanan of
Augusta County to rely on the specially recruited rangers for defense and not call out the militia except in emergencies.[11]

The most serious problems in the militia were desertion and
refusal to perform military duty. In 1754 Augusta leaders were
unable to raise even fifty men for an expedition to expel the French
from the Ohio Valley, and William Preston reported in 1757 that he
could not keep the men in his command on duty for more than a
week or two at a time.[12] During the summer and fall of 1774, officers
throughout the region found it difficult to raise and retain adequate
forces. In October, for example, James Thompson led fifty men
down the Holston River on what was planned as a ten-day march,
but half of the group deserted and returned home after only two
days. James Robertson's men told him that if he left their post on the
lower New River for a few days, they would desert immediately. As
Robertson reported to Preston, "I dare say you have a great deal of
trouble getting hands to us and I am sure I have a vast deal of
Trouble in keeping them in [illeg] as they are a distracted enough
party I assure you."[13] Recruiting for the Point Pleasant expedition
that fall proved particularly difficult: at least twenty-five men in the
Staunton area refused to join the army even after being drafted, and
officers throughout the southern part of the region encountered
serious difficulties.[14]

Both inside and outside the militia, popular violence toward
friendly Indians led to conflicts with elite values. Upper valley
leaders carefully distinguished between friendly and unfriendly
Indians and avoided provoking hostilities with the former, whom

they valued as allies in the struggle against the French. Popular groups, however, often doubted the worth of such distinctions. In 1742, for example, an Iroquois party traveling through Augusta County disturbed local residents by killing livestock and stealing provisions. On orders from the county lieutenant, Captains John McDowell and James Buchanan provided food to the Indians and raised a militia party to escort them out of the settlements. The captains' restrained behavior, however, provoked criticism from their men. Eventually a fight with the Indians broke out, and one account suggested that it was started by the insubordinate militiamen. Popular resentment also appeared in rumors that before the militia party was raised Captain McDowell had entertained the Indians and provided them with whiskey. Five years later, one person even alleged that McDowell had incited the Indians to attack the settlements.[15]

The actions of the "Augusta Boys" in 1765 illustrated the depth of popular support for violence against friendly Indians. A group of twenty whites attacked a Cherokee party traveling from Staunton to Winchester under protection of a pass from Andrew Lewis. Although one of the instigators was imprisoned, a group of one hundred or more men, calling themselves the Augusta Boys, forcibly released him and issued a proclamation offering rewards for the capture of Lewis and several other local officials. The proclamation also charged that Lewis was in collusion with the French and had knowingly issued the pass to a group of hostile Indians.[16] A few months later Virginia officials were alarmed by reports that another group of Augusta men planned to ambush a friendly Cherokee party returning from meetings in Williamsburg, and two years later Governor Fauquier admitted that there was "not the least probability" of bringing the Staunton murderers to justice.[17]

Public support for such violence was evident when a Cherokee Indian was killed in the Watauga settlements in 1774. Although the incident threatened to provoke a war, many people continued to protect the probable murderer, Isaac Crabtree. Arthur Campbell reported that "it would be easier to find 100 men to screen him from the law, then 10 to bring him to justice." Despite the disapproval of authorities, Crabtree and his followers continued attacking isolated Indians in the area. When witnesses against him unexpectedly appeared at his murder trial, William Christian felt it necessary to order that a large militia party guard the prison to prevent any rescue attempts.[18]

Although the upper valley gentry often saw popular defiance in the militia as irrational and self-destructive, a network of interests and values did provide an underlying cultural rationale. The material interests of small farmers often encouraged attacks on friendly Indians and resistance to military duty. In some measure popular resistance to military discipline reflected the prevalence of less hierarchical and authoritarian, more consensual and democratic ideals of leadership among nonelite groups. In this resistance, and in a variety of efforts to obtain greater protection for their communities and greater local control over defense activities, upper valley settlers showed a stronger attachment to their local neighborhoods than to county and provincial authorities. Finally, both members of the elite and popular dissidents often perceived their clashes as manifestations of persisting and predictable conflicts of values rather than as discrete adaptations to individual situations.

Even so despicable an act as the killing of friendly Indians often was motivated not only by racism but also by the economic interests of popular groups.[19] As they traveled through settled areas, Indian parties frequently destroyed livestock and property, particularly in areas where game had become too scarce to provide an easy source of food. John Craig noted this problem in the Staunton area in the 1740s, and in 1753 James Patton reported popular resentment of the property damage done by traveling Cherokee Indians on the southern frontier of Augusta County.[20] The elite could tolerate such thefts as a necessary expense of Indian diplomacy, but for less wealthy settlers the immediate material losses could be disastrous. Resentment of such property damage played an important role in the Augusta County incident of 1742 and probably was a factor in other cases as well. Moreover, on some occasions, as in 1742 and 1765, hostility also developed toward leaders who refused to protect local settlers from these damages.

For small farmers whose only labor force was their families, military service during critical periods of the crop cycle was a serious burden. Thus in July 1774, some of James Robertson's men insisted on delaying their departure for the Point Pleasant expedition for several days so that they could put up their grain. Arthur Campbell reported in October that a group of militiamen on the Holston refused to stay on duty for more than a few days, "the saving of their own crops being a general cry." Perceptive leaders often took steps to alleviate these grievances. Arthur Campbell, for example, asked William Campbell to replace some of the men serving under him, "particularly Charles Bowen as his wife told me his crop would suffer if he did not return." Similarly, William Russell sought compensation for several men who served as scouts and messengers, noting that they had been obligated to hire other men to work their farms.[21]

Much of the indiscipline in the militia arose from conflicts between elite and popular ideals of leadership. While the gentry stressed the traditional eastern Virginia virtues of dignity, restraint, and concern with status and authority, common settlers often placed greater emphasis on dramatic action and a close identification with the men. The implications of these conflicting ideals can be seen by contrasting popular attitudes toward Andrew Lewis and toward other officers who recognized the need to appeal for popular support on the Sandy Creek expedition of 1756 and the Point Pleasant expedition of 1774. Lewis's embodiment of the gentry's concern with dignity and authority was evident in the admiring description of him by an associate: "His independent Spirit despised sycophant means of gaining popularity, which never rendered more than his superior merits extorted. Such a character was not calculated to win much applause by commanding an army of Volunteers. Without discipline experience or gratitude, many took umbrage because they were compelled to do their duty."[22]

Popular resistance to Lewis's authoritarian style of leadership contributed to the failure of the Sandy Creek expedition. During this campaign Lewis and the officers under his command struggled unsuccessfully to prevent desertions as their army exhausted its food supply. Although the other officers admired Lewis, many of them recognized the need to appeal to popular values in dealing with the men. Thus when William Preston's company attempted to desert, he argued that if they left before Lewis arrived with another part of the army, he (Preston) would be blamed for it, and his character would suffer. This emphasis on his close identification with and dependence upon the men succeeded, and they agreed to remain. Lewis, by contrast, conducted himself in an aloof and authoritarian fashion. According to Preston, when first informed of the threats of desertion, Lewis "said he had often seen the like mutiny among soldiers and it might be Easily settled &c &c." After arriving at Preston's position, he called the soldiers together, warned them of the ill consequences of desertion and mutiny, and urged them to continue the expedition. At the conclusion of his speech, almost the entire army immediately deserted, many of them marching off in company formation. The men's marching off in formation may suggest that many of the sergeants and other low-ranking officers identified so closely with the common soldiers that they supported the mutiny, especially since in Preston's company the sergeants had been early spokesmen for the men who wished to return home.[23] In any case, it clearly indicates a strong sense of solidarity, common purpose, and shared opposition to the leadership of Lewis.

A similar conflict between popular ideas and Lewis's standards of leadership occurred on the Point Pleasant expedition in 1774. John Stuart recollected that Lewis, who commanded the expedition, had much difficulty in controlling the soldiers, who rejected his emphasis on order and discipline.[24] Antagonism to Lewis apparently crystallized in a ballad about the battle of Point Pleasant which portrayed him as not merely aloof but also cowardly:

> And old Andrew Lewis in his tent he did set
> With his cowards around him alas he did sweat
> His blankets spread over him, and hearing the guns roar,
> Saying was I at home I would come here no more.[25]

Lyman Draper collected three versions of the ballad during the 1840s in West Virginia and Tennessee, and it may well have originated soon after the battle. In any case the popular critique of Lewis spread quickly. When he was mentioned in the Continental Congress the next year as a possible commander of the American army, one Virginian suggested that criticism of Lewis by his former troops made his appointment inadvisable.[26]

Though Lewis met with harsh criticism, other officers on the expedition, particularly his brother Charles, appealed more successfully to the values of their men. Even before the expedition, Charles Lewis had become a popular leader, largely because of his reputation as a brave, skillful, and dramatic Indian fighter.[27] The circumstances of his death in the battle of Point Pleasant increased his popularity. He was shot while standing in an exposed position and urging his men to move forward. Although seriously wounded, he gave his gun to a soldier and walked back to the encampment, encouraging the men he passed to fight bravely. Accordingly, the ballad praised him for bravery, self-sacrifice, and closeness to his men:

Charles Lewis our colonel was first in the field
He received a ball but his life did not yield
In the pursuit of honor he did animate
All those that fought near him or on him did wait.

The ballad also emphasized the virtues of bravery and empathy with the men in praising two other wounded officers, William Fleming and John Fields. Fields, who died of his wounds, was said to have told his men: "Fight on brother soldiers and don't be dismayed," thereby evoking a strong sense of his comradery and closeness to the common soldiers. The depiction of Fleming was strikingly similar to that of Charles Lewis: Fleming "received three balls but did not expire. / He animated his men and to camp did retire."[28]

Other upper valley leaders also gained support by partially rejecting traditional elite standards of leadership and authority and expressing their sympathy for the common people and their values. Thus when Indian hostilities threatened the Holston River frontier in September 1774, William Cocke tried to discourage settlers from evacuating the area by stressing his personal devotion to them and suggesting his distance from the established leaders of the militia. He ordered his sergeant to mobilize all available men for local defense and promised to go to North Carolina to recruit reinforcements. Although he hoped that the leaders "that is at the Helm of affairs" would approve these measures, he promised to pursue them with or without such approval. Cocke's efforts earned him much popularity on the Holston, but his Fincastle County superiors disapproved of his North Carolina recruiting and alleged that he sought to advance himself through improper means.[29]

Popular opposition to military duty often resulted from an overriding concern with defense of families and neighborhoods.[30] Thus in planning for the Point Pleasant expedition, Botetourt County officers recommended that help with local defense be obtained from other counties to the east. They felt that upper valley settlers would not volunteer for the expedition without assurances of protection for their own communities. In September 1774 Arthur Campbell found it impossible to persuade Holston River militiamen to assist in protecting the Clinch River, "as they look upon themselves in equal danger," and the next month John Montgomery reported similar difficulties in getting New River settlers to serve on the Holston. On several other occasions militiamen's concern for their own communities led to their threatened or actual desertion.[31]

Neighborhoods exposed to attack often pressured elite officials for more help with local defense, and in some cases those officials promised assistance to discourage settlers from fleeing their homes. Thus William Preston met with a group of Bullpasture settlers in March 1757 to decide on the location for a fort. Nine of the twelve people attending agreed on a fort site and signed a statement promising not to flee as long as a company of men was maintained there. Similarly, William Russell had his Clinch River militia company vote on the locations for construction of two forts in June 1774, and he informed Preston that a promise of reinforcements from the Holston had prevented the flight of local settlers.[32] Militiamen and settlers frequently protested ammunition shortages, especially when caused by the allocation of such supplies away from their neighborhoods. On the middle New River, for example, popular resentment developed when William Christian insisted on saving fifty pounds of gunpowder for the Point Pleasant expedition rather than using it for local defense. At one point, Christian feared the people would forcibly seize the powder.[33] To members of the elite, concerns with neighborhood defense sometimes seemed narrow and misguided, for in 1774 Arthur Campbell reported from the southern end of the valley that "the most of the people in this country seem to have a private plan of their own for their own defense." He then described the attitudes of each neighborhood, noting for example that "the Head of New River will have it that the Cherokees will fetch a Compass around Wautauga Settlement, and come down New River on a particular search for their scalps." He concluded, "You may thus see what a task one would have to remove every ones fears."[34]

Popular efforts to obtain local militia companies also reflected a strong attachment to neighborhoods. In 1742, for example, inhabitants of the Forks of James and the southern portion of the Borden tract petitioned Governor William Gooch to establish a company in their area.[35] In 1774 some men from an outlying part of a company on middle New River refused to attend the company muster, saying that since they lived ten miles away they should have a company of their own.[36] A group of men living on Madason Creek, a tributary of Clinch River, not only demanded their own company but also nominated officers and sent out their own scouts to provide warnings in case of Indian attack.[37]

The same spirit appeared in attempts to obtain commissions for locally popular officers. In 1774 a group of lower Clinch River settlers petitioned William Preston, their county lieutenant, to appoint Daniel Boone to command the forts in their area and asked that Boone be empowered to act without orders from the Holston River officers. This request was motivated by the settlers' belief that an officer living among them would be more concerned with their safety than one who lived in another area. They particularly resented a Captain Looney for being absent from his post during a recent Indian alarm, an absence occasioned by Indian attacks in Looney's own neighborhood.[38]

In recruiting men for the Point Pleasant expedition, popular support for local leaders proved particularly important. Several ambitious men with local popularity attempted to raise their own companies for the expedition, leading to serious frictions within some militia training companies. In several companies on the upper Holston, Joseph Drake and his associates recruited a large number of men who agreed to enlist under him. Although Arthur Campbell tried to persuade the men to serve under the officers sanctioned by valley leaders, Drake ultimately insisted that he would lead the men to the expedition's rendezvous point in direct defiance of orders from the county lieutenant. Moreover, for a time many of the men who opposed Drake refused to associate with any of his supporters and insisted that they be commanded by officers from their own companies. Similar problems occurred in Captain James Thompson's company on Holston River when some of the men refused to serve if John Read was their ensign, and James Robertson reported to William Preston that he had experienced recruiting problems in two New River companies because "there is some precarious gentlemen amongst us who makes mutiny amongst the men because they wants companies."[39]

In several cases the gentry were compelled to compromise with these dissidents and their followers. Thus despite his opposition to Joseph Drake's efforts, Arthur Campbell encouraged all volunteers from that region to march to the expedition's rendezvous point under any officers they chose, hoping that the conflicts between the officers could be resolved once the army was assembled. Although Campbell hoped that Drake's fear of punishment by valley leaders would deter him from joining the expedition, he agreed to furnish provisions to Drake and the men who followed him to the rendezvous.[40]

Ironically, even the recurrent mass flights from areas threatened with Indian attack showed some elements of popular attachment to local neighborhoods. Although such flights often began as spontaneous reactions to reports of Indian attack, in some cases neighborhood groups made deliberate collective decisions on whether to flee, suggesting a sense of communal cohesion and identity. After General Edward Braddock's defeat in the Seven Years' War, some members of John Craig's congregation near Staunton urged removal to a safer part of the country and called upon Craig to support them. When he opposed their proposal, they agreed to remain and defend the community only after Craig himself contributed much of his property to local defense. Once the consensus was reached, the congregation united in these defense efforts.[41] Similarly, the sense of community cohesion among Alexander Craighead's congregation shaped their flight from the Cowpasture River that same year. In September 1755, Hugh McAden encountered a large company of men, women, and children from that congregation who had fled into North Carolina.[42] Although McAden did not specify whether this group had made a collective decision to flee, their traveling together at such a great distance from their homes suggests that they may have made such a decision and implies at least a strong sense of common identity. Two years later, a group of Bullpasture settlers met with William Preston and agreed not to flee from their area as long as a company of men was maintained at a local fort. In 1774 the inhabitants of Bryce Russell's Holston River neighborhood debated among themselves whether to flee before an anticipated Indian attack. Brief references in several other letters of the colonial period suggest that similar collective decisions may have occurred elsewhere.[43]

Most important of all, both the upper valley gentry and the popular dissidents often saw their conflicts as indications of persisting and predictable cultural confrontations rather than as pragmatic adaptations to individual situations. In particular, upper valley leaders saw flight from areas exposed to Indian attack as a persistent and irrational pattern of popular behavior. Thus in 1774 Daniel Smith lamented that on the Clinch and Bluestone rivers "the people are so scary & . . . there are so many propagators of false reports in the country . . . Those reports which ought to stir us up to common Defense, by passing thro the mouths of imprudent people do more damage than their not coming at all, by causing timorous people to run away." In reporting recent flights from the Holston River, George Adams told William Preston, "I imagine you have such accounts too frequent." On the New River William Christian obviously considered such evacuations a recurrent phenomenon, for he referred to them as "races" in which the people fled "as the reports [of Indian attack] come in & so goes home in a day or two." During the Seven Years' War, such reports shaped even the perceptions of Governor Fauquier in Williamsburg, for he urged Preston to "inspire the people with a little courage" and dissuade them from fleeing "at every appearance of 20 or 30 Indians."[44] Militia officers consistently predicted that reports of impending attack would bring flight from local communities, and they considered it a significant victory to prevent such evacuations.[45]

Upper valley leaders similarly perceived other forms of popular disorder as representative of recurrent and predictable patterns of behavior. Following the murder of a friendly Indian in the Watauga settlements during the summer of 1774, both William Christian and Arthur Campbell feared further incidents of such violence.[46] Christian also noted apprehensively that some of the "most worthless" and undependable New River settlers actually hoped for a war and were disappointed when the news of an Indian attack proved false. When William Preston wrote the Cherokees in hopes of preventing them from avenging the Watauga murder, he stressed the recurrent conflicts in both white and Indian societies between restrained, peaceful leaders and lawless, "hotheaded" individuals.[47] In planning the Point Pleasant expedition later that year, Preston, Christian, and other leaders not only anticipated widespread resistance but sought to meet the underlying popular concern with protecting local neighborhoods by calling on the militia of Bedford and Pittsylvania counties to help with local defense. As noted earlier, Arthur Campbell bitterly criticized the recurrent and irrational fears of various neighborhoods, which were myopically concerned with their own protection rather than the defense of the entire region.[48]

Although generalizations regarding popular perceptions are inherently tenuous, dissidents apparently saw many of their clashes with valley leaders as representative of persisting differences of values and interests. They often suspected that members of the elite had selfish and improper motives in mobilizing militia for active duty outside their immediate communities. Before an election of Augusta burgesses in 1761, a report that William Preston had improperly drafted militiamen for frontier defense aroused much popular resentment. The incumbent burgess, Israel Christian, allegedly circulated this rumor. In 1774 John Bowyer apparently reduced enlistments in Andrew Lewis's Point Pleasant expedition by charging that Lewis had no authorization to raise men, that those who served would not be paid, and that Lewis was organizing the expedition in order to get his western land claims surveyed.[49] The success of such charges, especially the patently implausible accusations of Bowyer, suggest substantial and persistent popular suspicion of elite motives in mobilizing militia. On the abortive Sandy Creek expedition of 1756, popular suspicion of militia leaders developed when scouts returned to the starving army with a report of abundant game in the territory just ahead. Although the officers welcomed the news, William Preston noted that it "Rather increased the Mutiny among the Men for they Looked upon the report to be formed only to Draw them so much farther from home."[50] Problems in receiving pay for military duty also encouraged suspicions of the valley elite and the provincial government. Thus in 1774 Joseph Drake apparently maintained support for his disruptive efforts to raise his own company for the Point Pleasant expedition by insinuating to his men that if they abandoned him for the company commanders sanctioned by upper valley leaders, the government would not pay them for their service.[51]

These alternative popular values appeared to a lesser degree in areas of upper valley life beyond the militia and local defense. The authority of the gentry was also defied in the functioning of constables and other law enforcement efforts. Land disputes with prestigious leaders, especially with surveyors and major speculators, encouraged popular resentment of the elite in many communities. Attachment to local neighborhoods and alienation from county and provincial authorities were further stimulated by the settlement patterns and the shared middle colony backgrounds that prevailed in much of the region.

Upper valley leaders often found it difficult to impose their will on the populace through the operations of constables and other minor officials. In 1762, for example, Robert Reaburn drew a knife on Augusta constable Hugh Ross and forcibly took a horse and saddle which he had seized in performing his duties. Three years later a constable reported that he had been prevented from executing a court order "by cause of a hay fork."[52] In addition, constables, road overseers, and other minor officials often neglected their duties, and the valley courts found it difficult to keep these positions filled.[53] Turnover among constables and road overseers was especially frequent, and many incumbent constables actively petitioned for their own removal.[54]

Popular resentment of the gentry appeared more conspicuously in connection with land disputes. Upper valley leaders often quarreled with squatters who had settled on their land without obtaining title. In 1772, when preparing to move his family to lands they had purchased in the southern valley, William Christian discovered two families already living there. He reported to his mother that one family "after wrangling a while, agreed to go off." Although the other family refused to leave, Christian hoped he would "be able in a little time to drive them off."[55] In at least one part of the frontier, squatting became so prevalent that land magnate Thomas Walker instructed his associate William Preston not to disturb such people unless necessary to facilitate a sale, noting that if squatters were removed from unsold property "others may settle on the land & make a second & third Ejectment necessary." Perhaps significantly, upper valley leaders frequently required in the contracts for leasing of land that their tenants explicitly renounce any claim to that property based on improvements they made during their residence.[56]

The activities of county surveyors brought them into conflict with local settlers in various ways. Because they patented so much land in their own names, popular suspicions often arose regarding their ethics. In April 1770, for example, Thomas Lewis warned his fellow surveyor William Preston against acquiring a small plot of unclaimed land. Lewis noted not only that certain other gentlemen might challenge the legality and propriety of Preston's actions but also that the rest of the populace was always ready to believe and support such charges "without being justly informed of the merits of the Cause." Moreover, throughout Virginia, surveyors were accused of favoritism in reserving the best lands for their friends and associates.[57]

Common settlers often felt that the operating practices of surveyors threatened their landholdings. Surveyor's errors in entering and surveying lands could endanger ownership.[58] The employment of assistants and deputies to make surveys also endangered land titles, sometimes by leading to conflicting surveys for the same property and sometimes because the assistants lacked legal authority to do the surveys. On several occasions Thomas Lewis warned William Preston against allowing an unauthorized apprentice to make surveys on his own, noting how easily others could question the propriety of such practices.[59]

Perhaps the most widespread resentment against surveyors arose from their refusal promptly to survey land already occupied by settlers. Thus Augusta resident Thomas Turk complained that for over ten years county surveyor Thomas Lewis had refused to survey a tract of land for him, resulting in his loss of the property.[60] In 1774 Botetourt deputy surveyor Francis Smith angered William Preston by surveying land close to Preston's home on the New River. Preston, the head Botetourt surveyor, had delayed making surveys in that area, and this apparently worried local inhabitants. As Smith explained it, he had set off on a surveying trip to the Holston River but stopped to make two previously promised surveys in the New River region. Before he could finish these surveys, however, another local settler persuaded him to make two more in the area the next day. By this time, word had spread through the neighborhood, and one person after another prevailed on him to survey their lands, drawing him closer and closer to Preston's home.[61] That so many settlers were eager to have their lands surveyed suggests the extent of the anxiety created by Preston's refusal to survey in that community. Moreover, several months after Smith's misfortune, Peter Hog teased Preston by suggesting that "if you lose your Election you may thank your fat Sides & lazy Humour that you grumble at climbing the hills of Botetourt for tobacco at 1d [per acre] when the surveyors have 2d for walking over the plains below the ridge" (i.e., in eastern Virginia).[62] Thus Hog insinuated the existence of significant popular resentment of Preston's efforts to have the fees raised and apparently of his reluctance to make surveys.

Quarrels with individuals and groups speculating in large tracts of land also generated popular resentment. Augusta land magnate Benjamin Borden developed a reputation in the 1740s for deceptive practices in selling his land. A Roanoke valley settler, James Calhoun, caused trouble by spreading a rumor that speculator James Patton could not give legal title to the land he was selling.[63] In the 1770s Holston River settlers became uneasy over the uncertain location of the land claims of surveyor and speculator William Preston. Preston apparently was slow in completing his acquisition of this land, possibly to avoid quitrent payments and to enable him to select the most valuable tracts available. As Robert Doack informed Preston, the people "would give anything Reasonable to know where your Surveys are that they might Either purchase or move Immediately."[64] Some speculators and their agents angered settlers by refusing to sell small pieces of particularly valuable land which would decrease the salability of surrounding acreage.[65] In some cases, speculators restricted settlers' freedom of action by stipulating that they could not sell or transfer their rights to the land for at least six months after the purchase was completed and by requiring that they post bonds for double the price of their land to guarantee their eventual purchase.[66]

When speculators challenged the land titles of their rivals, common settlers could become particularly resentful, for such controversies threatened not only the titles of speculators but also those of other individuals who had purchased land from them. In 1753 James Patton noted that the caveats entered against his land grants by James Powers, John Lewis, and their associates had greatly alarmed local settlers. According to Patton, the people were "very uneasy not knowing but what they may have as many Proprietors in time as many of them had who had Lived in the Jerseys, Where when they had Paid six Proprietors was obliged to pay a seventh and [illeg.] off in Poverty at Last." Thomas Lewis described the unrest caused among Staunton area settlers by an apparently well-organized caveating scheme in 1767. Lewis and other local leaders circulated a petition against the conspiracy which they planned to present to the Governor's Council.[67] For several years in the late 1760s and early 1770s, the caveats of John Madison, Jr., and his associates threatened hundreds of land titles in the upper valley. To pay for additional surveying and legal services to defend their claims, many settlers made agreements with William Preston, Thomas Lewis, and other leaders who opposed the Madison group's efforts. Lewis, however, encountered problems in collecting the agreed-upon fees and suggested to Preston that "it will be of great Service To many your way that it be taken notice of that Johnston [an associate of Madison] first Caveated their Lands."[68] Thus many settlers came to resent not only the local leaders who challenged their land titles but also the men who defended them and sought to collect surveying and legal fees. Perhaps in such cases popular groups recognized that it was the negligence of these defenders, from whom they had purchased their lands, that made such litigation possible.

The circumstances of initial settlement in much of the region may have encouraged popular rejection of the elite-sanctioned system for purchasing land. Because of the difficulties of acquiring secure titles, some settlers not only squatted on land without purchasing it but also asserted such settlement as a basis of ownership. Claims of ownership derived from settlement and cultivation of land or even from "blazing" trees with a hatchet or tomahawk apparently received popular support in many parts of the eighteenth-century backcountry from Pennsylvania southward. In some Pennsylvania communities local settlers established extralegal "fair play tribunals" which enforced such claims and settled disputes. By the end of the colonial period, Pennsylvania law allowed squatters the right of first claim to their land.[69] In the early years of settlement in the upper valley, speculator Benjamin Borden, Sr., may have appealed to such traditions to encourage occupation of his land in present-day Rockbridge County: he promised to give each settler one hundred acres of land for each cabin built, and residents later described this land as having been distributed by "cabin rights."[70] Upper valley landowners often required that settlers renting from them renounce any right to ownership based on settlement and improvement of the land. And during the Revolution, Tory insurgents on the New River promised free land to their supporters and expressed defiance of William Preston and other patriot leaders by blazing trees on their land to mark the planned redistribution of property.[71]

In many upper valley areas the patterns of settlement also enhanced the social cohesion among local residents. Settlers often arrived in extended family groups and established homes near their kinsmen. Thus Reverend Samuel Houston recollected that his grandfather John Houston had migrated south to the valley with his own family and those of three other kinsmen. All four families settled in the adjacent Presbyterian congregations of New Providence and Timber Ridge southeast of Staunton. Houston also noted other kinship groupings among the early settlers. Walkers Creek, a Maury River tributary, was named for the four families of Walkers who settled on it, and four families of Lyles settled in Timber Ridge congregation.[72]

In some cases persons from the same congregations in Pennsylvania settled together in the upper valley. New Providence Church south of Staunton, for example, was named in recognition of Providence Presbyterian Church near Norristown, Pennsylvania, from which many of the New Providence leaders had come.[73] A group of settlers from another Pennsylvania congregation founded Windy

Cove Presbyterian Church on the Cowpasture River.[74] Many early residents on the upper New River along the North Carolina border settled near their former neighbors from middle colony communities, and one geographic analyst has suggested that this pattern was common throughout the region.[75] In other parts of the backcountry clustering of residents by kinship groups, former congregations, and earlier neighborhoods also shaped the patterns of life in local communities.[76] Even without strong residential clustering, kinship, ethnicity, and church affiliations could bind together settlers who were spacially dispersed throughout a particular community or region.[77]

Clearly, although the upper valley gentry accepted the values and priorities of eastern Virginia, they did not fully impose them on the society in which they lived. In the county courts and other elite-dominated sectors of public life, the values of deference, hierarchy, and devotion to the greater good of Virginia and the British Empire predominated. Yet the problems of indiscipline in the militia, desertion, and violence toward friendly Indians show the widespread popular defiance of these elite standards. Indeed, these circumstances suggest the development of an alternative popular political culture that reflected the realities of small-scale agriculture, the preference for less hierarchical, more consensual styles of leadership, and an attachment primarily to local neighborhoods rather than to county, colony, or empire. This culture appeared in other areas of upper valley life to a lesser degree, and the processes of land acquisition and settlement often furthered its development. In maintaining its control of the region, the elite was repeatedly forced to deal with these emerging popular political values.

CHAPTER FOUR

The Roots of Backcountry Order

Given the strength of popular dissent from the political values of the gentry, it is surprising that the upper valley experienced less disorder than many other parts of the colonial backcountry. In the Carolinas and Pennsylvania, the Regulator movements and the Paxton Boys threatened established authorities at the regional and provincial levels. The upper valley's greater political stability may be partially attributed to the presence of an elite group that was recognized and supported by provincial leaders and attained sufficient economic and moral stature to command at least the grudging respect of local settlers. Yet such a contrast between the region's leaders and their backcountry counterparts in other colonies does not completely explain the maintenance of order in the upper valley. Both the limited social cohesion of upper valley neighborhoods and the elite's willingness to compromise with popular dissidence played larger roles than did the characteristics of the elite itself. In particular, many of the subsidiary leaders in direct contact with local communities and militia training companies learned to act as intermediaries between the conflicting interests and values of their superiors and popular groups.

On first examination, the differing degrees of stability in the upper valley and the backcountry regions of other colonies seem to reflect the external contacts and social status of the local elites. In contrast to their counterparts in South Carolina and Pennsylvania, the upper valley gentry obtained the support of provincial leaders and thus successfully replicated the political institutions established elsewhere in their colony. Unlike the situation in western North Carolina, local leaders also possessed the economic and moral standing needed to obtain the respect of the common people.

For much of the colonial period, South Carolina authorities ignored their colony's frontier, refusing to establish local governments and thereby denying the region adequate law enforcement and legislative representation. Despite requests from the backcountry, the legislature failed to pass a vagrancy act until 1767. The lack of local courts and jails led to the use of extralegal means to meet the problems of pervasive crime and disorder. During the mid-1760s South Carolina's Regulator movement struck out against the outlaw bands, dissolute hunters, and other groups who threatened the moral, social, and economic order. Not surprisingly, the movement's leaders included many of the backcountry's emerging elite of prosperous planters, for it was they who suffered most from the problems of crime and disorder.[1]

The absence of an established political elite sanctioned by eastern authorities was still more striking in Paxton and the surrounding townships of backcountry Pennsylvania. Since Pennsylvania leaders had no substantial relations with any group of prominent local officeholders on the frontier, they dealt with defense and other problems in the region by contacting Presbyterian ministers, prominent merchants, and other inhabitants with significant outside connections. Paxton's inhabitants met the lack of stable community leadership by immediate, extemporaneous, and often illegal responses to crises. The Paxton Boys' massacre of friendly Indian groups and their march on Phildelphia were part of this recurring pattern.[2]

The upper valley gentry enjoyed much closer relations with provincial authorities. Virginia leaders generally authorized the creation of new counties in the region when sufficient population and a desire for local government developed. New counties, in turn, made possible the establishment of county courts and facilitated the development of the deferential political values that surrounded those courts in eastern Virginia. Moreover, the Patton-Preston and Lewis family groups developed extensive ties with prominent eastern Virginians, as did the Christian family to a lesser degree. Consequently, these families dominated the county surveyorships and other positions appointed by the provincial government, and they used this power, along with their replication of the Virginia county court and its political culture, to maintain control of the region.

Examination of the low economic and moral stature of the elite in backcountry North Carolina suggests another useful contrast with the upper valley. Throughout the eighteenth century, North Carolina's political leaders lacked sufficient wealth to overawe their neighbors decisively. Often they were newly prosperous men, who sought to advance their fortunes with little concern for the restraints of morality or law, and this further reduced public respect for their office. Misbehavior by local officials was especially serious in the backcountry. Fraud and incompetence interfered with the orderly sale of land to new settlers, and many sheriffs and other officials embezzled tax monies, assessed excessive fees, and otherwise abused their offices. These circumstances played a major role in stimulating that colony's Regulator movement.[3]

Upper valley leaders, by contrast, displayed both the economic and moral attributes needed to win some measure of respect from their communities. As noted in chapter 2, justices of the peace possessed substantially more land than the average settler. The more senior justices of the quorum and the region's legislative representatives were still more obviously wealthy. Moreover, despite some significant moral and legal transgressions by individual leaders, the county courts' attention to offensive behavior by justices, lawyers, masters of indentured servants, and other prominent individuals strengthened the moral standing of the upper valley gentry in the eyes of the region's population.

Nevertheless, the attributes and external connections of the upper valley elite do not completely explain the area's relative political stability. Upper valley leaders did use those assets to create a viable set of political institutions and to replicate the deferential culture of their eastern Virginia counterparts. Moreover, they successfully compelled at least a passing acquiescence to those deferential values by common people who came into contact with their institutions. Yet though the absence of integrity, wealth, and cosmopolitan connections may decisively weaken local respect for a ruling class, their presence does not automatically create popular acceptance.[4] To understand why the popular localism of upper valley neighborhoods failed to generate a more decisive clash with elite values, several additional factors must be considered.

Much of the upper valley's relative political stability derived from two sources. First, despite the strength of popular dissidence, the local communities in which it developed possessed only limited social cohesion. Second, in a variety of ways, the gentry compromised with popular groups and partially defused their grievances.

Indeed, the importance of these factors in stabilizing the upper valley suggests a need for closer examination of the internal structure of local communities and the interaction of elite and popular groups elsewhere in the southern backcountry.[5]

Although the residents of upper valley neighborhoods shared common interests and values and a measure of common identity, those neighborhoods lacked sufficient internal unity to provide a basis for sustained opposition to elite authority. Many communities, for example, often proved unable or unwilling to organize cooperative agricultural labor, a common practice at harvest and other times in much of eighteenth-century America.[6] On several occasions militia commanders assumed that the crops of men performing active duty would not be cared for unless those men were allowed to return home or someone was hired to work their farms.[7] In at least one case, frontier settlers refused to work in large groups at harvest time, even though doing so might have protected them from Indian attack.[8] Moreover, though squatters in other parts of the colonial backcountry often created extralegal "fair play" tribunals and used other informal practices to enforce their land claims, no evidence of such communal enforcement efforts in upper valley neighborhoods has come to light. Indeed, in ordering the surveying of his extensive landholdings, speculator Thomas Walker felt it necessary to encourage the squatters living there to resolve any conflicting settlement claims by some form of arbitration. Walker expressed his own disinterest in the specific results of these proceedings, simply hoping that the disputes might be settled amicably.[9] If many local communities lacked enough internal cohesion to cooperate in harvesting crops, defending their land claims, or even protecting themselves from attack, their failure to sustain concerted long-term opposition to elite authority becomes more understandable.

These elements of disunity in upper valley neighborhoods reflected the newness and instability of their populations. As late as the Revolution, settlement in much of the region was still relatively new. Moreover, out-migration to the Carolinas and other frontiers began in the 1750s. The movements of William Preston within the upper valley suggest the possibilities for similar mobility by less prominent settlers. Arriving with his parents and other relatives in 1740, Preston first settled in Beverley Manor in the northern part of the upper valley. In the late 1760s he moved to the south side of the James and in 1774 to the middle New River. Such instability in neighborhood populations obviously impeded the growth of wide-spread networks of social relationships within local communities: many newly arrived settlers fell outside the bounds of those networks, and the networks were weakened by the departure of established members. The turnover in population also inhibited the development of sets of overlaying relationships between individual settlers. In more established communities the gradual accumulation of social relationships—each for a different purpose—strengthened the ties between pairs of longtime residents.[10] In the constantly changing population of upper valley neighborhoods, these sets of relationships had little time to develop. In effect, although the neighborhoods were the primary focus in the social life of common settlers, that social life remained relatively weak, inchoate, and disorganized.

Although the lack of neighborhood cohesion inhibited the development of opposition to elite authority, the willingness of upper valley leaders to make concessions and compromises that diffused popular grievances proved still more important. Even in the elite-dominated county governments, the gentry took measures to reduce popular discontent. The county courts frequently pardoned individuals who offended the courts' dignity when those persons gave indications of penitence and renewed deference. The Augusta court-martial may have had similar intentions in 1747 when it proclaimed that it would fine no one except "those who out of contempt will not comply with the law."[11] In their land investment activities, upper valley leaders often avoided conflicts with squatters living illegally on lands they had purchased. In particular they avoided making new entries for unclaimed land on which squatters already lived.[12] These leaders clearly realized that litigation against a recalcitrant squatter could be more trouble than it was worth, especially if others settled on the land after the first ejection. Some land speculators also recognized that allowing squatters to remain on their property ultimately increased its value.[13]

Compromises and concessions by the upper valley elite were still more important in maintaining support for defense activities. The need for concessions proved particularly great in raising men for active military duty away from their local neighborhoods. Thus William Preston recruited men for the Sandy Creek expedition of 1756 by paying them in advance out of his own pocket. Throughout the colonial period, other officers extended credit to their men or made efforts to expedite their pay.[14] During the raising of the Point Pleasant expedition of 1774, the gentry encouraged enlistments by denying positions of leadership to men who had incurred the enmity of potential recruits. Similarly, regional leaders permitted popular men whom they found personally obnoxious to raise companies.[15] Finally, upper valley leaders sought help with local defense from counties east of the Blue Ridge, hoping that this would reduce popular fears that the launching of the expedition would leave their communities undefended.[16]

Even in the defense of local neighborhoods, upper valley leaders found it necessary to make special concessions and appeals to the common people. The inhabitants of frontier areas often threatened to or actually did flee from their communities when Indian attack seemed imminent. Since such evaluations weakened local defense, militia leaders sought to discourage the flights, in some cases by personal confrontations with fleeing settlers and in others by promising help with local defense. Thus in 1757, William Preston convinced a group of Bullpasture settlers not to flee by promising that a fort would be built at a location of their choice and a company of men maintained there.[17]

During the summer of 1774, William Christian showed a particularly sophisticated perception of the need to deal sympathetically with popular defense attitudes. Settlers in several New River neighborhoods had been repeatedly fleeing from their homes. Most of these evacuees, however, were returning within a few days. Such flights naturally disrupted local defense efforts, and Christian felt they were motivated by unfounded fears. Nevertheless, he remarked to William Preston that it was better to tolerate such temporary evacuations than to risk provoking a more serious reaction by "overpersuading" or too vigorously cajoling and coercing the settlers.[18]

Although many members of the upper valley gentry made concessions to popular interests and values, those leaders who worked closely with local neighborhoods and militia companies often showed particular sympathy and understanding. Some of these local leaders directly challenged the authority of higher officials. Most, however, remained in an intermediary position, articulating the interests and values of their neighborhoods while esteeming and aspiring to the culture and social status of more prestigious members of the elite. Their superiors, in turn, often recognized and consciously exploited the intermediary status of these men in order to maintain popular support for their authority in defense efforts and other areas of public life.

Because they had to maintain local support for their administration of frontier defense, leaders in outlying areas frequently endorsed popular demands for increased protection of their communities. Many of them encouraged or personally financed the construction of forts.[19] At one point in 1756, Governor Robert Dinwiddie complained that Augusta's militia officers "all gladly w'd have forts at each of their Habitations."[20] In some cases frontier leaders tried to persuade county authorities to station soldiers in their neighborhoods.[21] During Dunmore's War and other conflicts, they attempted to obtain more public ammunition for local use, while their superiors often preferred to conserve it for long-range expeditions and other purposes. From the Holston River, Bryce Russell pointedly wrote to William Preston: "We are obliged to you for your advice to Stand our ground and to build forts for our defense. . . . But if we get not a Suply of men and ammunition I think it will be impossible . . . a timely Suply I think would be very necessary[.] A disorder prevented is worth two Cures."[22] Some local leaders openly sympathized with their neighbors' resistance to performing military duty in areas distant from their own communities. In October 1774, for example, Fincastle justice of the peace John Montgomery noted that most of the men from a local training company had left for the Point Pleasant expedition. Thus, he asserted, the community could not raise an additional party to help defend the Holston, "unless Men were to Leave their Wives and Children exposed to the Mercy of the Enemy, which we in reason Cannot Expect."[23]

More important, many of these local officials adopted consensual leadership styles to win popularity in their communities. Several militia officers allowed local settlers to choose the sites for forts.[24] In 1774 Joseph Cloyd stressed his reliance on popular support in assuming command of a militia company on the middle New River, explaining to William Preston that although he was inexperienced he would do his best because the men were "willing that I shod serve in the place." Presumably, if Cloyd acknowledged his reliance on popular support in communicating with Preston, the county lieutenant, he did not use a less consensual approach in dealing with the men themselves. As a captain on the Sandy Creek expedition in 1756, Preston had used the tactic of stressing his reliance on the men of his company to discourage their desertion. During the Seven Years' War, Governor Dinwiddie blamed the indiscipline of the Augusta militia on local officers who succumbed to the wishes of their men. And throughout the colonial period, the leaders of the upper valley militia complained of subordinate officers' failure to maintain authority and discipline and threatened severe penalties for those guilty of such lapses.[25]

Many of the most successful local leaders diverged from the elite culture's emphasis on restraint and dignity and moved toward more emotionally charged and spontaneous personal styles which appealed to popular groups. The Holston River leader William Cocke had a particular gift for gaining support by projecting a vivid self-image. In 1774 he won popular acclaim when he promised that with or without the approval of his superiors, he would raise men in North Carolina to help defend the Holston frontier. In a message to local residents, he pledged that "my life and little all is always Ready to be risked in your defense." Arthur Campbell described Cocke as imprudent and misguided, easily excited, and hungry for action. At one point he explained that he would attempt to pacify Cocke before presenting a disapproving letter from county lieutenant William Preston, since "he will put his own construction on it which is very often wrong ones. He is half-distracted heady." On another occasion Campbell suggested that Cocke be given a special assignment, "as he is so hot for the fatigues of marching." Throughout his life Cocke retained a reputation as an enthusiastic and emotional speaker.[26] Cocke's talent for self-dramatization may have contributed to the tradition that just before the Revolution the royal governor tried to entice him into support of the crown. According to the obviously spurious account, when offered a position as second in command of the British army, Cocke replied that he was a patriot and the king did not have enough money to buy him.[27] Although his colorful leadership style aroused the enmity of Campbell and other superiors, it also apparently contributed to Cocke's success in maintaining popular support.

Other popular leaders also demonstrated this flair for dramatic, spontaneous action. Although some officers in the Staunton area failed to raise full companies for the Point Pleasant expedition, Captain George Mathews quickly filled his. Mathews did his recruiting in his brother's tavern, appealing to the men's pride in their physical strength by ostentatiously marking the height of each recruit on the barroom wall.[28] At the same time, on the upper Holston River, Joseph Drake used dramatic popular appeals to thwart the efforts of other officers to discourage men from serving under him. As Arthur Campbell described it, he was on the verge of winning over Drake's men at a public meeting when Drake and an associate arrived and "according to their normal mode of Whispering one thing and speaking out another put things into confusion." Drake declared "in a clamorous manner he would march the men down [to the expedition's rendezvous point] himself." Ultimately Campbell acquiesced, even providing supplies for Drake's march.[29]

Some of these popular leaders openly confronted the authority of more prestigious members of the gentry. Joseph Drake obviously used his popularity with Holston settlers to challenge Arthur Campbell and other regional leaders. William Cocke not only promised to raise men in North Carolina for defense of the Holston, even if opposed by county officials, but also stridently voiced his resentment of criticisms and slights from superior officers. In 1774 he complained bitterly when he was not appointed to command a company on the Point Pleasant expedition. Later that year he charged William Preston with ingratitude and injustice for criticizing his unauthorized efforts to raise men in North Carolina, arrogantly concluding that "I shall not give my Self the trouble to Justify my Conduct to a man who Condemns me without a hearing." When Arthur Campbell and another official blocked the allocation of public funds to compensate him for provisions given to these unauthorized Carolina recruits, Cocke threatened to appeal the matter to the Virginia assembly.[30]

During the controversy in 1765 over the murder of several Cherokees by the Augusta Boys, another upper valley leader apparently sought to gain popularity by attacking his superiors. According to Andrew Lewis, Peter Hog wrote a proclamation for some of the dissidents, claiming that the murdered Indians were actually from enemy rather than friendly tribes, alleging that Lewis and other Augusta officials were secretly in sympathy with the French, and mockingly offering rewards for their capture. As Lewis saw it, Hog, an attorney and a former officer in the provincial military service, had aided the Augusta Boys "for the sake of making himself popular amongst the Disaffected with a view to increase the number of his clients.[31]

On the abortive Sandy Creek expedition of 1756, some of the

subordinate officers directly challenged the authority of their commander, Andrew Lewis. At least in William Preston's company, the noncommissioned officers served as spokesmen for the starving soldiers who wished to return home. Moreover, several of the company commanders may have supported the dissidents. According to Preston, following the mass desertion that doomed the expedition, "Captain [Obediah] Woodson kept his Company together all Day under a pretense of Marching Down the Country some other way, which was only to Draw one Days Provisions for them." Another officer, Captian John Smith, was later accused of desertion. Perhaps significantly, during the initial organizing of the expedition, Smith and some other men apparently expected that Woodson rather than Andrew Lewis would be appointed the commander.[32]

Because of their dependence on county and provincial authorities for appointments, however, local leaders in the upper valley generally remained in an intermediary position, maintaining divided loyalties to the interests and values of both their communities and their superiors. This was particularly clear in the case of Daniel Smith, a militia leader on the upper Clinch River. On several occasions during Dunmore's War in 1774, he demonstrated sympathy for the localist orientation of the area's residents, appealing in May for gunpowder to be provided more quickly than was being done and requesting in July that additional men from outside his area be brought in to help with local defense. More important, he endorsed the efforts of lower Clinch settlers to have Daniel Boone placed in command of local forts, independent of any control by Holston River superiors. Nevertheless, Smith remained fundamentally loyal to the interests and values of the elite. He repeatedly sought to prevent local settlers from evacuating their neighborhoods when threatened with Indian attack, and he harshly criticized such flights. In the letter requesting more ammunition for his community, he expressed his determination to enforce discipline in his training company by using the provisions of a new militia law if necessary. When he endorsed the petition for Boone's commission, Smith carefully acknowledged to county lieutenant William Preston that the appointment might be improper because another Clinch River officer had greater seniority.[33] Thus, even as he supported popular sentiment, Smith reaffirmed his respect for the gentry's traditional concerns with hierarchy and status.

Ultimately a series of economic and political favors tied Smith to

Preston and other major leaders. By 1773 he had become a deputy surveyor in Fincastle County, an appointment normally requiring the support of county and provincial leaders. During the late colonial and revolutionary years, he often surveyed and collected money for William Preston and the influential land speculator Dr. Thomas Walker of Albemarle County.[34] Throughout those years, Smith moved upward in the militia and civil government of the region.

Another frontier leader, William Russell, also maintained divided loyalties to popular and elite values. Serving as captain of a Clinch River training company and performing active duty in the area, he clearly recognized the need to deal with popular interests in maintaining community support for his defense efforts. To discourage flight from the area, he allowed his company to select the sites for local forts and sought outside help with defense. He also tried to secure active duty with pay for settlers who wanted it. In raising a company for the Point Pleasant expedition, he requested that his soldiers be authorized "to take Horses proportionable to what has been granted to Captain Shelby, *as the Men look for the same Indulgence.*"[35]

In many of his activities, Russell combined the advocacy of popular interests and values with his own pursuit of traditional elite goals. Thus in the spring of 1774, he dispatched several scouts to provide warnings of Indian attack, recognizing that this might appease the fears of local settlers and discourage evacuations. At the same time, he ordered that if no hostile Indians were discovered, the scouts should determine the location of Virginia's border with the Cherokees, information of value to Russell and other upper valley land speculators. Moreover, he instructed the men to avoid provoking a war with nonhostile Indians, not only because of the consequences for the existing settlements but also because such a war would "blast our fairest hopes of Settling the Ohio Country."[36] Similarly, Russell voiced the resentment of Clinch River inhabitants against settlers and leaders from the Holston. In July 1774 he urged that when militiamen were mobilized to defend his area, Clinch rather than Holston settlers be allowed to volunteer for active duty with pay. In advocating these popular interests, however, Russell also expressed his personal disappointment at not receiving an appointment for active duty and his resentment of leaders "with such powerful Connexions as are upon Holston, and New River Waters."[37] Like Daniel Smith, Russell moved into increasingly prestigious military and civil positions in the late colonial and revolutionary periods.

Other local leaders mediated between the interests and values of popular and elite groups in a variety of ways.[38] Indeed, since many men who began their careers in this way ultimately advanced into the upper levels of the gentry, upper valley leaders may well have viewed this intermediary role as an initial stage in a typical career progression within their social class.

Upper valley authorities often recognized the utility of subsidiary leaders in maintaining support for their defense policies. In October 1774, for example, Arthur Campbell promised to allow Daniel Smith to modify or selectively enforce any regulations or orders he made regarding Smith's company. Campbell explained that he felt Smith could better judge the appropriateness of such local orders and regulations and tellingly urged him to "try to humour the Inhabitants as much as you can with justice to the service." Similarly, when William Preston negotiated with a group of Bullpasture settlers to prevent them from fleeing their homes in March 1757, he began these efforts by approaching several community leaders, extracting promises to support his efforts, and only then arranging a meeting of inhabitants to plan the construction of a local fort. Andrew Lewis, Preston's superior, shared this perception of the pivotal role of the Bullpasture community leaders, for he ordered Preston to arrange for the construction of the fort only if those leaders would otherwise remove their families. This reliance on popular local leaders became particularly clear during the organizing of the Point Pleasant expedition, as regional authorities promised commissions to lesser leaders who could deliver substantial numbers of recruits.[39]

Since popular interests and values diverged most decisively from those of the gentry in defense matters, the intermediary function of local leaders was limited in others areas of public life. Nevertheless, on several occasions they played such roles in land disputes between common settlers and major speculators who refused to clarify and thereby limit the extent of their holdings. Thus Robert Doack, who was acting as agent for William Preston, informed Preston of Holston settlers' uneasiness about their land titles and their desire that Preston clarify the location of his own claims in that area. Deputy surveyor Francis Smith found himself drawn unwillingly into similar frictions between Preston and New River settlers when he acceded to demands that he survey a number of claims in the immediate area of Preston's own home.[40] The early New River leader James Calhoun, however, apparently chose to exploit such popular insecurities for his own purposes in the late 1740s and early 1750s when he spread rumors that land magnate James Patton could not give good titles to purchasers of his land. Calhoun was a relatively new member of the elite, being installed as a captain of militia in November 1750 and recommended for membership in the Augusta court the next day. Patton responded with several prosecutions against the Calhoun family, and, for whatever reasons, they ultimately moved to South Carolina, where the family attained political prominence, particularly in the career of John C. Calhoun.[41]

The efforts of the upper valley courts to maintain a network of constables and justices of the peace in all parts of their counties also indicated a recognition of the importance of such intermediary local officials. In their values and leadership styles, some of these office-holders were closer to the populace than to the leading men of the region. Valentine Sevier, for example, was a well-to-do merchant, tavern keeper, and farmer who served as a constable on Smith Creek in the northern part of the upper valley. Yet he was often in trouble with the county court, being arrested in 1747, for example, for inciting a riot in the court yard.[42] Several traditional accounts suggest his flair for dramatic and spontaneous gestures in maintaining his authority, a technique used by William Cocke and other popular militia leaders. When a local bully challenged his authority as constable, Sevier allegedly intimidated the man by lifting both him and his horse over a fence. Similarly, in Sevier's tavern, customers drank from pewter or crockery mugs called noggins, and they ordered drinks by asking for "a noggin to crack." Sevier used the mugs to strike unruly patrons, or as local tradition put it, he "cracked noggins with one of his noggins."[43]

A variety of disparate factors, then, contributed to the upper valley's political and social stability in the colonial period. The economic and moral stature of the region's elite, as well as its connections with provincial leaders, obviously played a part. Yet the willingness of the gentry to compromise with dissidents proved more important in preventing serious disorders. The role of local leaders in mediating between the conflicting values of elite and popular groups proved particularly crucial. Although such men generally respected and aspired to the culture and social status of their superiors, they were willing to compromise with the interests and values of local communities in order to maintain support. When the Revolution came, bringing both growing demands for public support of the war effort and a new republican ideology which legitimized political appeals to the common people, the need for such compromises would become greater still.

CHAPTER FIVE

Toward the Republic

Despite its slow and conservative beginnings in the upper valley, the Revolution transformed the region's political culture. For a time in 1775 and 1776, the discrediting of royal authority threatened to undercut the local structure of power as well. The more lasting changes, however, arose from the continued strength of popular localism and from the growing social and economic demands imposed by the war effort. To maintain their own authority, upper valley leaders made more substantial compromises with popular dissidents than they had before. Eventually they moved toward a new political ethos centering on the values of regionalism, voluntarism, and republicanism.

As the patriot movement emerged in eastern Virginia in 1774 and 1775, upper valley leaders gradually moved to active support of it.[1] Until the end of Dunmore's War late in 1774, they generally followed events from a distance. During the early months of 1775, they began to organize local support for the patriot movement and to articulate that movement's ideology in terms reflecting the distinctive heritage and concerns of their region. Most important of all, upper valley leaders constantly sought to maintain respect for established and legitimate authority.

Throughout 1774, the upper valley gentry followed the developing imperial crisis,[2] but generally with a sense of inability to affect the course of events. Thus Thomas Lewis reacted with helplessness and despair when Governor Dunmore dissolved the Virginia assembly for its condemnation of the Coercive Acts. In reporting Dunmore's action to William Preston, Lewis expressed himself in uncharacteristically millennial terms: "Trusting in prayer in this age of refinement is like to be attended with Ill Consequences[.] I think everything is like to be inverted[.] vices are growing into vertues[.] These seems to be the times foretold when Satan was to be let loose for a certain time." In similar fashion, Reverend John Brown suggested that the British taxation measures, together with an impending Indian war, indicated the unavoidable wrath of God.[3]

The coming of Dunmore's War also reduced the elite's involvement with events to the east. Fincastle legislator William Christian, for example, left Williamsburg as the assembly's confrontation with the governor over the Coercive Acts approached. He did so, moreover, at the direct request of Governor Dunmore, who sought his help in defending the frontiers against Indian attack.[4] When Fincastle County leaders formally pledged their loyalty to the patriot cause in January 1775, they apologized for their delay by explaining that the Indian war had absorbed all of their energies until recently.[5] In February, similar sentiments were expressed at a meeting in Botetourt.[6]

Early in 1775, upper valley leaders began actively to support the patriot movement. Augusta settlers had sent flour to relieve the poor in blockaded Boston the previous summer.[7] On 20 January 1775, a meeting of Fincastle inhabitants endorsed the boycotts and other measures of resistance taken by the Continental Congress, and they elected a committee to enforce those measures within their county. By late February Augusta also had a committee.[8] Although the upper valley apparently sent no representatives to the first Virginia convention in August 1774, all three counties elected delegates to the second convention in spring 1775.[9]

Throughout the upper valley, committees and public meetings not only endorsed the ideology of the patriot movement but also expressed that ideology in ways that reflected the region's background and its special concerns. In the language of the commonwealth tradition, a meeting of Fincastle freeholders denounced the "hand of unlimited and unconstitutional power" which sought to usurp their liberty and property. While affirming their loyalty to the crown and other lawful authority, they refused to submit to "the power of a venal British parliament or the will of a corrupt minister." The Fincastle freeholders also emphasized the special way in which they had won their liberties, enduring the hardships of a mountainous wilderness surrounded by hostile Indians to gain the rights denied to them in Ulster. They listed prominently among their rights "the free exercise of our religion as Protestants," placing it before "our liberties and properties as British subjects."[10] This ranking presumably reflected the concerns of a largely Presbyterian region with an Anglican colony.

Resolutions passed in Augusta and Botetourt counties also showed both the acceptance of patriot ideals and the integration of the upper valley's frontier background and Presbyterian concerns into that ideological perspective. A month after the Fincastle meeting, the Augusta committee drew up instructions for the county's delegates to the second Virginia convention, stating their refusal to surrender their rights "to any minister, to any parliament or any body of men upon earth by whom we are not represented." Like the Fincastle resolutions, the Augusta instructions emphasized that the inhabitants had endured the hardships of a "once savage wilderness" to gain their rights, prominent among which was "the free exercise of the rights of conscience." A meeting of Botetourt freeholders asserted: "A set of miscreants unworthy to administer the laws of Britain's empire had unjustly, cruelly & tyranically . . . invaded our rights." As did Fincastle and Augusta, the Botetourt affirmation of principles reflected a consciousness of the region's historical background. The freeholders requested their representatives to tender "my gun, my tomahawk, my life . . . to the honor of my King and country; but my LIBERTY to range these woods on the same terms my father has done . . . is sacred."[11] By relating the patriot ideology to their region's special experiences and values, the upper valley gentry gave that ideology a heightened relevance for their communities.[12]

During the spring of 1775, upper valley leaders actively supported the Virginia convention's organization of resistance to royal authority. In ordering local militia officers to drill their companies, Andrew Lewis and William Preston cited not only colonial laws but also the extralegal authority of the patriot convention. More important, at the convention's request, Lewis and Preston ordered subordinate officers to collect funds from their men for the expenses of Virginia's delegates to the Continental Congress and for the encouragement of salt-making.[13] In July the Fincastle County committee endorsed Patrick Henry's use of force in his attempt to recover the public gunpowder seized by Governor Dunmore in Williamsburg.[14] In June one traveler described the men at an Augusta militia muster as undisciplined and disorderly but "most thirsty for News . . . from poor Boston" and vociferously committed to the defense of freedom.[15] All of this occurred before the outbreak of fighting in Virginia.

Throughout this period the patriot movement repeatedly expressed its respect for established leaders and legitimate authority. In all three upper valley counties, the leaders of local government dominated the patriot movement.[16] Though these leaders presumably shaped the decisions at all public meetings, in February 1775 the Augusta freeholders explicitly deferred the selection of their convention delegates to "the judgment" of an elite committee. The Botetourt freeholders' resolutions of March 1775 included profuse and deferential expressions of gratitude to their county delegates and to Virginia's representatives at the Continental Congress. Moreover, the resolutions of upper valley patriots all affirmed their support for British authority when exercised within constitutional limits. As late as April 1775, a meeting of Fincastle freeholders lavishly thanked Governor Dunmore for his leadership in the recent Indian war. They noted: "Notwithstanding the unhappy disputes . . . between the Mother Country and the Colonies, in which we have given the publick our sentiments, . . . justice & gratitude, as well as a sense of our duty, induce us collectively to return your lordship our unfeigned thanks."[17]

In much of America, the ideology of revolution unleashed a "contagion of liberty" in which defiance of British dominion encouraged opposition to other forms of established authority.[18] Despite the efforts of upper valley patriots to minimize this subversive potential by constant expressions of respect for local and provincial leaders, the revolutionary ideology provoked challenges to the local power structure. Various groups declared that if British injustice should be resisted, so should injustice originating at home. More important, defiance of royal officials facilitated challenges to local leaders who acted under their authority. During 1775 and 1776, there emerged such a challenge to the authority of William Preston as Fincastle County surveyor.

Several upper valley groups seeking concessions from local and provincial authorities asserted a correlation between their own situation and the patriots' struggle to secure their liberties. In February 1776, for example, settlers living on land which Virginia authorities regarded as belonging to the Cherokees sought recognition and protection from the Virginia government. In explaining that they had chosen a committee "to supervise their publick affairs," they cited as justification "the Pattern of the several Virginia counties" that had formed committees to resist British oppression.[19] Later that year, Fincastle leaders encouraged settlers living beyond the Cherokee border to move back within the settlements to avoid an Indian war. In defending the reluctance of such people to abandon their homes, William Cocke noted that Americans were presently fighting for "the glorious Cause . . . of Liberty & property." Consequently, he hoped that "the good people of Wataugah & Holston would Stand acquited by Every unbiased mind for following so good an Example."[20]

When Augusta freeholders addressed their legislators on the issue of religious freedom in 1776, they revealed the disruptive potential of patriot ideology. Earlier that year the Virginia assembly's Declaration of Rights had removed the legal penalties and restrictions imposed on religious minorities. The declaration, however, failed to eliminate tax support and other advantages given to the Church of England and thus failed to satisfy religious dissenters in the valley and elsewhere. The Augusta address began with a deferential statement of respect for its representatives, commending the legislature's declaration that all men were entitled to the free exercise of their religion. The freeholders also hoped that the legislature's proclamation would lead to full legal equality for all religious denominations. In closing, however, they declared that they would not be bound by any unjust laws the legislature might pass. These last remarks drew criticism when the statement was published in Williamsburg so the freeholders again declared their refusal to acquiesce in unjust laws. They further affirmed that to repeal such laws, measures "beyond a simple remonstrance addressed to the legislators" could be justified.[21] Although these resolutions had no immediate practical consequences in the upper valley, the episode suggests that much of the region's population, both leaders and common people, recognized the potential challenge of revolutionary ideology to the structure of authority within their own society.

In a much more immediate way, the challenge to William Preston's position as Fincastle County surveyor in 1775 and 1776 demonstrated that resentment of royal officials could be turned against local leaders who acted under their direction. The controversy stemmed from Preston's collaboration with Governor Dunmore in a dispute over land claims in Kentucky. Although crown policy since

1763 had restricted settlement beyond the Appalachians, in 1774 several groups began efforts to purchase much of Kentucky from the Cherokees. One such group of Virginia speculators included Fincastle leader William Christian, whose family had often opposed Preston in the past. For a time Christian belonged to another group led by Richard Henderson of North Carolina, and Arthur Campbell, who was emerging as another important rival to Preston, also assisted Henderson's efforts. In March 1775, the Henderson group bought much of Kentucky from the Cherokees.[22]

Preston encouraged Dunmore to block the Henderson group's purchase, informing him of their plans several months before they met with the Cherokees. He warned the governor that settlers on the Henderson tract might not pay quitrents and might not acknowledge the jurisdiction of Virginia or the authority of the crown. Preston also urged Dunmore to provide for sale of the land within the Henderson tract by officials of the Virginia government.[23] Presumably, Preston's concern stemmed in part from fear that he and his assistants would lose the fees to be made from surveying in Kentucky if the region fell outside his jurisdiction as Fincastle County surveyor. He also apparently feared that Henderson's claims would endanger his own unregistered claims and surveys in Kentucky, as well as those of his friends and associates.[24]

In March 1775 Dunmore declared the Henderson claims invalid and instructed Preston to begin surveying in Kentucky according to a system that overturned existing Virginia land practices. Under the previous policy, the individual purchaser paid specified fees and personally selected the land to be surveyed. Dunmore now directed Preston to survey tracts of one hundred to one thousand acres and then auction them off to the highest bidder. This meant that purchasers would lose the power to select the most valuable tracts, and the open auctions would presumably lead to higher prices. Preston had known since at least June 1774 that the crown would insist on these procedures when western surveying was resumed. Thus his motives in promoting Kentucky surveying remain unclear. He may have assumed that through his role in the auction process, he could protect the prior claims of his friends and himself. Or he may have hoped to delay returning the surveys to the provincial government and ultimately dispense with the auctions.[25] In any case, although the Virginia patriot convention condemned Dunmore's actions, Preston dispatched his assistants to begin surveying.[26] Moreover, as late as June 1775, Preston wrote to the Cherokee chiefs indicating

Dunmore's displeasure with their sale to the Henderson group and expressing his own support of crown policy and authority.[27]

Since the actions of Dunmore and Preston threatened both to undermine the claims of the Henderson group and to raise the price of western land through the new auction process, several upper valley leaders launched a vigorous opposition. William Christian and William Russell urged Kentucky settlers to prevent surveying by Preston's assistants. In July the Fincastle patriot committee, which Christian chaired, petitioned the Virginia convention to stop the surveying. They not only complained that selling the land at auction was unjust but also charged that Preston's assistants were making private surveys for favored individuals.[28] In making these accusations, the committee apparently deceived Preston in several respects. They gave him no notice that they planned such measures, and Christian actively discouraged him from attending the meeting at which the petition was approved. Although Christian later claimed not to have known of the proposal prior to that meeting, he also failed to consult with Preston before sending the petition on to the convention.[29] Apparently Arthur Campbell, also a Preston rival, supported these efforts, for his close associate Reverend Charles Cummings played a central role in the committee's actions.[30] Ultimately the Virginia convention refused to condemn Preston, but it also ordered that no surveys be made under Dunmore's proclamation.[31]

Although this controversy centered around surveying policies, it broadened as various rivals exploited Preston's ties with royal authority to undermine his standing with the upper valley populace and the Virginia patriot government. Rumors spread in several neighborhoods that Preston continued to support the crown and that he was forwarding dangerous correspondence from the royal governor to the Cherokees. From the Staunton area, Reverend John Brown reported that these rumors had reached him and that he was searching his correspondence for letters demonstrating Preston's patriotism.[32] Similar reports circulated on the Cowpasture, and in September 1775 one county's patriot committee felt compelled to investigate Preston's conduct.[33] A year later Arthur Campbell was still spreading rumors of Preston's disloyalty to the patriot cause, probably to advance his successful campaign against Preston for the state senate.[34] As late as 1796, rumors of Preston's disloyalty retained sufficient currency that a political rival could use them against Preston's son Francis in a campaign for the U.S. House of Representatives.[35]

Nevertheless, these attacks on William Preston did little lasting damage to his political standing. Within a year he was back on relatively good terms with two of his principal antagonists. William Christian made plans for social visits with Preston on at least two occasions during the summer of 1776.[36] In August William Russell, another former antagonist, agreed to deliver to Preston some crucial information dealing with the efforts to block Henderson's claims to Kentucky lands. The rapprochement was particularly striking because the Henderson controversy had originally provoked the campaign against Preston.[37] In 1776 Preston decisively defeated another rival, Arthur Campbell, by obtaining the position of Washington County surveyor for his newly arrived Irish relative Robert Preston. Several years earlier, William Madison, an Augusta County leader and brother of a professor at the College of William and Mary, had obtained the college's promise of a surveyorship whenever a new county was created. Although the Prestons obtained the position from Madison by promising to pay him part of the surveyor's fees, William Preston's connections made the deal possible and allowed Robert Preston to keep the position once obtained. Arthur Campbell and the Washington County Court strenuously protested after the announcement of the appointment, submitting several petitions to the provincial government. Although such protests by a county court normally would have prevailed, Robert Preston was able to retain the surveyorship. For a man who had arrived from Ireland only in 1773 to obtain so lucrative a post against the wishes of Washington County leaders clearly indicates the continuing prestige and influence of William Preston in the upper valley and in eastern Virginia.[38]

Despite this moderate beginning, the Revolution ultimately transformed the upper valley's political culture. Once the war began to affect the area directly, popular attachments to local neighborhoods and localistic defense priorities again challenged the gentry's ability to implement the policies of state and regional authorities. During the Cherokee hostilities in 1776 and following the murder of a friendly Shawnee leader by militiamen the next year, this challenge became particularly acute. By the end of the 1770s, the growing human and economic costs of the war effort had greatly intensified popular resentment.

During the Cherokee war of 1776, outlying communities used the threat of evacuation to obtain greater assistance in local defense. In May the Cherokees warned settlers on the valley's southern frontier to abandon their communities or face attack.[39] Despite the efforts of militia leaders to dissuade them, many inhabitants in exposed areas began preparations to flee. In several of these cases, settlers promised to stay if county and state authorities would supply them with gunpowder, and local leaders urged their superiors to meet these demands to prevent the evacuation of their neighborhoods. Anthony Bledsoe, for example, reported to Fincastle County lieutenant William Preston that "the Inhabitants generally agree to stay if Powder can be procured though I really fear the people will brake if we cannot give some encouragement of that kind. . . . If it is possible to spair this Quarter any more powder, pray do it."[40] In July settlers collected at Fort Chiswell on the New River criticized William Russell's insistence that all public gunpowder of usable quality be reserved for militiamen serving on active duty in the area. According to local leaders, if more powder was not provided to the settlers themselves, they were likely to flee.[41]

As valley leaders mobilized forces to defend the frontier and to launch an expedition against the Cherokee towns, popular resistance developed in communities less directly exposed to attack. In June William Christian warned Preston to order at least a third of Fincastle's militiamen to be ready for immediate service, pointing out that "if you order a third perhaps not more than a fourth can be had." The next month William Russell and other officers encountered resistance to frontier duty in many Fincastle militia companies.[42] As during the colonial period, much of this opposition arose from commitments to local neighborhoods. Even in areas removed from the frontier, settlers were reluctant to leave their homes unprotected while they performed military duty. Militiamen from Fincastle and Botetourt counties feared that if they marched south to meet the Cherokees, Shawnee and Delaware war parties would attack from the northwest in their absence.[43] On the New River in September, James Robertson felt it was best not to draft men from two militia companies that were close to the Holston River because of recent Indian attacks on the Holston frontier. Many settlers also refused to remain on duty during harvest time. William

Russell reported on July 7 that the New River militiamen serving with him were about to return home to harvest their crops. Two weeks later he encountered similar problems with another group serving on the lower Holston.[44]

The next year a clash between elite and popular attitudes toward Indian diplomacy developed when upper valley militiamen murdered Cornstalk, a friendly Shawnee leader. In an effort to prevent war between his tribe and the United States, Cornstalk was visiting the garrison at Point Pleasant on the Ohio. During his stay, other Indians killed a Rockbridge militiaman who was hunting across the river. Cornstalk claimed that he knew nothing about the attack, and Matthew Arbuckle, the fort commander, tried to protect him. Nevertheless, the slain militiaman's comrades killed Cornstalk and two other Indians in cold blood.[45] Hoping to avoid war with the Shawnees, the Virginia government condemned Cornstalk's murder and insisted that upper valley leaders bring the murderers to justice.[46] Although state authorities identified James Hall and several other men as the instigators of Cornstalk's murder, no witnesses would testify against them in the upper valley courts. Apparently Rockbridge County leaders recognized the strength of popular sentiment and the futility of these prosecutions, for the court records indicate no attempt to summon witnesses beyond having the sheriff stand at the courthouse door and call for all persons who would give evidence to come forward. Ultimately the crime went unpunished.[47] Thus, as they had in the colonial period, popular groups refused to accept the gentry's distinctions between friendly and unfriendly Indians: common settlers sought to prevent or avenge attacks on their communities and their neighbors regardless of the implications for Indian diplomacy and defense beyond their local neighborhoods.[48]

Throughout the early years of the Revolution, upper valley leaders struggled against popular resistance to their defense policies. In 1777, for example, Augusta and Botetourt leaders could raise only three or four companies for an expedition against the Shawnees. The Greenbrier settlements recruited a full company only because John Stuart and other officers agreed to serve as enlisted men on this occasion.[49] When a large Indian party marched up the Greenbrier River the next year, both William Fleming in Botetourt County and William Preston in Montgomery found it necessary to ask the counties east of the Blue Ridge for reinforcements. Preston and Fleming clearly recognized the futility of efforts to mobilize substantial numbers of their own militia. At one point Fleming wrote despairingly to Preston, "Will not self-preservation induce Your People on this pressing occasion to turn out . . . I am afraid nothing will."[50]

In many cases resistance to military duty reflected a primary commitment to local communities rather than to county, state, or nation. Holston residents refused to aid in the defense of the adjacent Clinch valley in 1778, and at least one Holston leader complained when similar drafts were attempted the next year.[51] Drafting men during critical periods in the crop cycle also remained difficult: during spring planting in 1780, Walter Crockett predicted that New River settlers would refuse to make even a short march to disarm the Tories in several neighboring militia companies.[52] Much of the opposition to the war effort apparently stemmed from distrust of state and national authorities. Thus in July 1776 William Preston reported that settlers on the Fincastle frontier were reluctant to sell supplies for an expedition against the Cherokee towns because they remembered the Virginia government's delay in paying them for the Point Pleasant expedition of 1774.[53] In Botetourt County in 1780, a rumor spread that the British were retreating into Charleston and that the American army in the Carolinas therefore needed no reinforcements. The rumor, which greatly hampered recruiting efforts in Botetourt, apparently indicated a widespread belief that state and national authorities would needlessly draft men for service far from their homes.[54]

By the end of the 1770s, the costs of the war effort in taxes, manpower, inflation, and food shortages further weakened popular support for it. Throughout the colonial period the Virginia government had relied almost exclusively on per capita taxation. In 1775, however, a new law placed taxes on carriages and land and increased the poll tax rate. The state imposed additional taxes in 1777, 1779, and 1781.[55] Upper valley settlers particularly disliked the new per capita taxes, payable in grain and other commodities. In 1779 and 1780, groups from Rockingham, Montgomery, and Botetourt counties petitioned the legislature, arguing that poor harvests and the destruction of crops by Indians made payment impossible. Perhaps significantly, in 1780 the Rockbridge court refused to appoint collectors for the commodity taxes, claiming that it had received no notice of the new legislation until after the deadline for making the appointments.[56]

By 1780 the war's demand for manpower created severe problems as the Virginia government attempted to draft one out of every fifteen militiamen throughout the state for the Continental army. These efforts had particularly serious effects in the upper valley, where the militia was also responsible for frontier defense.[57] Moreover, since many people fled from exposed parts of the frontier, military obligations bore still more heavily on those who remained. Even as early as 1777, Botetourt leaders protested that they could not comply with a request for two hundred men to serve in an expedition to the west "as the County has been considerably drained of men."[58]

Further difficulties arose from the inflation created by the war. In 1778 many Montgomery militiamen who refused to perform active duty claimed that the pay was not enough to support them.[59] By 1779 circulating currency had so thoroughly lost its value that, according to William Christian, "None will buy but as distress drives them to it & none will sell but at the highest Rates; and every sale of any Property makes it dearer."[60] The next year a Greenbrier County group petitioned the legislature to raise the pay of scouts sent out to provide warning of Indian attack. According to the petition, inflation had so devalued the current wage levels that scouts could no longer be hired. This inflation may have been particularly alarming to small farmers who had only recently entered the market economy. Hemp cultivation had produced this transition in the northern part of the upper valley only in the 1760s. With its growing demand for hemp and other products, the Revolution brought the initial stages of commercialization to the rest of the region. Not surprisingly, some settlers insinuated that wealthy creditors who heavily discounted revolutionary currency were traitors to their country.[61]

In many frontier communities the destruction of property by hostile Indians led to severe food shortages. Following the Cherokee warfare of 1776, three upper valley leaders asked Governor Henry to send food to settlers on the Holston and Clinch to avoid famine, and food from Augusta County and elsewhere was distributed in some distressed portions of Washington County. Daniel Smith reported from the Clinch frontier in June 1778 that there was not enough food in his area to supply the small number of militiamen helping with local defense. In May 1780 Montgomery settlers asserted in a petition that Indian attacks, combined with bad weather, had prevented them from raising good crops for several years. In November, William Preston argued that food shortages in

Montgomery made it impossible for that county to maintain the prisoners taken at Kings Mountain. Settlers and leaders from less exposed areas often complained that the provisioning of expeditions against the Indians and the British had seriously depleted food supplies in their communities.[62]

In a letter to the governor in November 1778, William Preston summed up the problems facing the upper valley's wartime leaders. General Lachlan McIntosh of the Continental army had asked Preston to mobilize two hundred Montgomery militiamen for six months of service in an expedition against the Delaware Indians. Preston argued that the request was beyond his capacity, pointing out that his county had recently been unable to raise fifty men for service at Fort Randolph on the Kanawha. Single men, he noted, refused to perform active duty and fled to either the Carolinas or the nearby mountains "from whence they cannot be drawn." Married men could not be expected to leave their families defenseless for six months. According to Preston, several years of warfare had produced such food shortages that soldiers' families would go hungry in their absence. Nor could the county provide the men with clothing, tents, and other supplies for their march. Most important of all, Preston feared that attempts to enforce the order would lead the drafted men and their relatives into armed resistance, which "would be too formidable to quell with the remainder of the Militia if they even could be prevailed on to engage in the Business." While urging the governor to countermand these orders, Preston promised to use his greatest efforts to raise the men until he received new orders "to which I shall Pay the most implicit Obedience."[63]

In response to these problems, the upper valley gentry made frequent concessions to popular localism. Many leaders increasingly relied on voluntarism in their attempts to maintain support for the war effort. They also became more critical and contentious in their dealings with state authorities. Ultimately, upper valley leaders would fuse these new attitudes and values into a more comprehensive republican political ethos.

Substantial concessions to popular dissidents began early in the war. During the first four months of 1776, the Fincastle County committee showed particular sensitivity to the problems of outlying neighborhoods. In January and again in April, they created new militia companies in communities that found it difficult to muster with their assigned training units.[64] In February they decided that the hardships imposed by distance and terrain, along with the threat of Indian attack, made it advisable to postpone the coming general muster of the county militia.[65] The Cherokee hostilities of 1776 led many officers in frontier areas to support popular demands for men and ammunition to assist in neighborhood defense.[66] Upper valley officers also dealt perceptively with the local orientations that prompted militiamen to resist performing active duty.[67] William Campbell suggested evacuating women and children from the frontier to relieve militiamen's anxieties about leaving their families undefended. During the planning of the campaign against the Cherokee towns, William Preston urged state authorities to assign troops to guard the frontiers while the expedition was gone. In September 1776 James Robertson made a striking compromise with popular attitudes on military leadership. During Dunmore's War in 1774, Robertson had bitterly criticized undisciplined militiamen, referring to them in his correspondence as troublesome, "distracted," "Hulking young dogs," and "Sons of Bitches." Apparently insubordination among his soldiers was increased because of his rigidly authoritarian style of leadership. Now Robertson informed William Preston that he had drafted a number of New River militiamen for frontier defense but had not appointed their officers "as I could not Imagine who would be most agreeable to the soldiers."[68]

These concessions in defense matters continued in the following years. In 1777, for example, Evan Shelby criticized a plan to position soldiers and public ammunition in areas well inside the frontier. According to Shelby, settlers on the Clinch frontier deserved to have the ammunition and soldiers placed among them, and they should not be forced to abandon their families and crops to perform active duty themselves.[69] In 1779 John Coalter pointed out the threat of Indian attack against his community and argued that local citizens should not be drafted to defend other areas. When he dispatched Montgomery militiamen to assist in suppressing the Tories of western North Carolina in 1780, William Preston realistically warned a Carolina leader that the men could not remain long on duty during harvest time.[70]

As popular support for the war effort declined, militia leaders increasingly tried to minimize opposition to military service by using volunteers rather than conscripts.[71] Thus when his neighborhood received reports of a threatened Cherokee attack and the impending evacuation of nearby communities, Captain Aaron

Lewis mustered his upper Holston River militia company. Rather than ordering preparations for war, Lewis "made a motion for Men," and thirty settlers volunteered to be ready for immediate service whenever necessary. The rest of Lewis's company promised to serve if needed. The next year, William Preston directed William Buchanan to raise a company for active duty by recruiting volunteers if possible. Although he promised a draft if necessary, Preston felt that Buchanan and his subordinate officers had sufficient popularity to raise volunteers. Significantly, Preston appointed Joseph and Ephraim Drake as Buchanan's lieutenant and ensign.[72] In 1774 Joseph Drake had exploited his local popularity to raise an unauthorized company for the Point Pleasant expedition in direct defiance of upper valley leaders. Now, to obtain volunteers, regional leaders were compromising with this popular rebel. For a time in 1779, Montgomery patriot leaders apparently tried to use voluntary popular support as a means of combating groups of horse thieves and counterfeiters who were at least loosely tied to the loyalist cause. They did this by drawing up a statement to be signed by the members of particular militia training companies. In the statement, the signatories promised to inform against such criminals and to provide all possible assistance in their capture. Furthermore, they pledged to require that all strangers who came to live among them give satisfactory evidence of their allegiance to the law and the patriot cause.[73] By 1780 the war's manpower demands had become so heavy that the Augusta court-martial began to require the captains of training companies to obtain the consent of a majority of their men before exempting anyone from military duty.[74] Thus the redistribution of military obligations was made dependent upon the voluntary consent of the men affected.

As important as this preference for using volunteers was upper valley leaders' growing realization that, by celebrating the voluntary devotion of their men to the cause, they could strengthen the discipline of their troops and the support of the general public. In 1778 the campaign to raise a small military force for service along the Ohio River demonstrated the multiple uses upper valley leaders had found for voluntarism. Each of the young men who agreed to perform this duty signed the group's Articles of Association, thus affirming the voluntary nature of the service. Moreover, each man explicitly agreed to suffer the loss of public reputation if he broke his pledge to serve. Before the company marched, William Preston instructed the commander to report any offenders so that they "may be known to their country & suffer that Infamy which such Delinquents deserve."[75] Thus revolutionary leaders used the dignity of voluntary pledges not only to attract recruits but also to maintain their discipline once recruited. In addition, they relied on the public's respect for voluntary devotion to the patriot cause to sustain their enforcement efforts.

The war experience also transformed the upper valley gentry's relations with state authorities. As the Virginia government confronted the threat of British invasion in the east and contributed to the national war effort, it became more critical of requests for assistance with frontier defense. Thus Governor Henry informed William Preston in September 1777 that if new hostilities began, the state would order no expedition against the Indians. He added that militia from neighboring counties could provide assistance only if upper valley forces proved too weak. Henry's insistence that the frontier militia "must fight if invaded" presumably reflected his low opinion of their past performance.[76] The cold-blooded murder of the Shawnee leader Cornstalk by upper valley militiamen the next month provoked especially strong criticism from Williamsburg. Not only did Governor Henry announce that the killers deserved no protection from Indian violence, he also warned that the rest of the upper valley population could expect no assistance from the state in the future if the murderers were not punished. Finally, Henry refused to authorize offensive operations against the Shawnee territories, saying that under the circumstances such measures could not be justified.[77]

In response to this criticism, upper valley leaders became more insistent and contentious in dealing with the state government. After Cornstalk's murder, Preston appealed to Virginia authorities for defense assistance, noting that if frontier inhabitants fled their homes, Shawnee raiding parties would penetrate farther east, perhaps even across the Blue Ridge. In March 1778 Preston and William Fleming sought several measures from the state government to facilitate regional defense efforts. They asked that an additional fort be established on the Kanawha River beyond the Greenbrier settlements and that the militia to man it be drawn from counties less exposed to Indian attack than their own. Recognizing the reluctance of upper valley settlers to sell provisions to the government on credit, they also requested the appointment of commissaries with adequate money to purchase food for the militia serving at the new fort and on the Montgomery County frontier.[78] On several occasions that year Preston, Fleming, and other regional leaders opposed the state's efforts to draft local men for expeditions in the Ohio valley.[79] Stephen Trigg, an upper valley legislator, also put pressure on Virginia officials in defense matters, as a letter to Preston in May 1778 reveals:

The Letter you Wrote the Governor by McClenachan Was laid before the Council, I waited on the Govr afterwards to know their determination, which was that you must depend on your own Mill[a] for that it was thought too hard to draw Militia Men from this Side of the Mountain in the Spring of the Year to Guard those on the Other Side, When there own Might do the business. But after talking to the Govr on the Subject, he agreed to try it again, & today laid it before the Council, who heard What I had to say on the Subject, but Wou'd not even then Say whether you were to Call on those Counties or not but rather said Nothing at all. I this evening waited on the Governor again & he has promised me that he will write tonight empowering you to Call for Men from the Adjoining Counties if you find the Necessity of the times require it which Letter I shall wait on him for tomorrow morning.[80]

Trigg made three separate appeals but apparently won his point.

These changes in the attitudes and values surrounding frontier defense apparently encouraged the upper valley gentry to greater acceptance of the Revolution's new republican values. Their growing hostility toward state authorities could now be rationalized by portraying their region as a more virtuous republican society than eastern Virginia. Moreover, reliance on volunteers as the basis of military security became an asset in a political order that celebrated the people's uncoerced devotion to the public good. William Preston's proposal for recruiting a corps of volunteer riflemen in 1780 and 1781 epitomized the new political ethos.

According to revolutionary Americans, their country exemplified a particular form of polity and society: the republic. In a republic, they affirmed, political power belonged to the entire people rather than to a monarch or an aristocracy. Since all power lay with the people, however, the preservation of liberty created special problems. According to eighteenth-century Anglo-American political thought, the attempts of rulers to gain more power threatened liberty in all polities. In a republic, this problem was greater still: the selfishness and contentiousness of the entire population who shared power tended to produce chaos and undermine political order. This disorder, it was believed, would eventually lead the people to accept a dictatorship in order to regain stability. Therefore, republics could survive only when their people remained devoted to the public good rather than to divisive private interests and only when they remained vigilant in defense of their liberties.

In wartime, such thinkers argued, republics should rely on untrained but public-spirited citizen-soldiers. Despite its inefficiencies, the militia system was preferable to the dangerously authoritarian discipline of a professional standing army. Standing armies, moreover, were normally recruited from the poorest, least virtuous, and most politically manipulable social classes. The exacting ideal of the republican citizen-soldier was most easily achieved in societies that shunned competition, luxuries, and individual self-enrichment. Past history suggested that this was most often accomplished in small mountainous polities like the cantons of Switzerland.[81]

As frictions with state authorities grew, upper valley leaders increasingly used this republican ideology to portray their mountainous region as politically and morally superior to the east. Throughout the continent, revolutionary Americans lamented their devotion to private interests and their evasion of taxation and military obligations, seeing these failings as threats to republican virtue and the patriot cause.[82] Although upper valley leaders frequently criticized their militia's refusal to serve, they most often described the loss of virtue as an eastern phenomenon. Thus when Thomas Lewis acknowledged in a letter of July 1779 that "disipation and a wanton abuse of Public credit" were common in the valley, he reserved his most severe condemnation for the Continental Congress's alleged betrayal of trust: "In a future state no duration of fire & Brimstone to which they can be consigned can burn out the Criminal Stain[.] O! Honesty, Integrity O! Love of Country, whither hast thou fled." Many upper valley militiamen failed to serve in the Carolina campaign in 1780, but regional leaders more often noted the moral dimensions of such failures in eastern Virginia. Thus John Brown, Jr., reported from Williamsburg in March that public spirit was "almost exhausted & a sordid spirit of gain possesses the public attention." In July he lamented that "the want of Men, Money & Provisions & still more of Public Virtue & Patriotism is universal[.] a melancholy lethargick disposition pervades all Ranks in this part of the Country; they appear as if determin'd to struggle no more." In a letter to Martin Armstrong of western North Carolina in August, William Preston expressed the hope that recent military defeats would arouse "the Neighboring States . . . from their late languor." In any case, Preston added, he and Armstrong should continue their own efforts to defend the patriot cause.[83] Thus Preston too believed that the primary moral failures were occurring not in the backcountry of Virginia and North Carolina but in the more developed parts of America.

Especially after the victory won by backcountry militia at Kings Mountain in October 1780, upper valley leaders identified with and celebrated their region, asserting that its mountainous frontier environment was particularly conducive to the spartan virtues demanded by a republic at war. Thus Arthur Campbell promised Governor Thomas Jefferson in February 1781 that Washington County would "turn out with its usual ardor" to support General Nathanael Greene's army in the Carolinas. Campbell went on to lament the eastern Virginia militia's failure to "act in the same manner."[84] State and national leaders also began to praise the bravery and virtue of the frontier or mountain militia, presumably as an appeal to regional pride, when they requested upper valley officials to send them reinforcements.[85] In the spring of 1781, William Preston and other upper valley leaders urged the recruiting of a corps of volunteer riflemen in their region, asserting in their proposal that "as Mountains has always been friendly to liberty, it perticularly becomes Inhabitants thereof to use that power which God, and the nature of their Situation, have providentially put into their hands."[86]

This regional pride also may have influenced the creation and preservation of an anecdote that later appeared in a memoir of Reverend William Graham. During the British invasion of 1781, after the Virginia legislature had fled from Charlottesville to Staunton, they received word that Banastre Tarleton's British troops were advancing toward them again. The legislature immediately dispersed, taking no measures to repel the invaders. Graham happened to be traveling into Staunton that day, and he encountered several fleeing assemblymen. When he learned what had happened, Graham insisted that the men separate and notify all militia officers along the roads to the south. By the next morning a sizable body of Augusta and Rockbridge militia had assembled at Rockfish Gap, "determined to allow no hostile foot to enter their borders with impunity." When word arrived that Tarleton was retreating, some of the men went to another gap which they suspected the British might try to use. Others advanced in pursuit of the enemy and joined the marquis de Lafayette's American forces, "but finding the campaign was likely to be a protracted one, they did not continue with him very long."[87] Thus the anecdote portrayed the superiority of western to eastern Virginia, contrasting the cowardice and indecision of eastern legislators with the determination and bravery of Graham and the western militia. Other similar stories about this episode apparently circulated in the upper valley in the postrevolutionary decades.[88] Strikingly, in the Graham anecdote, the militia's refusal of long-term service with Lafayette appeared not as a failing but rather as proper behavior for the mountain country's citizen-soldiers.

Upper valley leaders also increasingly associated voluntarism and other aspects of their defense efforts with the moral attributes required in a virtuous republic. Anticonscription petitions, presumably written by literate leaders, affirmed their devotion to the patriot cause and emphasized that other forms of military service were preferable for them and their republic. Serving as riflemen, they could provide their own clothing and weapons, and since the "exact discipline" of a standing army would be unnecessary in such service, shorter tours of duty would be effective. Laws that authorized conscription and the hiring of substitutes for military service gave unfair privileges to wealthy persons and were "repugnant . . . to the Nature and spirit of a Republican Government." Such a polity was best maintained by encouraging in its citizens the virtue of voluntarily contributing to the defense of their country.[89]

The efforts of William Preston and other upper valley leaders to raise a corps of volunteer riflemen for the Carolina campaign showed how fully they had absorbed the new republican values. In August or September of 1780, Preston and a group of Montgomery militia officers proposed that the upper valley counties recruit five hundred volunteer riflemen to serve as an independent body of light infantry, responsible only to their own leader and to General Horatio Gates, who commanded the American forces in the Carolinas. The Montgomery officers sent the proposal to the state government for approval. Such regional leaders as George Skillern, William Fleming, and Andrew Lewis also endorsed the plan.[90]

Several features of the proposal evoked the ideal of the public-spirited citizen-soldier produced by a mountain republic. An enlistment statement drawn up by the leaders proclaimed that the recruits were "motivated by an utter abhorrence for slavery and an innate Love of liberty." Significantly, the quoted phrase replaced the more innocuous original wording: "having the sanction and approbation of our own government."[91] Not the authorization of government but their own love of liberty would motivate the volunteers. Although the soldiers would be paid and supplied out of public funds, each one was to provide his own rifle and other weapons, again suggesting the ideal of the citizen-soldier who rushed quickly into service at times of public alarm.[92] Unlike the soldiers of professional standing armies, whose loyalty was maintained through discipline and intimidation, the upper valley volunteers pledged that if they failed to serve they would forfeit their honor and reputation in the eyes of their countrymen.[93] Pride in the upper valley's superior republican virtue appeared in the revised proposal for raising men in the spring of 1781 which asserted that "Mountains has always been friendly to liberty."[94]

Even the failure of the volunteer plan stemmed in part from the upper valley's new republican values. In approving the raising of men, the state government imposed several new conditions. Only two companies were to carry their own rifles; the rest would be furnished with muskets. Although upper valley leaders William Campbell and William Christian were to be the commanders, the corps would fall under the authority not only of the southern army commander but also of any other officers he might designate. Citing the press of "domestic affairs," Campbell declined the appointment.[95] William Christian's refusal, however, clearly showed his rejection of the requirements imposed by the state. In part Christian resented the state's insistence that he be under the authority of any officer specified by the southern commander. Since many of these officers had previously served under Christian's command or had held ranks inferior to his own, Christian considered this a personal insult. More important, he felt that this provision, combined with the state's requirement that muskets be issued to most of the men, would reduce the moral stature of the entire corps. Rather than being independent riflemen and virtuous citizen-soldiers, they would be forced into the authoritarian structure of the standing army and reduced to a position "no better than the mixed multitude picked up for the regular service."[96] Thus Christian's refusal reflected not only his concern with personal status but also his insistence that the upper valley's citizen-soldiers not lose their independence from and moral superiority to the dangerously unrepublican standing army.

The subsequent actions of state officials made it clear that they took these objections seriously. They quickly agreed that all of the upper valley recruits could serve as riflemen. In a letter to William Campbell, the most likely commander of the force, Governor Jefferson attempted to allay concerns about the soldiers being placed under the authority of Continental army officers, assuring him that the intention was simply to make the volunteers part of an independent corps of frontiersmen under the command of General Daniel Morgan.[97] When valley militiamen were mobilized to meet a British invasion of eastern Virginia the next year, state authorities promised that those who came as riflemen would serve as a separate corps under their own officers.[98] And before reassigning this force to Greene's army, Governor Jefferson insisted that the men consent to this change.[99] Despite the ultimate failure of the proposal for a volunteer rifle corps, these actions by state officials suggest their recognition of the growing support for the interrelated values of regionalism, voluntarism, and republicanism in the upper valley.

The transformation of values which the Revolution produced in the upper valley can be seen as the reverse of the changes experienced by many leaders of the emerging nation. Charles Royster has suggested that Americans began the Revolution confident in their ability to sustain the virtue required by a republic and to prosecute the war as citizen-soldiers. Yet as selfishness and corruption grew and the public devotion to the war effort waned, many national leaders moved away from the initial republican ethos. Increasingly, they acknowledged the need for a stronger, more coercive government and for the recognition of a republican elite, distinguished by ability, virtue, and dedication to the patriot cause. Ultimately their dismay at the popular betrayal of the Revolution would move many of these men into the Federalist party.[100]

In the upper valley, the war effort pushed backcountry leaders toward rather than away from the Revolution's republican ethos. The region's patriot leaders initially emphasized the maintenance of respect for traditional authority. Yet the continued strength of popular localism and the growing social and economic demands imposed by the war pushed these leaders toward more substantial concessions to popular dissidence, greater reliance on voluntarism, and increasing friction with state authorities. Ultimately the political and moral values of the republican ethos provided a unifying rationale for the new methods of governance.

The republican ideology's inherent ambiguities, however, limited the changes it had created by the early 1780s. Although power rested with the people in all republics, the relationship between the people and their rulers was less certain. Some revolutionaries felt that the decisions of their leaders should directly reflect the will of the people. Others hoped that the citizens of a republic would select the most virtuous and capable among them as leaders and leave most public decisions to their superior judgment. Such leaders might not be a traditional aristocracy of wealth and family, but they would be an aristocracy nonetheless.[101] For upper valley leaders who considered themselves a republican aristocracy of virtue and talent, traditional concerns with deference and status remained substantially consistent with the new political order.[102] Nevertheless, some men in the region espoused more radical conceptions of republicanism, and their influence would grow in the coming years.

CHAPTER SIX

The Tory Challenge

The most serious challenge to patriot authority in the upper valley arose from the Tory movement during the years around 1780. In its pattern of development, the magnitude of its support, and the ethnic composition of its membership, upper valley loyalism differed from the other popular unrest of the colonial and revolutionary years. Yet in the interests and values that shaped the movement, as well as the attitudes that contributed to its failure, loyalism shared many attributes of popular localism. As with other aspects of the war effort, defeating the Tories pushed upper valley leaders to greater acceptance of popular political values.

Little Tory sentiment appeared in the upper valley during the early years of the Revolution. By 1779 and 1780, however, a substantial and organized loyalist movement emerged along the New River and in other communities. The movement seems to have been centered among German and Welsh settlers rather than among the Scotch-Irish and English who dominated the region.

During the first two years of the war, loyalism appeared chiefly in minor isolated incidents. In October 1775 the Augusta County committee found Reverend Alexander Miller guilty of repeatedly slandering the patriot movement. Four months later, the Fincastle committee charged two men with opposition to patriot authority.[1] During the summer of 1776, Fincastle leaders accused several people of unfriendliness toward the American cause, refusal to perform militia duty, communication with Tories living among the Cherokees, and other offenses.[2] Patriot leaders paid particular attention to the German population, and reports circulated that outlaw bands and British agents were inviting outlying settlers to abandon their homes and the patriot cause and move into the Cherokee territory.[3]

More serious problems began in 1777, apparently caused by changes in Virginia law. The state now required that all free white males over the age of sixteen take an oath of allegiance. Those who refused to do so were to be disarmed, and they would lose the right to vote, hold office, sue for debt, or buy land. In addition, they would be liable for double their normal tax assessment.[4] By the end of the summer, a Williamsburg paper reported that about seventy-five Tories had assembled in Augusta County and "bid defiance to the militia." Similar incidents occurred in Botetourt and Montgomery counties.[5] In Montgomery Captain Thomas Burk and almost his entire company refused the oath of allegiance, and a large group in another company successfully resisted attempts to disarm them.[6] The next year, Montgomery authorities ordered that a suspected Tory be sent to the Augusta County prison. According to the Montgomery court, it would have been unsafe to keep the man in their county, even if they had a prison, because of the strength of Tory sentiment in the area.[7]

In 1779 and 1780, loyalist organizers began swearing sympathetic settlers into a conspiracy along the New River and in adjacent parts of the upper valley. Often they coerced support from reluctant individuals in strongly Tory neighborhoods. Groups, some as large as a hundred persons, met to plan the insurrectionary activity. These conspirators hoped to destroy the strategically valuable lead mine at Fort Chiswell, and on some occasions they proposed cooperation with British troops and Tories from outside the region. In several neighborhoods, loyalists threatened the lives, families, and property of local officials. For a time, state authorities responded by using soldiers initially recruited for service in Kentucky to guard the lead mine. Upper valley leaders sent reliable militiamen into Tory communities to disarm the inhabitants and arrest suspected insurgents. In July 1780 they infiltrated two spies into the Tory organization, learned of plans for a general insurrection, and suppressed the conspiracy.[8] Despite continuing patriot fears, a significant Tory threat never recurred.

Although upper valley Tories included members of all major ethnic groups, they apparently drew disproportionate strength from the German and Welsh minorities. Fincastle authorities feared disloyalty among the German population as early as 1776. In February of that year, William Preston asked Peter Muhlenberg, a German patriot leader from Frederick County in the lower valley, to write to several upper valley Germans.[9] The middle New River in general and Preston's neighborhood in particular had long been centers of German population, and the conspiracies of 1779 and 1780 drew great strength from these areas.[10] The Welsh miners at Fort Chiswell also actively supported the loyalist movement. Many joined the Tories after hearing that the English army would punish Welshmen and other British natives who produced lead for the patriot forces.[11] Ethnic frictions in the upper valley probably encouraged Welsh and German loyalism. One Welsh woman complained to William Preston that her husband had been arrested as a Tory because of "a misunderstanding between Colo. Lynch and the Welsh in General."[12] Friction between German and Scotch-Irish groups was common throughout the middle colonies and the southern backcountry.[13] As William Nelson has suggested, the Tory rank and file in all parts of the continent drew heavily from religious and ethnic minorities, especially those most conscious of their minority status.[14]

Although ethnicity played a crucial role, it is difficult to delineate additional attributes that separated the Tories from other upper valley settlers. The loyalists apparently were substantially poorer than the region's leaders, but they did not clearly differ from the mass of common settlers in their economic status. Given the small number of identifiable Tories and the uncertain size of the total movement, more detailed quantification seems impractical.[15] One analysis of loyalism in southwestern Virginia has suggested that many Tories had only recently arrived in the area and therefore felt little loyalty to the established leaders. Yet the Tory dominance of many German neighborhoods, including some that had been among the earliest settlements in the upper valley, casts doubt on this argument.[16] In any case, the factors that distinguished upper valley Tories from other settlers reveal less of the movement's origins and character than do the localist interests and values which the Tories shared with many of the common people who supported the patriot cause.

Despite its differences from other instances of unrest, upper valley loyalism shared much of the spirit of popular localism. Like the dissidents of the colonial era, the Tories had little involvement with county courts or the provincial government; they identified primarily with local neighborhoods. Although they expressed loyalty to the crown and opposition to the Revolution's political principles, the Tories directed much of their hostility against valley leaders.

Moreover, upper valley loyalists clearly shared the economic grievances that had contributed to popular localism throughout the
colonial and revolutionary eras.

For many upper valley Tories, the county courts were an alien
world. Thus in explaining his reticence during a previous examination, Robert King noted that he had "Never been Brought before a
Cort in my Life Before[.] I was very much Danted and Could not
Recullect my memory as would wanted to Do." According to William Preston, even the Tory "Ringleaders" in his area did not attend
court, bring suits, or vote in elections." A Montgomery proclamation of 1779 attributed the loyalism of many citizens to "the remote
and scattered situation" of the population, which prevented many
people from receiving "full and ample information" on the quarrel
with England. Perhaps significantly, Preston expressed the hope
that the suppression of a Montgomery Tory conspiracy by Washington County militia would prevent further disturbances by con-
vincing "those stupid Wretches that they have more counties than
one to contend with."[17] And in offering a pardon to penitent
loyalists in November 1779, the Montgomery authorities required
them to post bond with any local justice of the peace rather than
insisting that they appear before the county court.[18]

For Tories as for other settlers, the local neighborhood generally
provided the focus of social and political cohesion. Patriot accounts
repeatedly made it clear that loyalist sentiment was concentrated in
particular communities. During the summer of 1780, for example,
William Campbell and a Washington County militia party marched
to the lead mine on the New River in Montgomery County. Shortly
after Campbell's arrival, two scouts returned from a reconnaissance
into the Tory area up the river. These men reported being held
prisoner by more than one hundred insurgents who had assembled
near Captain John Cox's home. If this group was predominantly
from the immediate neighborhood, it obviously would have included an overwhelming majority of the able-bodied male population. In any case, two days later Campbell's party marched through
the most densely settled part of the area and found only women,
children, and old men at home. Thus, when forced to a decision,
virtually all the adult males in the neighborhood chose to flee and
thereby visibly side with the Tories.[19] For a time during the previous year, Captain Cox himself had been suspected of loyalist
sympathies. According to Cox, however, he had been afraid to
inform authorities of the Tory activities in his community. The

insurgents had threatened his life and property and had kept him under constant surveillance. Most important of all, Cox had felt that outside of his own family, "there was no person near him, in whom he could confide."[20]

In other Tory neighborhoods similar forces were at work: community ties apparently encouraged unified support from the sympathetic and helped to intimidate the uncommitted. In December 1777 William Preston reported that all but four or five of Captain Thomas Burk's militia company had refused to take the oath of allegiance, as had nearly forty of Preston's own neighbors. Two years later James McGavock lamented that Tories dominated both his own and Preston's neighborhoods.[21] When Montgomery leaders offered to pardon penitent Tories in September 1779, they were able to delineate precisely those parts of their county where loyalism was strong: "up New River betwixt the River and the Flower Gap and also on the Two Reed Islands and Greasey Creek and Walkers Creek." The next March Preston informed Governor Jefferson that about seventy-five inhabitants of one Montgomery County neighborhood had sworn allegiance to the king. Preston believed Tory sentiment to be so strong in another neighborhood that he ordered patriot militia to make a sudden sweep through the area, disarming all inhabitants. Four months later Preston called for similar action in two other communities. Captain James Byrn was to assemble a militia party, feign a march toward Fort Chiswell, and then sweep through the settlements on Walker and Wolf creeks "with all imaginable Secresy and Dispatch." Any inhabitants who could later demonstrate their patriotism to civil authorities would have their firearms returned, but for the moment Byrn was to disarm everyone except Captain Thomas Ingles.[22]

In many Tory communities the individual and collective hostility of their neighborhoods intimidated uncommitted residents. Even William Preston sometimes feared to leave his family alone because of the hostility of local Tories.[23] As noted earlier, Captain John Cox also was intimidated by the loyalist community in which he lived. At one point in 1779, a Tory party took him prisoner, tried for several days to persuade him to support them, and finally told him that "if he would not join them . . . he must Swear he would not lift arms against them or their Party, or disclose any of their Secrets which he might have discovered."[24] The next year James Duggless reported that another settler had threatened to kill a neighbor if that neighbor revealed the loyalist conspiracies. Duggless may have described this intimidation in an attempt to excuse his own passive support of the Tory cause: the rest of his statement emphasized the strength of Tory sentiment in his area and his earlier belief that many of the upper valley's leading men supported the loyalists.[25] In any case, such threats by individual Tories often depended for their effectiveness on the tacit support of the larger loyalist community. Coercion within many Tory neighborhoods became so effective that in July 1780 patriot leaders turned to the use of agents who posed as British officers to obtain information on the loyalist conspiracy. As Preston explained to Peter Muhlenberg, the Tory "Combinations were carried on with such amazing secrecy that we were apprehensive they could not be fully discovered until some desperate Blow would be struck."[26]

Thus several aspects of upper valley loyalism reflected its localist orientation. The movement's concentration of strength in particular communities and its successful suppression of opposition within those communities suggest that for Tories the local neighborhoods were the primary unit of social and political cohesion. Admittedly, ethnic loyalties also helped to bind German and Welsh settlers to the Tory cause. Yet those ethnic loyalties operated within the context of particular local communities. There were, after all, substantial numbers of German patriots in the upper valley. A predominantly German militia detachment from the New River served in North Carolina in 1781, and the Germans of northwestern Augusta County formed an entire company for active duty.[27] The Tory movement's localism also appeared in its primary hostility toward regional rather than state and national authorities and in the role played by local economic grievances in motivating individual loyalists.

Not surprisingly, upper valley Tories often expressed their loyalty to the crown and their hostility to the national leaders of the Revolution. Recruits to the movement pledged their support for George III, and loyalist gatherings huzzahed the monarch and drank to his health.[28] Rockbridge authorities jailed one Henry Bowman for "Speaking words Injurious to the Independence of America to Wit God Dam the Country & General Washington & . . . God . . . Bless . . . King George."[29] Some loyalists charged that the revolutionaries had virtually sold America to the French, and John McDonald of Montgomery County reportedly argued "that there would soon be a king in every County. That We had been f[i]ghting for Liberty, but Slavery was the Consequence."[30] At various times,

Tory organizers attempted to coordinate their efforts with the broader strategy of the British army, proposing to destroy the lead mine at Fort Chiswell, free the British prisoners across the Blue Ridge at Charlottesville, or march their supporters to join the royal army.[31]

Upper valley Tories, however, generally directed their primary hostility against regional leaders whose personal actions directly impinged on their local communities. Thus several patriot leaders warned William Preston in April 1779 that his life was in danger.[32] In a memorandum prepared the next year, Preston listed six separate threats against himself and his family, including several instances of rewards being offered for his death.[33] Loyalists also menaced the lives and property of other upper valley leaders. In 1779 a group of Tories hid for several days near James McGavock's home in the Fort Chiswell neighborhood, killing his sheep and apparently trying to burn down the house. William Phips, who lived in the same part of Montgomery County, received similar treatment: shots were fired into his house one night, and someone tried to set the building on fire.[34] The next year Tories stole six horses from another New River leader.[35]

Probably because of his reputation for imposing lynch law, upper valley Tories made particularly vehement threats against William Campbell of Washington County. In August 1780, several men apparently captured and threatened to hang one of Campbell's slaves, telling the man "that his Master injured them, therefore they would destroy his Property wh[enever] found."[36] On another occasion loyalists threatened sevenfold vengeance if Campbell executed one of their men whom he held prisoner. At one point someone left a message along a public roadway for "Cornl Will the bloody tyrant of Washington County and Court." The message proclaimed that Campbell ruled "by an arbetrary power" and warned him "to Prepare your Self for deth . . . for the Scripture Saith that whosoever spilleth mans blood by man shall his blood be Spilt."[37]

Upper valley loyalists also shared the economic grievances that had provoked unrest throughout the history of the region. Like other small farmers they wanted access to more land and resented big landowners. Thus Tory organizers frequently promised 450-acre grants to men who agreed to support the crown.[38] In seeking support for a projected insurrection, John Griffith acknowledged that his followers would lose their property but promised that "they would be made good again out of the Forfeited Estates."[39] Another

Tory organizer reportedly threatened a man who refused to join the conspiracy, saying "that if that was his sentiments he never would enjoy a foot of land in America, and what little he had gathered would be taken from him."[40] In July 1780 William Preston complained that Tory leaders in his neighborhood had promised to divide his land among their followers, even blazing trees to mark the planned boundaries.[41] Apparently in response to the upper valley's chronic shortage of circulating currency, Tory leaders frequently promised cash payments to men who would join the insurrection. Assurances of exemption from taxes and quitrents also drew many recruits to the loyalist movement, and Tory John McDonald allegedly threatened to kill William Preston if the Montgomery sheriff collected taxes.[42]

The localist roots of upper valley loyalism not only shaped its interests and values but also contributed to its ultimate failure. Despite the sympathy it won in many communities, the loyalist movement failed to generate a sustained and concerted challenge to patriot authority. Within particular neighborhoods Tory leaders gained limited support for small-scale and short-term acts of defiance, as well as the passive loyalty of larger numbers of people. It proved impossible, however, to win the active commitment of sympathetic settlers to larger organizations and campaigns, at least in part because those organizations and campaigns transcended local communities.

Upper valley Tories often showed distrust or even ignorance of the loyalist organization beyond their own locality. The Holston River Tory leader John Griffith encountered such distrust in 1780 when he attempted to enlist sympathetic settlers from several New River areas in a planned insurrection. Many of these people already had taken oaths to keep the secrets of the Tory conspiracy and oaths of allegiance to George III. Yet almost all of them refused to take oaths promising military service, claiming that Griffith lacked proper authorization to enlist them. In the end Griffith had to conciliate these men by promising to return in a month with a properly authorized officer from the British army.[43] Another Tory, Robert King, freely admitted his involvement with the conspiracy but could not remember his own rank within the insurgents' military hierarchy.[44] Thus King was ignorant not only of the loyalist organizational structure but also of his own most fundamental ties to that structure.

The localist orientation of upper valley Tories hampered efforts to hold meetings among supporters from different neighborhoods. In 1779 or 1780 a meeting at the head of Peak Creek, a New River tributary, drew only fifteen to twenty people from Walker's Creek and other Tory communities.[45] Andrew Thomson reported that he traveled part of the way to the meeting with several other men. According to Thomson, however, some of his companions seemed reluctant to attend the meeting, and Thomson himself "went Back under Pretence of being unwell." Internal divisions disrupted a larger assembly near John Cox's house in 1779, and Tories from Elk Creek refused to attend because they felt that the men from other neighborhoods at the meeting had assembled without proper authorization from their superiors.[46]

Finally, many settlers who passively accepted loyalist activities in their own communities refused to support the movement more actively or in ways that transcended the bounds of local neighborhoods. Thus Tory leaders found it necessary to distinguish between those supporters who had promised military service in an insurrection and those who had merely sworn to keep the loyalist conspiracies secret. In some cases Tories forced the oath of secrecy upon men who sympathized with the patriot cause but feared to turn against their loyalist neighbors. This apparently occurred with the New River leader, John Cox.[47] In other cases new supporters voluntarily took the oath of secrecy but later refused to make stronger commitments. Morrison Lovell, for example, was sworn into the secret by John Henderson and subsequently attended the meeting at the head of Peak Creek. At the meeting a leader "asked him if he wou'd list & swore [another] oath to be true to king & hold himself in readyness &c to which he answer'd he wou'd be Dam'd if he wou'd."[48] Thus although community ties helped to buy passive support, they did not encourage and may indeed have discouraged greater levels of commitment. Even among those who promised active support for insurrection there must have been many like George Pemberton of Elk Creek. According to James Duggless, Tory organizer John Griffith told him that Pemberton "was hal[f] and half that is to signify that every wind will turn him."[49]

In the end upper valley loyalism's most prominent characteristic was its deep roots in the circumstances of life in local communities. Its primary enemies were not the leaders of the United States or even of Virginia but rather "Cornl Will the bloody tyrant and murderer of Washington County" and William Preston, whose lands the Tories promised to divide and whose life and scalp they frequently threatened.[50] The loyalists' grievances included not only the severance of ties to England but also the allocation of wealth, prestige, and power within upper valley communities. Despite frequent threats to assemble large forces and take decisive actions to aid the British cause, the Tories' principal tactics were anonymous threats against local leaders, theft of livestock, and firing on houses at night.[51] Ironically, this localist orientation common to so many Tory and patriot communities in the upper valley may have been the biggest single barrier that separated them.

As with the measures taken to maintain support for the war effort, the methods used by upper valley patriot leaders to defeat the Tory threat revealed both the continued attachment of regional leaders to traditional political values and their increasing acceptance of popular attitudes. William Preston and other leaders preferred restrained, fully legal methods in dealing with Tory offenders. Fundamentally they hoped to reintegrate these men with a harmonious and largely deferential social order. Yet popular hatred of Tories forced even Preston to modify this policy, and William Campbell and other leaders regularly employed harsh and illegal measures against the loyalists.

The legalist orientation of Preston and other leaders was particularly clear in their treatment of Tories in the county courts. These officials repeatedly allowed suspected loyalists to post bond for their future good behavior as an alternative to prosecution and imprisonment.[52] In trying men accused of disloyalty, Preston's Montgomery court scrupulously followed the requirements of the law. One Montgomery justice articulated this concern in April 1779, calling for some arrested Tories to be given "a fair cool and Impartial tryal." He also urged Preston to attend that court session because his judicial experience would be invaluable.[53] In examining William Ingles for treason the next year, a group of Montgomery and Botetourt justices decided to defer final determination of the case, noting that the charge of treason had not been fully proven but that further evidence seemed likely to appear. Despite this uncertainty, they released Ingles after he posted bond guaranteeing his appearances in court if summoned in the future.[54] Although Governor Jefferson commended Preston and his colleagues for their care in prosecuting Tories, he apparently feared they might be too lenient. Thus he suggested that in many cases in which sufficient evidence of treason was lacking, convictions for the lesser offense of misprison of treason might be obtained.[55]

Outside the courts Preston also preferred to operate with restraint. Thus in dispatching militia to disarm suspected Tories in July 1780, he ordered them to avoid unnecessary cruelty and to operate within the law. The militiamen were not to mistreat women, children, or the elderly, and they were to take no property except from settlers who refused to give up their arms and ammunition peacefully. Nor was any confiscated property to be sold until the owners could defend themselves in court.[56] Not surprisingly, Preston protested when Colonel Charles Lynch of Bedford marched into Montgomery County and began arresting and apparently illegally punishing Tories near the lead mine at Fort Chiswell.[57]

Preston and his colleagues chose these cautious and restrained methods for several reasons. One modern scholar has suggested that Montgomery County's lack of an adequate jail encouraged the justices to allow suspected insurgents to post bond for their future good behavior. In addition, the manpower demands of the Carolina campaign made upper valley leaders reluctant to use militiamen to suppress local Tories when those militiamen were badly needed to strengthen American forces to the south.[58]

More fundamentally, Preston and other leaders hoped to reintegrate the Tories into a harmonious society, bonded by the voluntary loyalty of all citizens. In pardoning John Spratt for his expressions of disloyalty, for example, the Fincastle committee noted his penitence and promises of future loyalty and therefore restored him "to the Friendship and Confidence of his Countrymen."[59] Other loyalists were restored to the privileges of citizenship so long as they behaved appropriately, and the Montgomery court even made such concessions to three men whom it felt had not sincerely repented of their past offenses.[60] A proclamation of August 1780 seeking the voluntary surrender of Thomas Heaven and other loyalists declared that patriot authorities "would rather reclaim and pardon" than punish these offenders.[61] When compelled to employ military force against recalcitrant Tories, Preston expressed the hope that "humbling" the loyalists might be "a Means of reducing those unhappy People to reason and of bringing them to a Just Sense of the Duty they owe the Country, in which they Live, and by which they have hitherto been protected in the peaceable Enjoyment of their Lives Liberties & Property."[62]

For Preston and others, the duty the Tories owed to their country included by implication an obligation of deference toward established leaders. A Montgomery order of September 1779 invited penitent Tories to "throw themselves on the mercy of the . . . Court."[63] Repentant loyalists recognized this concern and filled their petitions to Preston and the Montgomery court with references to their own humility and ignorance and appeals to the superior wisdom, virtue, and compassion of patriot authorities. Robert King, for example, confessed that he had "been working in a Rong Cause" because "of my own Simple Notion and the Bad avise of Others that this was the Best Way." He begged "that Your Worships would look over it as Easily as you posablely Can" and promised to pay any fine or give security for his future good behavior. He protested only that it would be unjust to take away the property he had earned by his own labor, which provided his family's only support.[64]

A desire to maintain respect for established leaders may also have shaped the lenient treatment that William Ingles received from patriot authorities. Ingles had initially supported the Revolution: in 1775 he signed the Fincastle resolutions that endorsed the patriot cause, and in 1777 he became the sheriff of Montgomery and a colonel in the county's militia.[65] By 1780, however, patriot leaders suspected him of playing a leading role in the Tory conspiracies throughout the New River region. In August of that year, he was formally charged with treason. Yet when the evidence against him proved incomplete, a group of Botetourt and Montgomery justices allowed him to post bond and go free, even though they anticipated the appearance of further evidence.[66] By spring of 1781, Ingles had resumed a prominent role in the Montgomery militia, and by the end of that year he felt confident enough to attack Preston's surveying and land speculation practices in a petition to the state legislature.[67] Patriot leaders also dealt gently with Ingles's son, a captain in the Montgomery militia. In July 1780, a month before the elder Ingles's trial for treason, Preston ordered that young Captain Ingles be allowed to keep his weapons when the rest of his predominantly Tory militia company was disarmed.[68] This decision too may have reflected Preston's desire to encourage deference and respect for the established leaders of his region.

Preston and other like-minded leaders also recognized that the culture of deference required not only humility from the common people but also beneficence from the gentry. Thus the Montgomery court dealt kindly with those Tories whom it regarded as "proper

Objects of Mercy." On several occasions the justices ordered that officials and private individuals return property taken from men whose disloyalty had not been proven. In calling for the return of David Fulton's property in February 1781, they noted that he had apparently given no active support to the enemy and, more significantly, that he had a large family. A sense of obligation to protect his Tory neighbors may even have led Captain John Cox to intercede in their behalf with the county court, an action that may have added to suspicions about Cox's own loyalties.[69]

Although Preston and other leaders pursued these moderate policies, most common settlers felt far less conciliatory toward upper valley loyalists. Ethnic frictions presumably fostered hostility toward German and Welsh Tories. Personal resentments also apparently played a role. Montgomery resident Benjamin Cook, for example, cleared himself of charges of disloyalty. Yet as he told William Preston, he found "that it is the intention of some people to involve me in Troubles again, as it is an Old Saying to give a Dog an ill name and hang him." Accordingly, Cook asked for Preston's protection while he sold his property and moved out of the area. Although many leaders forgave William Ingles for his apparent disloyalty, other settlers may not have done so, for when Ingles resigned his militia commission in 1782, he felt compelled to declare formally that physical infirmity was his only reason for doing so.[70]

The demands imposed by the war effort also encouraged popular hostility toward Tories. Common settlers recognized, for example, that loyalists who refused military service imposed greater burdens on their fellow citizens. Thus Walter Crockett reported in May 1781 that the failure of militiamen from a largely Tory area to assemble for active duty had produced threats of similar refusals from otherwise loyal citizens.[71] On other occasions groups of militiamen hunted down loyalists and compelled them to serve as substitutes in the draft for the Continental army.[72] In many cases militiamen who were mobilized to suppress Tory activities demanded that the property of accused loyalists be confiscated and sold to benefit either the government or the soldiers themselves.[73]

Popular criticism of lenience toward suspected loyalists helped to compel even William Preston to accept harsher policies. As early as 1779, Preston informed his Tory neighbors that his indulgence toward them had "subjected my Character to the Tongues of the Malicious as an enemy to the Liberties of my Country."[74] The next year he again alluded to the "difficulty & Censure" which his moderation had brought upon him. By August 1780 these pressures forced Preston openly to accept the plundering of Tory property. As he reported to Governor Jefferson, upper valley militiamen insisted that such property be sold and the proceeds divided among them. Preston and other officers submitted to these demands, he explained, because "otherwise it would be almost impossible to get men on these pressing occasions."[75] In 1782 the state legislature included Preston on a list of Virginia leaders whom it protected from civil suits for illegal acts committed against the Tories.[76]

In Washington County, patriot leaders were especially sympathetic to popular attitudes in their treatment of loyalists. As early as May 1779, the Washington court confiscated the estate of a local Tory. William Campbell, an important Washington County leader, also implemented harsh measures against loyalists. By 1779 he apparently had executed at least one of them. According to a popular story, while returning home from church with his family, Campbell captured a suspected Tory. He quickly tried and hanged the man and continued homeward with his wife and children.[77] Whether or not this story was true, loyalists frequently accused Campbell of such illegal actions, labelling him "the bloody tyrant of Washington County" and threatening him with venegeance.[78] Another Washington County leader, Arthur Campbell, shared his kinsman's views, suggesting in June 1780 that an insurrection by upper valley Tories might at least have the good effect of ending the lenience often shown to them.[79] In 1783 he provoked a controversy by arresting a local citizen for allegedly aiding the British while a captive in Detroit.[80]

William Campbell and other leaders frequently used the same harsh methods against Tories outside Washington County. When he marched against the Montgomery County loyalists near the lead mines in 1780, Campbell seized the brother of a suspected insurgent and threatened to kill him unless he guided Campbell's scouts to a Tory encampment. At the camp Campbell's soldiers captured one man, whom they immediately shot. The next day the patriots hanged one captured loyalist and whipped two others. In proclamations addressed to the Tories, Campbell demanded that they promptly surrender on pain of having their property destroyed and "themselves held liable to suffer the Punishment which for their Crimes, they so justly deserve."[81] Fourteen of the captains and subaltern officers on the expedition explicitly endorsed the confiscation of Tory property by signing a statement directing Campbell and Walter Crockett of Montgomery County to arrange for its sale.[82]

Other expeditions against backcountry Tories also led to plundering and lynching. Arthur Campbell, for example, supported his men's demands for the sale of property taken from loyalists in a battle at Ramsour's Mill in North Carolina.[83] After forces under his command defeated a predominantly Tory army at Kings Mountain in the Carolinas, William Campbell attempted to prevent the killing and plundering of prisoners, but he apparently ordered that in case of an attack, all captives were to be shot.[84] Moreover, a few days after the battle, Campbell acquiesced to the demands of Carolina officers for the trial and immediate execution of nine Tory officers.[85]

In at least one case, William Campbell apparently used popular opinion to justify harsh treatment of a loyalist prisoner. As he explained in a letter of July 1780, Campbell and a force of Washington and Montgomery militia met a party of 130 North Carolina militiamen near Fort Chiswell. The North Carolinians had recently captured Zachariah Goss, who belonged to a band of Tory criminals. As Campbell put it, Goss "was immediately hung, I believe with the joint consent of near three hundred men."[86]

Admittedly, the Washington County justices, like their Montgomery counterparts, frequently treated suspected Tories with lenience. They often allowed men accused of disloyalty to post bond for their appearance at trial or for their future good behavior. In November 1780 two accused Tories, Jinkin Williams and John Robinson, served as each other's securities, and the next spring the court postponed the trial of another accused loyalist, based solely on Williams's testimony.[87] In part, however, this apparent lenience may reflect attendance patterns of the Washington justices: neither Arthur nor William Campbell was present at the court sessions at which the decisions were made. More important, the Washington court could afford to be conciliatory: loyalism was a much lesser threat in that county than in Montgomery, and the judges were not directly answerable to the popular will. Washington militia commanders, by contrast, often took action against Tories in Montgomery County, where support for insurgency was stronger, and they could not operate effectively in their own county or elsewhere without the acquiescence and active support of their men.

Thus in several respects upper valley loyalism reflected broader patterns in the region's political development. Although ethnic and other barriers separated the Tories from other upper valley settlers, the movement shared much of the localist values, interests, and orientations that fueled popular discontent throughout the colonial and revolutionary periods. Ironically, this localism also contributed to the Tories' ultimate failure to mount a well-organized and sustained campaign that united individual loyalist neighborhoods. Finally, the Tory challenge to patriot authority added to the wartime pressures that forced upper valley leaders into greater compromises with popular attitudes and values. During the final years of the Revolutionary War and the postwar years, these pressures would grow still stronger.

CHAPTER SEVEN

Finishing the Revolution

During the 1780s the growth of popular discontent and of support for republican political values continued in the upper valley. Until peace was finally achieved in 1783, the Revolution's military and economic demands clashed with the localist values of common settlers. Because of the war and its aftereffects, taxation and fluctuations in the value of currency remained volatile issues throughout the decade. By the early 1780s, moreover, republican political values were being widely espoused in disputes beyond those related to the costs of the Revolution. At mid-decade, the campaign by Arthur Campbell and other leaders to include southwestern Virginia in the proposed state of Franklin showed how fully they had learned to mobilize popular support and to exploit the republican values of popular sovereignty, liberty, virtue, and the public good for political purposes. By the end of the decade, these new political methods and values had begun to shape all areas of public life.

As in earlier years, the military and economic costs of the war created widespread popular opposition to the defense priorities of upper valley leaders. Outlying communities repeatedly pressed authorities for more protection, and attachments to local neighborhoods underlay much of the resistance to the elite's measures throughout the region. The war's economic demands added to these resentments, and the drafting of men for the Continental army provoked particularly vehement opposition. Although common settlers retained strong attachments to local communities, a growing awareness of the outside world helped shape their political attitudes and actions by the end of the war.

Throughout the latter part of the war, communities exposed to Indian attack urged state and county authorities to provide more help with local defense. In the fall and winter of 1781 and 1782, settlers who had abandoned their homes on the lower Kanawha River promised in petitions to the governor and the Greenbrier County lieutenant that they would return to the frontier if troops were placed in the area.[1] During the spring of 1782, inhabitants of the upper Clinch River threatened to flee unless militiamen were stationed among them.[2] In January 1783 Arthur Campbell reported that "the whole settlement of Clinch . . . have generally come to a resolution to abandon the river early in the Spring if some apparently effectual measures are not set on foot for their protection." Soon afterward William Preston responded to requests for assistance on the Montgomery frontier by sending out scouts and ordering militia captains to prepare their men for immediate action.[3]

In all parts of the region, the conditions of local life fueled resistance to military duty. County lieutenants regularly reported that militiamen would not join the patriot armies to the east and south when Indian hostilities threatened their own communities.[4] Upper valley leaders also stressed to their superiors that small farmers, especially those who had performed extended service in the past, needed time to produce food for their families.[5] It was particularly difficult to obtain men for active duty during harvest time. In June 1781, for example, the Botetourt County lieutenant reported that his efforts to mobilize men seemed likely to fail because reports had circulated that the militia of other counties had been excused from duty until after the coming harvest.[6] As in earlier years, common settlers often failed to share the concern of state authorities for maintaining good relations with friendly Indian groups. Thus Joseph Martin reported from the southwestern frontier in February 1781 that "some of our Disorderly men" had killed two emissaries from a Cherokee faction that hoped to avoid war with the United States.[7]

Once on duty, militiamen proved equally troublesome, especially when ordered to march far from their homes. In Powell's Valley in April 1781, both Aaron Lewis and Joseph Martin failed to convince their men to continue the hot pursuit of Indian raiding parties. According to Martin, he was "still on fresh sign" when the men refused to go farther, protesting that their party was too small, their provisions nearly exhausted, and their horses too tired. Although Martin claimed that they were within a few miles of an Indian settlement, the men charged that he was really trying to take them much deeper into Indian territory.[8] That same spring more than two hundred Botetourt militiamen deserted from a march to join Nathanael Greene's army in the southern campaign. Their reasons evidently included the inadequacy of their supplies, some confusion as to how many men were needed, and their reluctance to leave their farms during planting season. Not surprisingly, the county lieutenant decided against the prosecution of so large a group.[9] When a Rockbridge militia party marching to join Greene learned that his forces had advanced from Virginia into North Carolina, their commander had great difficulty in persuading them to cross the state line.[10] Similarly, William Preston acknowledged that most of the Montgomery County men who marched south with him eventually deserted. Yet he noted pointedly that his party "did duty on the Enemy's lines, as long as any other that went from behind the mountains, & much longer than some."[11] Augusta and Rockbridge militia serving in eastern Virginia also troubled their commanders. Sampson Mathews feared a mutiny among these troops in January 1781, and the men threatened to return home in April despite the wishes of state officials and their commanding officer, Peter Muhlenberg.[12] In July 1782, when drawing up defense plans for their counties, Montgomery and Washington officers tried to avoid bringing in men from other counties because such measures were "attended . . . too frequently with disorders on the march."[13]

Economic problems troubled the upper valley during the war and postwar years. The state government was often slow to pay for military service, food, and other supplies. Furthermore, both the state's currency and that of the Continental Congress rapidly lost value. Money of any sort was in desperately short supply in the region, especially after the state government began to withdraw its paper currency from circulation in the fall of 1781. Finally, the war led Virginia to impose a much higher tax burden on its citizens than it had before.[14]

These economic problems encouraged distrust and resentment of state and regional authorities. In all parts of the upper valley, the state's slowness in paying its obligations made settlers reluctant to sell supplies to the government on credit. In April 1781 Arthur Campbell found it difficult to recruit men for frontier defense in Washington County or for service with Greene's army because local settlers had not been paid for military duty performed the previous year.[15] Especially after the contraction of currency in 1781, money was scarce, and regional leaders often suggested that Virginia au-

120 GENTRY AND COMMON FOLK

thorities appoint a commissary provided with ready money to purchase supplies.[16] By 1782 an official in Staunton reported that there was "no such thing . . . as public credit" there.[17]

Tax collection proved difficult throughout the 1780s. Even before the state's currency contraction, shortages of money and other problems hampered collection in Montgomery, Botetourt, Rockbridge, and Augusta counties.[18] In at least four cases, county sheriffs lost their positions because they refused or failed to give the required security for their complete collection of taxes.[19] Although the legislature agreed on several occasions to accept part of the taxes in commodities, upper valley leaders and citizens protested that this provided little relief: the costs of transportation were too high, and harvests had been drastically reduced by military service, Indian raids, and other factors.[20] Throughout the decade, upper valley citizens petitioned for tax relief, and in 1787 a group of Greenbrier County inhabitants threatened to block the collection of taxes and other debts.[21] Not surprisingly, popular bitterness was often expressed against the local officials who collected taxes. Thus, when petitioning for relief from his collection responsibilities in 1789, a Montgomery County sheriff claimed that his own conduct had been scrupulously fair but acknowledged the justness of the "prejudice which generally prevails against Sheriffs, who act on the principle of inequity."[22]

The most serious challenge to the authorities in the late war years arose from popular resistance to conscription for the Continental army. Until 1780 Virginia allowed militiamen to avoid the Continental draft by capturing and turning in deserters to serve in their place. Many counties raised one-third to one-half of their quotas through this means. In October 1780, however, the state banned this practice.[23] Upper valley militiamen were performing an unusually large amount of active duty during that period. To add eighteen months of Continental service to this militia duty would work a particular hardship for men whose families depended on their labor at home, as numerous leaders and citizens pointed out.[24] The depreciation of the currency effectively reduced the state's bounties to recruits and draftees, which may have further increased resistance to conscription.[25] Scarcity of currency also affected the situation: one Montgomery militia captain reported that he and his men could not pay their share of the bounties because tax collectors and surveyors had "swept this Neborhood of all the half bits in it."[26]

For all these reasons, opposition to the draft grew and became violent during the spring of 1781. When Augusta officers met on April 30 to divide the county into districts for drafting men, a mob demanded that they not proceed. After the officers refused to stop, a group of armed men broke through the crowd, seized the documents needed to lay out the districts, and publicly destroyed them. According to county lieutenant George Moffett, the rioters "Said they were cheerfully willing to Spend their hearts blood in Defense of the Cuntery. Yet they would suffer Death before they would be Drafted eighteen months from their families and made Regular Soldiers of." Although he deplored the rioters' actions, Moffett felt they were "Good Whigs and despise[d] the name of a Tory."[27]

A similar riot occurred in neighboring Rockbridge County a few days later. After hearing of the Augusta disturbance, a group of about one hundred men seized and destroyed the documents needed to divide the county into districts for the draft. Like their Augusta counterparts, the Rockbridge rioters declared that they would gladly perform active duty with the militia "but would not be drafted for Eighteen months and be regulars." At least some of these men believed that existing laws forbade obstruction of the draft itself but not of the preliminary laying out of districts. Therefore, they expected no punishment for their actions.[28] By late May one leader estimated that a majority of Rockbridge and Augusta inhabitants supported resistance to the draft. Eventually the state offered the rioters full pardon.[29]

Draft resistance continued the next year. By then the state had responded to the depreciation of its currency by beginning to withdraw it from circulation. Leaders and citizens in the upper valley argued that the resulting scarcity of money prevented the payment of bounties required by the conscription law.[30] In Augusta George Moffett feared more riots, and he noted that many people believed that the previous state legislature had intended to block completion of the draft. Moffett postponed his county's draft and urged that further concessions be offered to the people.[31] Perhaps prudently, the Montgomery court refused William Preston's request that it levy a tax to pay the bounty for the county's draftees.[32] In Greenbrier County a mob prevented officials from laying off conscription districts, and apparently few men were raised elsewhere in the upper valley.[33]

In March 1782 Arthur Campbell suggested several reasons for opposition to the draft in Washington County. He noted the unfortunate effects of currency fluctuations, heavy military service in the past, and the failure to pay men who had performed active duty. Campbell also asserted that local draft resistance resulted from the past failure of other counties to raise their quotas of men while Washington had more than met its obligations. Like other upper valley settlers, Washington County residents strongly preferred active duty with the militia to service in a standing army. As Campbell put it, "some how there is a general disgust taken place for what bears the name of a Regular."[34]

In the end, the draft resistance showed that despite the continued strength of localism, a growing awareness of the outside world also affected popular political perceptions, attitudes, and actions. The Rockbridge draft rioters knew of the earlier incident in Augusta and used essentially the same justification for their own conduct, proclaiming their willingness to serve in the militia and their refusal to join the standing army. However incorrect they may have been, popular perceptions of state legislation influenced the riots in both these counties and probably the Greenbrier disturbance the next year: in all three cases, rioters blocked the laying off of districts rather than the actual draft, apparently because they believed state law did not clearly prohibit resistance at this early stage.[35] Similarly, in 1782, many Augusta citizens alleged that the state legislature opposed continued imposition of the draft, and in 1781 the Augusta mob initially offered to petition the legislature if local officials delayed the conscription process.[36] Like other upper valley dissidents, the draft resisters cited events and circumstances in neighboring areas to justify their actions. Arthur Campbell, for example, noted that the past failures of other counties to fill their own quotas fueled draft resistance in Washington County.[37]

To a limited degree, these popular groups had absorbed from the outside world the new republican ideology and its dislike of standing armies. The Augusta and Rockbridge rioters proclaimed their willingness to fight for their country but also their refusal to be "made regular soldiers."[38] In Washington County Campbell noted similar sentiments. Yet for these popular dissidents, other more immediate and practical objections were as important as the republican aversion to standing armies. The Augusta rioters, in Moffett's portrayal, were as much opposed to a prolonged separation from their families as they were to the discipline and control imposed by a regular army. In issues farther removed from the war effort and in the politics of the postwar era, the republican ideology would play a stronger role in mobilizing and influencing popular groups.

Even before 1780, the Revolution had begun to transform upper valley political methods and values in areas beyond defense issues. During the colonial period, surveying and land acquisition practices had created popular discontent. Now this discontent increased, and ambitious leaders learned to mobilize it and to exploit the new republican political values for that purpose. Moreover, by intensifying the controversies over county divisions and religious liberty, the Revolution also encouraged greater participation in the political process.

The struggle for independence brought dramatic changes in American political values. The revolutionaries believed that in a republic such as theirs, political power derived from the people as a whole rather than from a monarch or an aristocracy. Therefore, it was argued, the people themselves should determine the fundamental structure of their government, and they should elect as many of their public officials as possible. This principle of popular sovereignty also came to mean that elected officials should submit to the opinions and desires of their constituents rather than expecting those constituents to defer to the judgment of their leaders. Since this new conception of representation departed radically from the deferential tradition, its acceptance came slowly and met with strong resistance in many parts of America. In addition, revolutionary Americans believed that the preservation of liberty in a republic required scrupulous protection of the rights, liberties, and fundamental equality of the people. Since a population of virtuous, independent small farmers formed the best foundation for a republic, the material welfare of such people should be especially carefully protected.[39]

During the revolutionary era upper valley leaders became increasingly adept at using this republican ideology to mobilize opposition to county surveyors. In 1777, when Robert Preston secured his appointment as Washington surveyor, the county court initially rejected his commission, arguing that it was based on the prerogative power of the English crown. Then Preston's antagonists circulated a petition calling for surveyors to be nominated by the people or the county courts, rather than by the College of William and Mary. The petition argued that the proposed selection process was more consistent with the "present Form of Government" in which most officials were "chosen or nominated by the suffrages of the people Collectively or by their Substitutes."[40] Admittedly, the petition's endorsement of popular sovereignty was partial at best because it considered nomination by the oligarchic county court an acceptable alternative. Nevertheless, in attempting to undermine an entrenched leader, the petition did proclaim that power derived from the people, and it held out the possibilty of popular election of local officials.

Several years later a group of upper valley leaders exploited popular resentments in a controversy over illegal surveys made by John Buchanan during the colonial period. Under pressure from land magnate James Patton, the Augusta County surveyor had appointed Buchanan as an assistant. Buchanan then began surveying for Patton on the upper valley frontier without obtaining the required commission from the College of William and Mary.[41] Rumors of this illegality may have circulated during the colonial period.[42] In any case, in 1781 William Ingles and others raised the issue in litigation challenging the land titles held by Patton's heirs, associates, and clients.[43] Ingles and his allies also circulated petitions in Montgomery and Washington counties. The petitions called Buchanan's surveys illegal, charged that his work was often inaccurate, and claimed that Patton and his associates refused to provide proper titles to settlers who purchased tracts of land from them. The petitions further alleged that Patton's heirs and executors had circumvented the Virginia government's efforts to provide redress to the inhabitants of Patton's grant. By September 1782 William Preston reported that the charges of illegal surveying had been "industriously propagated through every part of the Country."[44]

New political methods and values also appeared in campaigns against Thomas Walker's Loyal Company and other groups of land speculators. Before the Seven Years' War, the colonial government had made large but poorly defined grants of land in southwestern Virginia and the Greenbrier valley to the Loyal and Greenbrier companies respectively. The war prevented the companies from completing the acquisition of their land, and afterward the royal Proclamation of 1763 forbade settlement in these and other frontier areas. Nevertheless, many people moved onto the company lands, and company agents surveyed tracts for some of these settlers and for speculators. Although the surveys did not fully establish ownership, it was generally assumed that survey holders would have primary claim to their tracts when the government again allowed the private acquisition of western land. In some cases, company surveyors exploited this assumption to force reluctant settlers to agree to purchase their lands from the companies. Since the companies could survey the land for someone else if the occupants refused, this tactic was often effective.[45] By removing royal authority, the Revolution reopened the questions surrounding the sale of western land and the claims of the land companies.

In 1779, after several years of controversy, Virginia passed comprehensive western land legislation which favored wealthy speculators at the expense of common settlers. Under these laws, all previous surveys would be honored. Individuals without titles or surveys who had settled their farms before 1 January 1778 would receive four hundred acres at a nominal price, as well as the option of purchasing another one thousand acres at the newly established rate of forty pounds per one hundred acres. Settlers who had arrived since 1 January 1778 could purchase up to four hundred acres at that price. The statutes also empowered special commissioners to resolve disputed claims. After all these demands were met, the remaining land was to be sold at the rate of forty pounds per hundred acres, with no limits on the quantity any individual could purchase, a provision that clearly favored major speculators.

The legitimation of the land companies' earlier surveys particularly antagonized upper valley settlers. It meant that men whose land the companies had surveyed for someone else would lose their property. Moreover, settlers who had allowed such surveys of their land now had to complete their payments to the companies. Since these people could have purchased their land more cheaply from the state had they not authorized the earlier surveys, they deeply resented both the new laws and the land companies.[46] Because of continuing appeals to the legislature and the courts, the controversies arising out of these laws continued into the nineteenth century.

Throughout the revolutionary and postrevolutionary periods, upper valley leaders on all sides of these land controversies solicited popular political support. Leaders allied with the Loyal and Greenbrier companies pressed settlers to sign petitions supporting the companies' claims.[47] Arthur Campbell and other men circulated petitions against the land companies throughout the region.[48] They were motivated by political opposition to the men who supported the companies and probably also by a desire to secure independent title to land the companies claimed.[49] As late as the 1790s popular opposition to the Loyal Company remained so strong in southwest Virginia that its agents were often threatened with violence.[50]

In Augusta and Rockbridge counties, even the long-established Beverley and Borden tracts came under attack. The provincial government had made these grants in the 1740s, and land sales there had not been interrupted by the Proclamation of 1763. Nevertheless, at least three petitions condemned the grants as unjust monopolies, charging that the proprietors had unfairly raised prices on the land they still controlled and had not paid taxes on this property. The petitions demanded that the state collect all unpaid taxes and confiscate the property for resale if the proprietors failed to pay.[51]

Petitions attacking land speculators combined practical arguments with appeals to the republican values sanctioned by the Revolution. Pragmatically the petitioners argued that by monopolizing land, speculators exploited the common people, slowed the pace of settlement, and thereby weakened frontier defenses.[52] Evoking republican values, many petitions emphasized that the Revolution had created a polity committed to equality, liberty, and the rights of all citizens. Therefore, they asserted, the grievances of settlers deserved a fuller hearing than before, and the obvious injustices created by the monopolization of land should be remedied.[53] A group of Greenbrier residents proclaimed that tamely surrendering their lands to speculators would be "unbecoming [of] Citizens who have arrived to the dignity of free, sovereign, and independent States." The Greenbrier group also warned that men unjustly deprived of their property would come to loathe their government.[54] Another petition pointedly stated that the activities of land speculators were as injurious to the backcountry as the proposed British taxes would have been throughout America.[55]

Because it emphasized the conflict between mankind's insatiable drive for wealth and power and a free society's need for devotion to the public good, republican ideology also added a moral dimension to attacks on land speculators.[56] Upper valley petitioners asserted that "artful Monopolizers" of land had accumulated their present wealth by pursuing private advantage at the expense of the public good. Such conduct contrasted sharply with that of "the virtuous Citizen who has been kept in Poverty by faithfully adhering to the Interest of his Country." Moreover, under the tenets of republican social thought, it was logical to assume that those who had gained a measure of wealth would seek to increase it further at the expense of fellow citizens. Thus a Botetourt petition asserted that the monopolizers of land "have it in their power and no doubt also in Contemplation, to engross the greatest part of the vacant lands on this Side of the Ohio." Finally, since republican liberties were most easily sustained in societies dominated by small independent farmers, petitions attacking land speculators could assert that a policy which provided moderate amounts of land to settlers at low prices best suited the present form of government.[57]

In addition to its impact on land controversies, the Revolution led to greater agitation for the creation of new counties in the upper valley. Although such proposals had been common in the colonial period, after 1763 the crown discouraged the creation of new counties on the frontier in order to curtail westward expansion. By removing this royal restraint, the Revolution encouraged a dramatic surge in the creation of new counties. As late as 1769, Augusta County had encompassed the entire upper valley. By the beginning of the Revolution, only two more counties had been created. Then in 1777, Fincastle County was subdivided into Montgomery and Washington counties. When the war ended in 1783, there were seven counties in the region, and by 1790 four more had been added.[58]

Throughout the revolutionary and postrevolutionary years, competing groups circulated petitions for and against the creation of new counties. Proponents argued that the distances to county courts and the intervening geographic barriers required the creation of a new county or the adjustment of existing county lines.[59] Opponents minimized these charges, often asserting that the existing county and its court site better served their local communities. They also frequently charged that the proposed changes would create new counties with populations too small to maintain the militia system and to pay the taxes required for county government.[60] In 1777 alone the state legislature received at least eight petitions from the upper valley relating to county division proposals.[61]

Because the Revolution undermined the privileged position of the Church of England, controversies over religious freedom also arose in the upper valley. As early as 1776, Augusta freeholders passed two sets of resolutions endorsing the state's proclamation of toleration for dissenters and calling for full religious liberty. In Botetourt an Anglican clergyman, the Reverend Adam Smyth, found it impossible to collect his overdue salary from county taxpayers. The incumbent vestrymen protested in May 1777 that the vestry did not have enough active members to authorize such a tax. In response, the state legislature ordered that a new vestry be elected and that they collect money for the minister's salary.[62] Yet a year later nothing had been done, and William Fleming reported that there appeared little hope for the selection of a new vestry or the collection of Smyth's salary because most inhabitants wished "that every trace of the late established Church might be done away."[63] In 1780 the state permanently dissolved vestries throughout the upper valley, and as late as 1793 Botetourt's debt to Smyth remained unpaid.[64]

Sentiment against the religious establishment climaxed in 1784 and 1785 after the Virginia legislature solicited public reactions to a proposal for taxation to support all Christian denominations. This general assessment proposal would have allowed each taxpayer to choose which religious group should receive his payment.[65] At their meeting in the fall of 1784, Virginia's Presbyterian clergy had passed resolutions endorsing such a plan.[66] Nevertheless, the upper valley's largely Presbyterian population was strongly opposed. Even before the appearance of the state's proposal, Rockingham and Rockbridge citizens submitted petitions to the legislature which opposed any general assessment for religion. By the end of 1785, similar petitions had arrived from Augusta, Botetourt, Montgomery, and Washington counties.[67] When the state's Presbyterian clergy met in the valley in spring 1785, an Augusta congregation demanded an explanation of the clergy's earlier endorsement of religious taxation. The clergymen quickly reversed their position, unanimously passing a resolution opposing the general assessment. In August a meeting of representatives from Presbyterian congregations throughout the state met in Augusta and denounced any contacts between church and state. As James Madison informed Thomas Jefferson, the general assessment proposal had produced "some fermentation below the Mountains & a violent [reaction] beyond them."[68]

To some degree the Revolution's republican ideology shaped the opposition to the general assessment. Several petitions condemned the proposal as a threat to individual freedom of conscience and a violation of the revolutionary heritage and Virginia's Bill of Rights.[69] While supporters of assessment argued that religion promoted the public virtue required by a republic, upper valley opponents asserted that a republican government might regulate conduct but not individual consciences.[70] This concern with individual freedom and the revolutionary heritage was not, however, the chief source of upper valley opposition to the general assessment. More important was the fear, shared with many evangelical Protestants, that state subsidies would debase true Christianity. Early Christianity, it was argued, had survived and prospered for centuries before being corrupted by imperial Roman support.[71] Several upper valley petitions noted that reliance on voluntary contributions had strengthened Christianity in Pennsylvania and in their own region during the colonial period. Other petitions asserted that compulsory support for religion would reduce all denominations to the corruption of the Anglican establishment: mandatory assessments would weaken the faith and commitment of church members, and financial independence would morally degrade ministers by improperly separating them from their congregations.[72] Finally, many opponents of general assessment saw the proposal as an attempt at de facto reestablishment of the Anglican church.

By mid-decade, the Revolution and its republican ideology had encouraged several direct assertions that the entire citizenry rather than any select group of leaders or officials possessed the ultimate right to make political decisions. As early as 1779, a Washington County meeting directed its legislative representatives to oppose any law that would facilitate the monopolization of unappropriated western land. The meeting also ordered the assemblymen to support an increase in legislative salaries and recommended that they promote several changes in the militia laws.[73] Another set of resolves drafted in 1784 declared that people were not free unless governed solely by laws to which they had consented. This popular consent could come either directly or through the people's representatives "freely chosen, *subject to the controul* and frequently returning into the common mass of constituents."[74] In several cases upper valley groups proclaimed that not only specific laws but also the fundamental structure of government should be approved by the entire body of citizens. Thus a Rockbridge petition of 1784 asserted that since the existing state constitution had been approved only by the legislature, "the people at large" should "choose a Convention for the express purpose of forming a [new] Constitution." The petition further stipulated that the election of convention delegates should be proposed by the assemblymen "not in their Legislative capacity but as a respectable body of Citizens."[75]

The practical implications of the new political values were extensively displayed in the effort to add southwestern Virginia to the proposed new state of Franklin. The exact methods of Arthur Campbell and the other advocates of this proposal remain shrouded in a mass of charges and countercharges. Nevertheless, these men clearly sought to mobilize public support by appealing to popular interests within the region and by exploiting the revolutionary heritage and the republican ideology. The opponents of the Franklin scheme denounced their adversaries as demagogues and traitors. Yet even these opponents found themselves forced to abandon the traditional politics of deference and to compete with Campbell in direct issue-oriented appeals to the common people. In the end the controversy showed that the political culture of the upper valley had been permanently changed by the developments of the revolutionary era.

Proposals for the creation of Franklin originated in the uncertainty regarding jurisdiction over the transappalachian west. In 1781 Virginia ceded the territory north of the Ohio River to the Confederation government on condition that Congress invalidate all purchases of land from the Indians. Not surprisingly, most such acquisitions had been made by speculators from other states. A congressional committee, however, recommended against accepting Virginia's stipulations and suggested that the Continental authorities simply assume control of the entire transappalachian west. Congress took no action, and by spring of 1782 the uncertainty had led to Arthur Campbell's unsuccessful call for a convention of western settlers to plan appropriate actions. At the urging of major speculators, North Carolina ceded its western lands to Congress in spring 1784 but reversed itself the next fall, whereupon settlers in North Carolina's transappalachian region organized a new state which they called Franklin. Campbell encouraged the Carolina secessionists by predicting that Washington and Montgomery counties in Virginia would join them.[76]

Within southwestern Virginia Arthur Campbell and other leaders began efforts to build popular support for Franklin in 1784. In November Campbell sent to the Continental Congress a Washington County petition requesting the creation of a new state.[77] Then in a series of meetings the next year, Campbell and his associates tried to arouse public sentiment for a union with Franklin. Apparently they also encouraged settlers not to pay state taxes or elect legislative representatives, and they may have endorsed armed resistance to Virginia authorities. Governor Henry responded to these activities by removing Campbell and several other men from their positions in the militia. Campbell, however, refused to step down as commander of the Washington County militia. By the end of the year, Campbell's opponents charged him with this refusal and other criminal offenses connected with his Franklinite activities. Campbell escaped punishment, largely through a combination of delaying tactics and legal technicalities, but the movement for union with Franklin was defeated.[78]

Whatever the uncertainty over their exact methods, Campbell and his allies clearly accepted the necessity for issue-oriented appeals to common citizens. They encouraged concern with taxation and other problems and urged settlers to make their own judgments on these questions rather than deferring to the opinions of the elite. Thus Campbell and Charles Cummings produced statistics allegedly showing that Washington County paid more than its fair share of state taxes. They asked citizens to consider this evidence, as well as the apparently tyrannical intentions of Virginia authorities, and to support appropriate measures of opposition. Campbell and his associates evidently urged nonpayment of taxes and resistance to forcible collections, and they openly argued that relief would be most readily obtained through the creation of a new state.[79] These secessionist leaders also exploited the anxieties of numerous settlers who had not yet received full title to lands upon which they had made some payments to surveyors and state authorities. They suggested that money thus paid should be considered as a tax payment, at least until the state produced an accounting of these fees.[80] Finally, Campbell addressed the chronic problem of currency shortages by suggesting that a new state in the west would keep within the region much of the money that now flowed eastward to the state government at Richmond.[81]

Throughout the Franklin controversy, secessionist leaders portrayed their efforts as a continuation of the revolutionary tradition. At one point Campbell charged that his opponents had "lost sight" of the ideals of liberty and republican government.[82] He also claimed that the taxation which Virginia imposed on the upper valley frontier threatened to recreate the sort of "British Tirany" from which the country had just escaped.[83] The secessionists imitated the earlier methods of the patriot movement, establishing local committees to organize popular support and shouting huzzahs for liberty at their public meetings.[84]

In their efforts to mobilize support, Campbell and his associates employed not only the symbols and methods of the Revolution but also its republican conception of the inherent antagonism between power and liberty. Thus a written address to the citizens of Washington County began by pointing out the tendency of many rulers to usurp more and more of the liberty and property of their people. The address then urged the citizens to consider if their own liberty and property were not threatened in that way.[85] Similarly, at Washington County's March 1785 court, Campbell charged that the actions of the last Virginia assembly suggested a plan to usurp the people's liberties and change the government into a monarchy or an aristocracy.[86]

As other American republicans had begun to do, secessionist leaders in southwestern Virginia appealed to the state constitution as a fundamental law which restricted the dangerous actions of government.[87] An address to Washington freemen, for example, proclaimed that "in free Communities the laws are only obligatory when made Consonant to the Constitution or original compact," and Campbell's indictment of the Virginia legislature in March 1785 included the charge that it "intended to brake the Constitution." When Governor Henry attempted to replace him as Washington County lieutenant, Campbell insisted that Henry's action was unconstitutional. Then, when William Russell attempted to assume the county lieutenancy, Campbell extended the concept of constitutional restraints still further, proclaiming that under the existing separation of powers, the county court rather than the governor had the authority to enforce the law. After Russell condemned this as unlawful disobedience of the governor and council, Campbell apparently asserted that when acting beyond the bounds of their constitutional power, the governor and council were "no more than an individual."[88]

The leading opponents of the secessionist movement denounced its tactics as dangerous exploitations of the limited capacities of the common people. In letters to state officials, they described Campbell and other secessionists as licentious and artfully deceptive.[89] At several public meetings, William Russell attempted to counter Campbell's arguments by warning the people that Campbell sought to deceive them and to turn them against the government, which, he asserted, would lead to rebellion and inevitable retribution by state authorities.[90]

Despite their misgivings about such tactics, the opponents of the Franklin proposal found themselves forced to compete with Campbell in urging ordinary settlers to make their own decisions on the issues being disputed. William Russell spoke to at least three of the public meetings called by Campbell. In addition to warning against Campbell's deceptive and seditious designs, Russell attempted to refute the argument of overtaxation. He charged that Campbell's statistics were inaccurate and noted the concessions already made to local taxpayers: they were to pay only half their assessments, the sheriff would accept payment in cattle, and the evaluation of such cattle would be scrupulously fair. Furthermore, Russell suggested, if taxes were paid now, the state government might be persuaded to excuse the region from payment of part or all of the assessments still due.[91] Apparently because of the Franklin controversy, two legislators from Montgomery and Botetourt found it necessary to circulate a broadside to their constituents, detailing the amounts of taxes owed to the state, arguing that the region was not overtaxed, and urging faithful payment.[92]

In the end the Franklin controversy showed that despite the ambivalence and uncertainty of many leaders, all public decisions were now potentially subject to the will of the entire citizenry. Despite his distaste for such tactics, William Russell found himself compelled to adopt the techniques of popular political appeal. Campbell and his associates were moving more quickly, if not entirely clearly, toward the full acceptance of popular sovereignty. As early as 1782, in his abortive plan for a convention to consider the future of the west, Campbell sought to put the delegates under popular control. The proposal insisted that the representatives' power and tenure of office be strictly limited. Moreover, William Christian urged that the delegates be "deputed by the People from whence all power flows." In 1785, when Campbell and his associates held a series of meetings to shape popular opinion, an assumption that such opinion should reign obviously underlay their efforts. At one point that year, Campbell explicitly asserted that although relatively few citizens possessed sufficient talent and education to direct the government, "all may, with some diligence and honesty, be capable of judging whether it be done right or not."[93]

Campbell's own ambivalence about popular sovereignty appeared in the struggle with William Russell over the command of the Washington County militia. When Russell tried to force the Washington court to swear him into the county lieutenancy in July 1785, Campbell insisted on delaying any action until the August court so that the will of the people could be learned. This appeal to popular sovereignty, however, was not Campbell's initial response to the dilemma created by Russell. According to several witnesses, Campbell first tried other tactics: suggesting that the order Russell carried might not be genuine, arguing that the order was unconstitutional, and insisting that state authorities had been deceived. It was only after these initial ploys that Campbell demanded that popular opinion be consulted and proclaimed his willingness to accept the public verdict.[94]

By the end of the Confederation era, then, the new political methods and values brought by the Revolution had become prominent in the agitation of specific issues that concerned popular groups. In campaigns for the legislature, however, many candidates continued the traditional appeals for deference and personal loyalty. They could do so, perhaps, because the issues surrounding legislative elections often seemed unimportant in the localist world of common settlers. Yet direct issue-oriented addresses to voters began to appear in political campaigns and would play a role in the controversy over ratification of the federal Constitution.

The election of John Breckinridge to the state assembly in 1784 showed the persistence of the traditional politics. In the Botetourt election, all candidates apparently used the customary methods of personal rather than ideological appeals for support. Initially, Breckinridge, who was then studying law in Williamsburg, hoped to be elected by simply notifying a few friends of his availability and making no personal appearances in Botetourt himself. By March, however, he knew that other candidates and their friends were soliciting support from the voters, and Archibald Stuart warned him that his appearance at the polls was essential.[95] When John Preston and Breckinridge's brother James attempted to save the election for him, they too adopted the traditional methods of personal appeal. On election day, the two men went to the polling place, securing promises of support from everyone they met on the way. Yet to the surprise of most persons present, George Hancock announced his candidacy at the polls and won the election. Significantly, James Breckinridge attributed the loss to a failure of individual loyalties, lamenting to his brother, "the behavior of some persons who I thought were your friends."[96] Then, without any apparent efforts on his behalf, Montgomery County elected John Breckinridge to the legislature. Breckinridge and his friends found this especially heartening, for it showed that he could command deference and respect even without direct appeals to the common people.[97] Thus Breckinridge and his supporters interpreted both the Botetourt defeat and the Montgomery victory as reflecting the traditional politics of deference and personal loyalty.

The election of Francis Preston in Montgomery a few years later showed at least the beginnings of more democratic and issue-oriented campaigning methods. Preston was studying law in Williamsburg when the initial political maneuvering began, and his brother John argued that a personal appearance at the polls was indispensable. Indeed, when his brother sought personal support for him from local leaders, these men insisted on strong assurances that the candidate would appear at the elections. John Preston, however, moved beyond the customary limits of campaigning and planned a more systematic appeal to the voters on behalf of his brother. Thus he accepted a post as commissioner for the land tax so that he could meet most of the voters himself rather than relying on the personal contacts of influential friends. More important, in several ways John Preston urged his brother toward an issue-oriented campaign. Apparently he tried to extract from Francis a set of specific promises that he could pass along to voters. He also warned Francis that popular opinion favoring a new county could not be defied: another candidate had badly weakened himself by opposing division of the county, and Francis should avoid this mistake. Francis, moreover, would be obliged to do "many other things . . . to make yourself agreeable, though not pleasing to you." Finally, John urged the preparation of a political speech for the voters. Although the speech could be chiefly "froth," John insisted that it acknowledge a representative's submission to his constituents.[98] Thus he explicitly accepted the fundamental assumption of the new politics, the principle of popular sovereignty.

A letter from Francis Preston to James Breckinridge in 1789 reveals how well established the principle of popular sovereignty had become. By this time, Preston, who still sat in the legislature, had firmly had publicly committed himself to support any petition signed by a majority of the inhabitants of the county it affected. Preston was very much disturbed that a political rival was spreading a rumor that he had endorsed an unpopular proposal for the creation of a new county. Consequently, he asked Breckinridge to obtain a statement from a man who had witnessed the conversation in question. This statement, Preston believed, would establish that he had not endorsed the proposal for a new county but rather had predicted that it would enjoy considerable support in the legislature. Preston plainly considered the rumor a threat to both his political survival and his personal honor, for he remarked to Breckinridge that he had seriously considered challenging the propagator to a duel and might make such a challenge in the future once his political credibility had been restored.[99]

When the proposed new federal Constitution reached the upper valley in the fall of 1787, the response of regional leaders was divided. As in eastern Virginia, men who feared the impotence and insolvency of the state and national governments saw the Constitution as a solution to these problems. Thus, after describing the fiscal difficulties of Virginia and the United States, Archibald Stuart proclaimed the Constitution "our only hope."[100] John Breckinridge feared that if it were not adopted, the prevalence of political conflict would give rise to "some entrepid, enterprising demagogue" who would "involve us in eternal anarchy and ruin."[101] On the other side, various upper valley leaders denounced the Constitution for its failure to protect states' rights and the liberties of individual citizens. In their eyes it threatened to create a dangerous concentration of power in the new federal government.[102]

During the campaign for ratification, at least one Antifederalist leader made a direct ideological appeal to public opinion. In Rockbridge County, William Graham aroused popular sentiment against ratification. For a time he considered publication and mass circulation of a pamphlet expressing his views. According to one observer, by November 1787 Rockbridge citizens almost unanimously opposed the Constitution, denouncing it "as one of the most villanous peases of arbitrary [as]sumption tending directly to the overthrowing of all liberty among Citizens & quickly terminat[ing] in absolute monarchy introduced by some blood thirsty Pre[si]dent."[103] The next March, Archibald Stuart reported that Graham had "raised an uncommon Commotion" in Rockbridge and seemed likely to be elected to the ratification convention. Apparently public opinion vacillated, for Rockbridge citizens ultimately selected two men who supported the Constitution. Nevertheless, a Lexington meeting, in which local resident William Graham presumably played a leading role, attempted to instruct the Rockbridge delegates to oppose ratification.[104]

In some respects upper valley public life was relatively placid by the end of the 1780s. The controversy over ratification of the Constitution seemingly had no lasting effect on the region. Some upper valley leaders were uncertain or mistaken as to the opinions of even their close associates. At least one Botetourt leader reported little popular interest in the issue in early 1788, and, as noted above, Rockbridge public opinion was quite fluid.[105] In Staunton the news of ratification led to public celebrations in which the "utmost harmony" prevailed, and one of the town's principal streets was renamed Federal Street.[106] Throughout the region, opponents as well as advocates of ratification promised to support the new Constitution. By July 1789 Arthur Campbell, who had earlier expressed serious misgivings, described its creation as "an event equally [as] friendly to liberty" as the Revolution itself.[107]

The operations of local government also appeared little altered by the revolutionary years. To be sure, some things had changed. The difficulties of collecting taxes made the office of county sheriff much less desirable than in the colonial period, and proposals for county divisions were a much more constant source of political controversy than they had been before the Revolution. Moreover, after 1787 the new district courts reduced the jurisdiction and prestige of the county courts.[108] Nevertheless, much of county government proceeded as before. Year after year, the justices supervised the delineation and maintenance of local roads, appointed constables, licensed ordinaries, and scrupulously upheld their own authority and dignity, as well as that of other local leaders. Year after year, the justices and the more humble citizens who served on the grand juries enforced the traditional legal and moral order of their communities.

Despite this apparent tranquillity, however, a future of political conflict was probably inevitable for the upper valley. As a series of Indian alarms in the late 1780s made clear, the old tensions between gentry and common folk on defense matters continued to trouble frontier communities.[109] More important, the Revolution and the succeeding years had made many settlers more concerned with events beyond their local communities, and upper valley leaders had learned to use popular support in pursuing their political objectives. Finally, the Revolution's republican ideology, with its celebration of liberty, virtue, and popular sovereignty, helped to make all citizens more suspicious of the holders of political and economic power.

CHAPTER EIGHT

John Stuart's History of the Greenbrier Valley

By the end of the revolutionary era, many upper valley leaders recognized that the rise of republican political values had fundamentally altered their lives. For John Stuart of Greenbrier County, the shift from a deferential to a republican culture provided the underlying structure for a narrative of his county's history. In effect, Stuart's awareness of this transformation shaped his explanation of the world in which he lived.[1] The techniques of structuralism make possible an analysis of this aspect of Stuart's text. This chapter will first summarize Stuart's narrative, then briefly discuss the principles of structuralism, and finally present a structuralist analysis of the text.

Both the "Memoir of Indian Wars" and its author were closely connected to the development of the Greenbrier area and the upper Valley of Virginia. Stuart played a prominent role in much of the region's early history, and in his narrative he attempted a straightforward, comprehensive chronology of Greenbrier's development. Yet in several important ways, Stuart's text seems confused and disorganized as it departs from its apparent purpose of narrating the region's history. Ultimately, this chapter will argue, these elements of confusion and disorder provide a clue to the deeper meaning of the narrative.

Stuart was born near Staunton, where his father was an important militia leader and a justice of the peace. The Stuarts were related by marriage to the influential family of John, Andrew, and Thomas Lewis. In 1769, at the age of nineteen, Stuart settled in the Greenbrier valley and soon rose to prominence, commanding a company in the Point Pleasant expedition of 1774 and holding important military offices during and after the Revolution. The first Greenbrier County Court met at his house in 1778, and he held the powerful position of county clerk for nearly three decades. Like other local leaders, Stuart maintained close social and political ties with his counterparts in the upper valley counties to the east.

The process of composing the narrative reflected Stuart's involvement with Greenbrier County and the upper valley. In 1798 he recorded a short local history at the end of the county's deed book. Sometime between then and his death in 1823, Stuart expanded this history into the fuller test that the Virginia Hstorical Society published in 1833. Stuart received much of his information on the colonial period from the prominent leader Andrew Lewis, and his own recollections were a major source for the discussion of the revolutionary years. Since Stuart and his friends frequently retold local historical events at informal gatherings, the narrative's material also may have been shaped by these social interactions among the Greenbrier elite.[2]

The "Memoir of Indian Wars and Other Occurrences" opens with several anecdotes about the beginning of white settlement in Greenbrier. The area was first discovered by a resident of Frederick County who often wandered through the wilderness during periods of lunacy. Attracted by his reports of a land abounding with game, two other men settled there, but after a quarrel one of them moved into a hollow tree near their cabin. They lived amicably under this arrangement until Andrew Lewis arrived in 1751 to survey land for the Greenbrier Company. Lewis continued surveying in the area until interrupted by the Seven Years' War in 1755, the subsequent royal restrictions on western settlement, and the American Revolution.

When fears of an Indian war arose in 1774, the Virginia government began planning an expedition against the Shawnee towns beyond the Ohio River. Provincial authorities ordered that scouts protect the Greenbrier settlements until the expedition departed. Because they ignored warnings from Greenbrier officials, several outlying settlers were attacked by Indians. One of these men was Colonel John Fields from eastern Virginia. After the Indians shot his companion, Fields ran into their cabin, picked up a gun, remembered that it was unloaded, and ran out into a cornfield, abandoning two children in the doorway. Thus, in Stuart's words, he "made his escape but never saw an Indian."

Colonial leaders originally ordered that the expedition against the Shawnees be conducted by armies from northwestern Virginia and the upper valley, to be commanded by Governor Dunmore and

Andrew Lewis respectively. The two forces were to meet at Point Pleasant on the Ohio River and advance together against the Indians. Upon arriving at Point Pleasant, however, Lewis learned that Dunmore had already crossed the Ohio, and the governor's messengers instructed Lewis to meet him at the Shawnee towns, a plan Stuart criticized as impractical.

The battle of Point Pleasant began when two soldiers who were out hunting brought word of an approaching Indian army. Lewis immediately deployed the companies commanded by his most senior captains. Then he gradually committed more companies to the battle until the Indians retreated. Charles Lewis, brother of the commander and an extremely popular officer, was mortally wounded as the fighting began. Several other officers were killed, including John Fields, who had escaped from the Indians on the Greenbrier frontier earlier that year. On the way to Point Pleasant, Fields had remained independent of Andrew Lewis, foolishly marching his company by a separate route. Only after Indians ambushed two of his men did Fields rejoin Lewis's army. Stuart emphasized that the Shawnee Indians who attacked at Point Pleasant were formidable fighters throughout the late eighteenth century; their leader Cornstalk was particularly impressive. According to Stuart, British officials had incited the Indians to wage this war to prevent the colonies from uniting in opposition to parliamentary taxation. Thus he claimed that the Point Pleasant battle actually began the American Revolution.

After noting Lewis's difficulties in preserving order and discipline on the Point Pleasant expedition, Stuart described his entire military career. In 1754 Lewis served in Washington's disastrous expedition to the upper Ohio. During Washington's surrender to the French, Lewis avoided the possible slaughter of the Virginia force by preventing a disorderly soldier from killing an Indian. Later in the Seven Years' War, Lewis accompanied a British officer, Major James Grant, on a reconnaissance mission that led the major to attack Fort Duquesne. Grant made this attack contrary to the prior orders of his commanding officer and against the urgent entreaties of Lewis. When Indians surrounded Grant's men, Lewis brought his Virginia troops into the fight, allowing Grant and a few others to escape but resulting in his own capture. Grant became lost in the woods, however, and surrendered to the French the next day. In his letters from prison, Grant blamed Lewis and the Virginia troops for his defeat. Stuart also noted that Grant served in Parliament in 1775, where he described the Americans as poor soldiers whom a small English army could defeat.

After his dramatic victory at Point Pleasant, Lewis lost the eminence he had gained there. His authoritarian leadership made him unpopular, as was noted in the Continental Congress when Washington suggested him for the command of the American army. Early in the Revolutionary War, Lewis served for a time as a brigadier general in eastern Virginia, and his troops drove the royal governor's forces out of Norfolk. When several less senior officers were promoted over him to major general, he resigned his commission and died of a fever on the way home.

Having summarized Lewis's career, Stuart described the rest of the Point Pleasant campaign. Following the battle, Lewis's army crossed the Ohio River. Before reaching the Shawnee towns, they were halted by a message from Governor Dunmore, who had made peace with the Indians. Dunmore thanked Lewis and his officers for their services and agreed to establish a garrison at Point Pleasant under command of Matthew Arbuckle. When the Revolution began the next spring, the Virginia government ordered Arbuckle to abandon the fort and join General George Washington's army, which he refused to do. Some of his men left, however, and served with the Continental army for the remainder of their enlistment.

In the summer of 1777, the government of revolutionary Virginia ordered another expedition against the Shawnee towns. It was to consist of a force raised by General Lemuel Hand near Fort Pitt and a second group from the upper valley. Hand failed to raise any troops, and upper valley leaders recruited only a few companies. In Greenbrier, Stuart and his associates succeeded in raising a company solely because most of the militia officers volunteered to serve as enlisted men during the campaign. When the soldiers from Greenbrier and the upper valley reached Point Pleasant, they found that Hand had not arrived. Despite their lack of supplies, the men decided to remain there.

This abortive campaign led to the murder of the Shawnee leader Cornstalk. During a visit to the Point Pleasant garrison, Cornstalk predicted that his people would be compelled to join the neighboring tribes in a war against the United States. Consequently, Matthew Arbuckle, the fort's commander, seized Cornstalk and his companions as hostages. Soon thereafter, other Indians attacked two upper valley soldiers near the fort, killing one. The man's comrades insisted on killing the hostages in retaliation, and they did so despite an attempt by Stuart and Arbuckle to stop them. General Hand arrived at Point Pleasant a few days later and disbanded the force from Greenbrier and the upper valley.

After Cornstalk's death, Indians attacked Point Pleasant several times. Following a fight in May 1778, one warrior entered the stockade peacefully, during which time a gun accidentally discharged. When the Indians outside began yelling, the visitor quickly leaped onto one of the bastions to show his companions that all was well. Finding that they could not overcome the garrison, the Indians marched up the Kanawha River toward Greenbrier to avenge Cornstalk's death.

After learning of this, Andrew Donnelly collected his Greenbrier neighbors at his home, which had been partially fortified. He also sent word to Stuart and Samuel Lewis, who attempted to raise men for reinforcements. Stuart and Lewis had little success, however, for local settlers were busy securing their property or fleeing to safer places. After waiting a day, they marched with the men they had collected and arrived during the battle.

According to Stuart, the real heroes of the fight at Donnelly's were Phillip Hammond and a black slave named Dick. Hammond and Dick were sleeping in the kitchen half of Donnelly's divided dog-run house when the Indians attempted a surprise attack. The two men held the door closed until the Indians were splitting it with their tomahawks, then suddenly let it fly open. Hammond immediately killed one of the attackers, and Dick fired a musket charged with swan shot into their midst. This commotion awakened the people in the rest of the house, whereupon the Indians retreated with heavy casualties. Stuart noted that Dick's owner later abandoned him and that the Virginia legislature refused him a small pension despite his poverty and the statements of prominent Greenbrier leaders attesting to his valor.

After Stuart's party arrived, there were no further assaults on Donnelly's house. One badly wounded Indian lay all day in the yard outside, suffering horribly and ignoring his comrades' calls to surrender and go into the house. That night another warrior approached and called out in English that he wished to make peace. The defenders invited him to come in and negotiate, but he declined and the next morning the Indians were gone. They made only two more minor incursions into the area, and Greenbrier's Indian wars ended with the last of these in 1780.

Although the "Memoir of Indian Wars" generally follows a

conventional pattern of organization, several striking divergences suggest that the narrative conveyed more than a simple summary of the community's history. First, Stuart departed abruptly from his chronological pattern of development to describe the career of Andrew Lewis, a divergence that occupied nearly a third of the colonial portion of the text. Second, although the narrative was intended to be a history of Greenbrier, the key episodes of both the colonial and revolutionary sections took place outside the region at Point Pleasant. Finally, in several respects, Stuart's interpretation of events differed from those of other contemporaries. The techniques of structuralism provide a method for analyzing these aspects of Stuart's narrative.

Structuralist analysis, as developed by Claude Lévi-Strauss and other theorists, depends on several analogies between the nature of meaning in language and in such cultural phenomena as myths, folktales, and formal literature.[3] First, both languages and cultural phenomena receive much of their meaning not from the inherent characteristics of their components but rather from values imposed by their users. Second, the underlying structure of relationships between their components creates much of that meaning. Third, there is often a hierarchy of such structured relationships within a single linguistic or cultural phenomenon. Finally, many users of both languages and cultural phenomena are not fully conscious of the underlying structures of relationships that generate meaning. Although the nature of historical narratives causes some problems for analysis, appropriate adjustments in methodology can make possible a meaningful examination of such texts.

Both language and many forms of cultural expression derive much of their meaning from values that are imposed upon them. In languages, there are relatively few causal links between particular sounds or sequences of sounds and particular meanings. The meaning attached to a phonetic sequence may vary between languages and often within a single language. In English, for example, the word *well* has several meanings, including "a deep hole or shaft sunk into the earth to tap an underground supply of water, gas, oil, etc." and "in a pleasing or desirable manner."[4] Since these meanings are quite different, there is clearly no connection between them and the group of sounds forming the word *well*. Instead, the meanings are imposed on the word by those who use it.

Similarly, the meaning of cultural expressions often is imposed on them rather than being inherent in their components. Admittedly, much of the meaning of a novel, myth, or narrative lies in its language. Yet many texts also have themes or meanings beyond the literal significance of the words that make them up. Understanding of these meanings frequently depends on familiarity with the cultural environment of the text. Similarly, many jokes and anecdotes have particular meanings for people who have shared certain experiences and perceptions. Outsiders who in a literal sense speak the language do not understand these meanings. Thus meanings are imposed on cultural phenomena both by those who create or perform them and by the audiences who receive and sanction them.

Language is also characterized by the transmission of its meaning through a system of relationships among its components. Individual phonemes do not have meaning until they are combined into words, and words acquire added significance as they are combined into sentences and larger units. Thus the words, *stop, car, the,* and *now* have meaning for English speakers, but *Stop the car now* acquires meaning not only from the component words but also from their combination into a sentence according to the rules of the language: *Stop the car now* makes sense; *The now stop car* does not.

In a similar way, the underlying relationship between component parts largely determine the messages conveyed by cultural phenomena. This is particularly clear in a poem by Emily Dickinson:

> I never saw a moor,
> I never saw the sea;
> Yet know I how the heather looks,
> And what a wave must be.
>
> I never spoke with God
> Nor visited in heaven;
> Yet certain am I of the spot
> As if the chart were given.[5]

The first stanza suggests a relationship between experience and knowledge: although she has not seen a moor or the sea, she knows what they are like. The second stanza suggests that the same relationship applies to her experience and knowledge of God and heaven: although she has not directly experienced them, she is certain of their existence. A second and contradictory meaning, however, arises from the juxtaposing of the two stanzas. At the end of the first stanza, the narrator claims to know the physical characteristics of several things, yet in the second stanza's conclusion, she asserts knowledge only of the location. Moreover, in the second stanza the narrator claims to be only as certain as she would be *if* she had a chart, substantially weakening her assertion of knowledge. Thus the relationships between the elements of Dickinson's poem both strengthen the meaning explicitly stated by its language and imply a second and contradictory level of meaning.

Both language and cultural phenomena often have hierarchies of relationships in which lower-level relationships between simple components themselves become components of more complex structures. In languages phonetic units combine into words, words into sentences, sentences into paragraphs, and so forth. In Dickinson's poem the relationships between the first and second halves of each stanza become components of a relationship between the two stanzas. Similar hierarchies of relationships occur in many literary works and, as Lévi-Strauss and others have suggested, in myths and other forms of cultural expression.

A final similarity between language and cultural phenomena is that their users need not be fully conscious of the underlying structures that create meaning. The speakers of a language or dialect often cannot recite the rules of proper form. Nevertheless, they can distinguish between grammatical and ungrammatical, logical and nonsensical sequences of words in ways that clearly imply such an underlying structure. Likewise, the members of a culture may not be able to explain the meaning of a popular narrative, myth, or other cultural phenomenon. Often even the creator of a particular text cannot fully and explicitly articulate its meaning.[6] Yet the popularity of these texts and artifacts, and especially the recurrence of similar patterns of meaning in other expressions of that culture, again suggests the existence of such an underlying structure.

The structuralist procedure for discovering the underlying meaning of a cultural phenomenon includes two steps: identifying its components and examining the relationships between them for suggestions of meaning.[7] There are no universal criteria for identifying the component units of a text. Many structuralists begin with a search for binary oppositions of characters, actions, concepts, or other elements. In "The Story of Asdiwal," for example, Lévi-Strauss points out a series of oppositions including high and low, heaven and earth, mountain and sea, men and women, and endogamy and exogamy. To insist that all analyses be based on binary oppositions, however, is overly restrictive; many texts are built on other types of cognitive structures.[8] Indeed, as some poststructuralist theorists have suggested, the most revealing feature of many texts may be the ways in which their apparent structure breaks down or is disrupted, for such disjunctures often illuminate warring patterns of construction and signification at work within the text.[9]

An alternative method of identifying the structural components of a text is to summarize it in a series of simple statements, which often serve as the components of more complex statements. Once the text has been summarized in this way, its meaning may be revealed by examining the relationships between these component statements. Two types of relationships, syntagmatic and paradigmatic, are of particular interest. Syntagmatic relationships are those between components which combine into a more complex sequence, often described as a syntagmatic chain. Paradigmatic relationships are those between components occupying analogous positions in different syntagmatic chains; these components form a paradigmatic class. The ways in which the presence of one or another member of a paradigmatic class affects its respective syntagmatic chain is an important identification of meaning.[10]

Several aspects of historical narratives such as Stuart's limit their susceptibility to structural analysis. Since facts as well as values influence the content of all nonfictional narratives, a single unified structure of meaning seldom shapes an entire text. Moreover, untrained historical writers often feel compelled to maintain a rigid chronological order and to leave no portion of their period unchronicled.[11] Such writers may also be attracted by particularly dramatic events regardless of their relation to the rest of the text.[12]

In several ways, however, historical narratives can convey meaning through their internal structures. Both fictional and nonfictional narratives often exploit the distinction between the *story*, or the pattern of events and actions, and the *discourse*, or narration of that story. For a narrative *discourse* to make use of flashbacks to earlier actions or events, for example, there must be an understood order in which the events are presumed to have occurred in the *story*. Similarly, although writers of historical narratives may strive to remain true to the "facts" of their *story*, they exercise considerable discretion in choosing which factual material to include or omit, emphasize or minimize in their *discourse*. Moreover, both nonfictional and fictional narratives are often decisively shaped by the narrator's desire to make his or her narrative appear significant.[13] All of these choices in composition and structure may create or enhance underlying meanings. Finally, a historical narrative's divergences from objective "truth" or from the conventional view of events held by the narrator's society, as well as the text's abrupt departure from its own apparent pattern of organization, merit close attention. For these disjunctures may indicate underlying structures of meaning that conflict with the narrator's inclination to produce a conventional chronology of events.[14]

Given these characteristics of historical narratives, structural analysis should begin by delineating the most significant and inclusive structured aspect of the text. This aspect can then be summarized in a series of short statements whose interrelationships may be examined for suggestions of meaning. In view of the writer's freedom to select the material to be included or emphasized in the narrative, even structural relationships between factually accurate textual components may convey significant meaning. Particular attention, however, should be given to instances of conflict with objective truth and with the prevailing view of events held by that society. Moreover, when a well-ordered narrative suddenly turns away from its apparent pattern of organization, that movement may suggest another level of structure and meaning within the text.

The most significant and inclusive structured element of Stuart's text is his description of authority and order. Contrasting depictions of authority and order underlie Stuart's apparent deviations from focus on the Greenbrier region and from his strictly chronological pattern of development. Ultimately a comparison of the maintenance of authority and order in the colonial period and the decline of those values in the revolutionary era shapes the entire narrative.

Although most of the text describes developments in the Greenbrier valley, the climactic events of both the colonial and revolutionary portions of the story occur outside the region, at Point Pleasant on the Ohio River. Lewis's victory there in 1774 marked the high point of his career, and the murder of Cornstalk by mutinous soldiers in 1777 began the Indian wars that dominate the revolutionary portion of Stuart's narrative. Several similarities in the two episodes underscore their analogous positions in the text and heighten the contrasts between them. Both episodes occurred while militiamen from Greenbrier and the upper valley awaited a rendezvous with forces from Fort Pitt before proceeding across the Ohio. In neither case did the reinforcements arrive, and on both occasions the dramatic action began when a pair of militiamen out hunting encountered hostile Indians. Most important, both episodes revolved around relationships of authority and order.

In Stuart's portrayal, Andrew Lewis won at Point Pleasant by maintaining effective hierarchical authority over his troops. As the battle opened, Lewis quickly took control and began deploying men against the Indians. Significantly, he started with the companies of his senior captains. Throughout the fight he remained behind the battle lines, directing the flow of reinforcements to the front. Although this aloof, hierarchical, and authoritarian style of leadership won the battle, it aroused resentment among the common soldiers.

Two of Stuart's deviations from other contemporary accounts of the battle reinforce his emphasis on Andrew Lewis's authority and control. First, although he mentions the popularity of Charles Lewis, Andrew's younger brother, Stuart says little of his part in the battle, simply stating that he was mortally wounded and then returned to camp. Other accounts emphasize the younger Lewis's unauthoritarian style of leadership and his battlefield role, noting that after being shot, he gave his gun to a soldier and walked back to camp, refusing assistance and encouraging the men he passed to go forward and fight bravely. A popular ballad about Point Pleasant directly contrasts Charles Lewis's bravery and closeness to his men with Andrew Lewis's aloofness and alleged cowardice.[15] Stuart also differs from other accounts by ignoring the disorderly consequences of Lewis's plan of battle. Because Lewis deployed his men company by company, without keeping each county's militiamen together, field officers at the line of battle were separated from the men they normally commanded and often failed to control the soldiers.[16] By ignoring these aspects of the battle, Stuart consciously or unconsciously places greater stress on Andrew Lewis's effective control of the situation.

In contrast to Lewis's control at Point Pleasant, Stuart and his fellow officers lost control of their men when Cornstalk was murdered at that site in 1777. After hostile Indians killed a militiaman who had crossed the Kanawha River, unruly soldiers murdered Cornstalk and two other friendly Indians inside the fort. When Stuart and Matthew Arbuckle, the fort's commander, tried to stop them, the men threatened to kill them too. Although Captain James

Hall joined the mob, Stuart makes it clear that the cries to kill Cornstalk arose spontaneously among the men. He also reduces the social distance between Hall and the militamen by noting that Hall was related to the man killed by the Indians across the Kanawha.

Thus the key episodes of Stuart's narrative can be summarized and compared in two simple statements: *Lewis maintained authority over his men. Stuart and Arbuckle failed to maintain authority over their men.* Moreover, within each half of the narrative, a series of analogous statements regarding authority and order summarize much of the rest of the text.

According to the narrative, constant maintenance of order and authority over his subordinates typified Andrew Lewis's career. As Stuart portrays it, Lewis's organization of the Point Pleasant campaign proceeded smoothly with little of the recruiting problems and popular resistance to conscription which William Preston and other leaders described. Moreover, Stuart departs from his otherwise strict chronological pattern of development to explain that Lewis had consistently maintained authority and order throughout his earlier career. During the surrender at Fort Necessity in the Seven Years' War, Lewis prevented a disorderly soldier from shooting an Indian and thus avoided the probable massacre of Washington's entire force. When Lewis represented Virginia in treaty negotiations with the Iroquois in 1768, the governor of New York remarked that even his personal bearing conveyed authority: "The very ground seemed to tremble under him as he walked along." Appropriately, Lewis ended his military career during the Revolution when he felt that the promotion of several inferior officers to ranks above his own violated his status. Stuart emphasizes that throughout his career, Lewis won his subordinates' respect and obedience through his own merits, not through any self-abasing appeals for popular support.

In contrast to Lewis's constant maintenance of authority, revolutionary leaders frequently failed to control their subordinates. When the war began, some of Arbuckle's men at Point Pleasant ignored his desire to maintain the garrison and joined Washington's army in Massachusetts. In 1777, when the Virginia government ordered an offensive against the Shawnee towns, upper valley leaders had little success in raising men. Augusta and Botetourt leaders recruited no more than three or four companies, and Greenbrier raised forty men only because most of the county's officers agreed to serve as common soldiers, thereby accepting a loss of status and authority to encourage popular support. General Lemuel Hand totally failed in his efforts to raise men in the area surrounding Fort Pitt. The next year Stuart and Samuel Lewis had trouble mobilizing a militia party to help defend Andrew Donnelly's home. They delayed their departure for a full day and even then raised only sixty-eight men.

As discussed thus far, Stuart's comparison of the maintenance of authority and order in the colonial period and the decline of those values in the revolutionary era can be summarized in the following statements:

Andrew Lewis maintained authority and order.

Lewis prevented a soldier from killing an Indian at Fort Necessity.

Lewis conveyed an air of authority at the Iroquois treaty.

Lewis recruited and organized effectively for the Point Pleasant expedition.

Lewis maintained authority and order during the Point Pleasant battle.

Lewis consistently refused to make self-abasing appeals for popular support.

Lewis ended his career when his authority was violated (by the promotion of interior officers).

Revolutionary leaders failed to maintain authority and order.

Matthew Arbuckle failed to keep all of his men at Point Pleasant.

General Hand and upper valley leaders failed to raise men for the 1777 expedition.

Greenbrier leaders made self-abasing appeals for popular support in raising men for the 1777 expedition.

Stuart and Arbuckle failed to prevent the soldiers from murdering Cornstalk.

Stuart and Samuel Lewis had great difficulty in raising a militia party to reinforce Donnelly.

Several other aspects of the narrative strengthen this contrast. The opening and closing portions of the text reiterate the difference between colonial and revolutionary patterns of order and authority. Stuart begins his narrative with the early settlement of the Greenbrier region: it was discovered by a wandering lunatic, and the first two settlers became so quarrelsome that one of them moved out of their cabin into a nearby hollow tree. Arriving in 1751 as a land company agent, Andrew Lewis brought order and authority to this disorderly region: he began surveying the land, thereby establishing both ownership of property and a relationship to the ultimate source of that ownership, the Virginia government. Moreover, according to Stuart, Lewis's arrival led to the naming of the Greenbrier River when his father became entangled in the briers along its banks. Lewis's arrival thus transformed the Greenbrier valley from a nameless region frequented by wandering lunatics and quarrelsome settlers into an ordered society characterized by ownership of property, ties to political authority, and a sense of geographic identity.

While the opening of the narrative deals with Andrew Lewis's creation of an ordered community, the conclusion depicts the salvation of that community not by its leaders but rather by a member of its lowest class. The last significant Indian attack in Greenbrier took place at Andrew Donnelly's home. According to other contemporary accounts, the arrival of Stuart and Samuel Lewis with reinforcements saved the settlers who were besieged there. In Stuart's portrayal, however, the real hero was a black slave who helped prevent the Indians from breaking into the house. Stuart further notes that the slave's owner abandoned him when he grew old and that the state legislature refused to grant him a pension despite statements by Greenbrier leaders attesting to his earlier heroism. Thus although a member of Greenbrier's lowest social class saved that community, he subsequently failed to receive even minimal support from the upper echelons of Greenbrier society, whose traditional role had been to provide such assistance.

The portrayal of Cornstalk in the two portions of Stuart's text also parallels the contrast between colonial success and revolutionary failure in maintaining authority and order. At the battle of Point Pleasant, Cornstalk appeared as a brave and forceful leader, encouraging his men to fight and constantly crying out, "be strong, be strong." At one point he killed a warrior who fled from the battle, and afterward he urged the Shawnees to fight to the death. In the revolutionary portion of the narrative, Cornstalk was much less forceful, stoically resigning himself to the consequences of forces beyond his control. Upon arriving at Point Pleasant in 1777, he announced that when the other tribes sided with the British in the future, he and his people would be forced "to run with the stream." In a speech to the American officers at the fort, Cornstalk foreshadowed his own death in a similarly fatalistic tone. Thus, although Stuart portrays him as a brave man who met his death calmly, he also stresses Cornstalk's acceptance of events as inevitable rather than as malleable by effective leadership.

A similar contrast between the colonial and revolutionary periods appears in Stuart's depiction of leaders who refused to respect established authorities. John Fields of eastern Virginia exemplifies this character type in the colonial portion of the narrative. In the summer of 1774, Fields was surveying land on the frontier beyond Greenbrier and ignored Stuart's warning of coming Indian attacks. As a result, the Indians killed his companion, and Fields got away only by disgracing himself. He abandoned two servant children and "made his escape but never saw an Indian." Fields also organized a volunteer company for the Point Pleasant expedition but insisted on his independence from Lewis and marched toward the Ohio by a separate route. Within a few days, however, Indians killed two of his men, and he rejoined the main force. Although Fields's reversals resulted from bad luck and his own foolishness rather than from any action by his superiors, Stuart's tone makes it clear that he regarded these misfortunes as Fields's just deserts. Stuart similarly depicts the transgressions of James Grant on the expedition against Fort Duquesne during the Seven Years' War: when Grant violated General John Forbes's orders by attacking the fort, not only was he badly beaten but he became lost in the woods and surrendered to the French to save himself. He further disgraced himself by unworthy behavior during the removal to Canada and by unjustly blaming Andrew Lewis and the Virginia troops for his defeat.

Although such disorderly leaders usually got their just deserts in the colonial period, circumstances changed in the revolutionary portion of the narrative. At the beginning of the war, Matthew Arbuckle refused to abandon the Point Pleasant fort when Virginia authorities ordered him to do so. Although some of his men left to join Washington's army, Arbuckle remained at Point Pleasant, and Stuart mentions no penalties being imposed upon him. More significantly, in Stuart's portrayal, little effort was made to punish Captain James Hall for his role in the murder of Cornstalk. General Hand arrived at Point Pleasant a few days after the crime but took no steps against Hall and the other murderers. Since the Virginia government *did* repeatedly if ineffectively try to prosecute Hall and the other men responsible for Cornstalk's death, Stuart's failure to mention these efforts is particularly striking.

The analysis thus far can be summarized in a series of short sentences contrasting the patterns of authority and order in the colonial and revolutionary periods. To the statements listed on p. 150 can be added the following:

Colonial Period
Lewis (a leader) creates a new society.
Cornstalk is a forceful leader.
Disorderly leaders receive their just deserts.
Revolutionary Period
A slave (the antithesis of a leader) saves that society.
(Moreover, its leaders cannot protect him later).
Cornstalk resigns himself to forces beyond his control.
Disorderly leaders do not receive their just deserts.

Structuralist analysis of Stuart's text can reveal not only its description of fundamental differences between the colonial and revolutionary periods but also its depiction of some of the causes and consequences of those differences. Simply grouping the statements, as on pages 150 and above, into paradigmatic classes summarizing the colonial and revolutionary eras shows Stuart's awareness of important changes between the two periods. His assessment of some of the sources and results of these changes can be suggested by an analysis of the summary statements as parts of syntagmatic chains, each chain implying a relationship between two aspects of either the colonial or the revolutionary period. The comparison of analogous colonial and revolutionary chains can then show the text's depiction of causes and consequences of differences between the colonial and revolutionary periods. The presence of these apparent causal connections in the narrative does not mean that Stuart and his audience were fully aware of them. And it certainly does not imply that they regarded these patterns as a total explanation of the events and developments described in the text. Yet the recurrence of such patterns in the narrative does suggest that the connections were made at some level of consciousness.

The syntagmatic relations between some of the summary statements indicate that in Stuart's eyes a simple loss of will power among revolutionary leaders contributed to their failure to maintain traditional standards of authority and order. In the colonial portion of his narrative, Stuart stresses that Andrew Lewis consistently refused to make self-abasing appeals for popular support. During the Revolution, by contrast, Stuart and other Greenbrier leaders willingly surrendered their own authority by volunteering to serve as common soldiers in the 1777 expedition. Although they hoped that this sacrifice would win popular support for the expedition, it also may have contributed to their inability to prevent their soldiers from murdering Cornstalk. Accordingly, two syntagmatic relationships may be suggested between the components of the narrative:

A1Lewis maintained authority and order	*in part because*	B1Lewis consistently refused to make self-abasing appeals for popular support.
A2Revolutionary leaders failed to maintain authority and order.	*in part because*	B2Revolutionary leaders made self-abasing appeals for popular support.

In effect the narrative implies that the difference between statements B1 and B2 contributed to the difference between statements A1 and A2: the willingness of revolutionary leaders to make self-abasing popular appeals contributed to the decline of the traditional order of their society.

Another apparent source of the decline of authority and order lay in the changing attitudes of Greenbrier leaders toward their superiors. Throughout the colonial portion of the text, Stuart emphasizes the abuse of the Greenbrier region and its leaders by British officials. He suggests that the British had incited the Indian attacks of 1763 and he repeatedly insists that Governor Dunmore had arranged the assault on Lewis's army at Point Pleasant in 1774.[17] Stuart also describes the relationship between Andrew Lewis and James Grant, a British superior during the Seven Years' War. In rejecting Lewis's advice against attacking Fort Duquesne, Grant insinuated that Lewis was a coward. Then when the attack failed, Grant unjustly blamed Lewis rather than acknowledging his own imprudence.

Despite this pattern of abuse, colonial Greenbrier leaders remained loyal to their superiors. At Fort Duquesne, for example, Lewis attacked the Indians to save Major Grant from the results of his folly, an action that led to Lewis's own capture. Similarly, despite Dunmore's failure to meet him at Point Pleasant as planned, Lewis complied with the governor's new instructions. After suffering

heavy battlefield casualties, he crossed the Ohio as quickly as possible and marched toward the Shawnee towns. When he received
yet another set of orders from Dunmore, Lewis halted his army
despite the soldiers' desire to defeat their enemy decisively, and
when the governor arrived at his camp, Lewis deferentially introduced him to the officers and then ordered his army home.

In contrast to Lewis's consistent support of his superiors, revolutionary leaders defied state officials, which in turn seemingly
undermined their own local authority. Matthew Arbuckle, for example, disobeyed the Virginia government's order to abandon the
Point Pleasant fort and join Washington's army. Arbuckle's defiance
apparently helped to erode his own power, for some of his men
decided on their own to leave Point Pleasant and join the Continental forces. Thus two additional syntagmatic relationships may suggest a partial connection between the declining power of Greenbrier
leaders and their declining respect for their own superiors:

C1Lewis maintained authority and order	in part because	D1Lewis respected superior authorities.
C2Revolutionary leaders failed to maintain authority and order.	in part because	D2Revolutionary leaders failed to respect superior authorities.

Stuart, apparently consciously or subconsciously felt that once the
Revolution had eroded authority at one point in his society, similar
erosions were likely elsewhere as well.

In addition to suggesting several causes for the decline of traditional patterns of authority and order, the structure of Stuart's
narrative implies that this decline in turn contributed to the loss of
virtue in Greenbrier society. Throughout the colonial period, Andrew Lewis and the Greenbrier settlers were morally superior to the
Indians and to the British officials who deceived and betrayed
them. The Indians who attacked Archibald Clendenin's home in
1763, for example, gained entry by posing as friendly visitors.[18]
Stuart also insinuates that the British had instigated this Indian war,
and he gives substantial attention to James Grant's attempt to blame
Andrew Lewis for their capture at Fort Duquesne. Lewis clearly

emerged as superior to Grant, dealing more bravely with adversity on their trip to Canada and receiving greater respect from their French captors. Finally, Stuart repeatedly asserts that Governor Dunmore had arranged the Shawnee attack on Lewis's army at Point Pleasant in 1774.

While Andrew Lewis and colonial Greenbrier remained morally superior to their antagonists, revolutionary militamen were guilty of betrayal in the murder of Cornstalk: the Shawnee leader was killed after entering the Point Pleasant fort as a friendly visitor. Several subsequent episodes contain implied references to the immorality of this action. Stuart relates, for example, that while an Indian emissary was in the Point Pleasant garrison the next year, a gun discharged accidentally. To reassure his alarmed companions outside, the visitor had to move quickly to a place in the fort where they could see him. Stuart notes that during the attack on Andrew Donnelly's house, a wounded Indian lay all day on the ground outside even though his comrades urged him to surrender and enter the house. After dark another Indian came close to the house and called out that he wanted to make peace, but he declined an invitation to come inside. Stuart's repeated descriptions of these minor episodes, with their underlying allusions to Cornstalk's death, suggest how important that betrayal and murder were in his perception of the Greenbrier region's history.[19] This aspect of the text can be summarized in two syntagmatic chains:

E_1Lewis maintained authority and order	*and this helped to ensure that*	F_1Colonial Greenbrier was morally *superior* to its adversaries.
E_2Revolutionary leaders failed to maintain authority and order	*and this helped to ensure that*	B_2Revolutionary Greenbrier was morally *inferior* to its adversaries.

Thus in Stuart's eyes, the decline of order also helped undermine the morality of his society.

The structure of Stuart's narrative suggests that for him and for many of his peers, a disintegration of traditional standards of au-

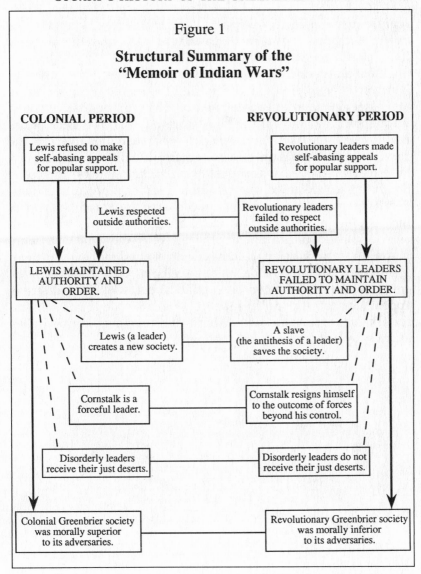

Figure 1

Structural Summary of the
"Memoir of Indian Wars"

thority and order characterized the revolutionary era. They attributed this decline in part to their own loss of the will to enforce the old ideals and to their own disrespect for higher authorities. Moreover, they ascribed much of their society's declining virtue to this growing political disorder. The structure of meaning underlying Stuart's narrative is summarized in Figure 1. The vertical lines represent causal relationships; the horizontal lines, contrasts between the colonial and revolutionary periods; and the diagonal lines, complementary relationships.

Most assuredly, the pattern of meaning embedded in Stuart's narrative oversimplified and distorted the reality of upper valley life. After all, disorder and defiance of elite authority had occurred throughout the colonial period. Andrew Lewis, the hero of the narrative's colonial section, encountered such defiance on the Sandy Creek expedition of 1756, when virtually his entire army deserted. Moreover, many postrevolutionary leaders, including Stuart himself, retained much of their traditional power and prestige. Stuart and other leaders who shared his apprehension of catastrophic decline failed to understand fully the forces transforming the political culture in which they lived. At the same time, more perceptive men, who often admired and aspired to the older ideals of authority and deference, were developing new styles of leadership which incorporated open political partisanship and strong appeals for active popular support. The ambivalent political and social values of such men would both reflect and shape upper valley life throughout the early national period.

Conclusion

This study of the eighteenth-century upper valley reaches two conclusions. First, although the members of the region's colonial elite recreated much of the political culture of eastern Virginia, they failed to fully impose their deferential values on the rest of the population. Second, despite the continued power and prestige of the gentry, the ideology and material circumstances of the revolutionary era combined to create a strikingly more republican political ethos by 1789. The developments of the colonial period cast light on events elsewhere in Virginia and the southern backcountry. Similarly, the experience of upper valley inhabitants in the revolutionary and postrevolutionary years may exemplify broader patterns in the myriad social, political, and cultural transformations of the era.

At least in the upper valley, Virginia's deferential culture was much less pervasive than Charles Sydnor, Edmund S. Morgan, and other scholars have suggested.[1] Although upper valley leaders maintained these values in the county courts and some other political arenas, the strength of popular localism limited their success. In contrast to the gentry, much of the upper valley population preferred more consensual styles of leadership and identified primarily with local neighborhoods rather than with their counties, the Virginia government, or the British Empire. These popular political attitudes appeared in the militia and in defense activities in general, as well as in some additional areas of public life. Several recent studies of other parts of western Virginia have revealed elements of the popular political culture that prevailed in the upper valley.[2]

Although many of the circumstances giving rise to popular localism were unique to the backcountry, substantial dissent from elite values also developed in eastern Virginia. James Titus's examination of Virginia's role in the Seven Years' War shows that many common people throughout the colony rejected both the deferential standards and the defense policies of provincial leaders.[3] As Timothy Breen and others have asserted, some aspects of the tobacco economy worked to divide rich and poor farmers. The "gentle" and "simple" folk differed in their use of credit, their methods of marketing their crops, and often in the type of tobacco they produced. Not surprisingly, poor Virginians failed to share the big planters' sense of economic and social crisis in the 1760s, and many ignored the patriot movement of 1774 and 1775 because they felt little concern with a dispute over tea, a luxury good that they seldom consumed.[4] Whatever the limitations of his analysis, Rhys Isaac's examination of the growth of evangelical religion makes clear that at least some Virginians saw this movement as a challenge to the values of the gentry.[5]

A number of studies of Virginia and other portions of early America suggest the need for more attention to local neighborhoods in the analysis of popular culture. In their examination of Middlesex County, Virginia, Darrett B. Rutman and Anita H. Rutman emphasize the importance of social bonds among the residents of particular sections of the county. Similarly, Mary Beth Norton notes the role of community networks in the development of social conflict through gossip and defamation in seventeenth-century Maryland. According to Paul D. Escott and Jeffrey R. Crow, popular opposition to both the Revolution and the Civil War in North Carolina arose in large part from the unwillingness of lower-class groups to reduce their independence from the elite-dominated outside world. Finally, Gregory H. Nobles and other scholars have suggested that strong ties to local communities and to relatively uncommercialized local economies separated the mass of western Massachusetts farmers from the more cosmopolitan leaders of their society in the late eighteenth century.[6] Clearly, the militia, which played a crucial role in the development of popular localism in the upper valley, was less important in the neighborhoods of eastern Virginia.[7] Yet other local institutions, including road gangs, dissenting churches, and local Anglican chapels, may have been more important than has yet been realized.[8]

The upper valley gentry's success in maintaining control of the region suggests several comparisons with less stable portions of the colonial backcountry. As was discussed in chapter 4, the relative political tranquillity of the upper valley resulted in part from the elite's greater economic and moral stature, which helped elicit popular respect. In contrast, the corruption and comparative poverty of western North Carolina leaders apparently contributed to the resentments that fueled the development of the Regulator movement. Upper valley leaders also enjoyed closer ties with provincial authorities than did their counterparts in backcountry South Carolina and Pennsylvania. The respect and support of these eastern leaders helped the valley gentry recreate the political institutions and values of Virginia's deferential culture in their frontier environment. These ties also enabled a few prestigious families to control the county surveyorships and other powerful and lucrative appointive offices.

Although the integrity, wealth, and cosmopolitan connections of the upper valley gentry enhanced their power, the limited social cohesion of local neighborhoods and the willingness of many leaders to compromise with dissidents also proved important in preventing serious disorders. Strikingly, Thomas P. Slaughter's recent analysis of the Whiskey Rebellion in postrevolutionary Pennsylvania underscores the role of some regional leaders in supporting but seeking to moderate popular discontent. These men dominated the conventions that condemned the whiskey tax and articulated the region's other grievances against the federal government. The conventions, however, gave no support to secession from the east, and the leaders worked to minimize illegal violence against tax collectors and other federal officials. Although the rebellion took a more radical turn after the outbreak of violence, the moderates appeared to be regaining control when federal troops arrived in the area.[9] The significance of these internal factors in stabilizing the colonial upper valley and in shaping the course of the Whiskey Rebellion suggests the need for more analysis of the structure of local communities, the interaction of elite and popular groups, and the role of mediators between the diverging interests and values of those groups elsewhere in the eighteenth-century backcountry.

As many recent studies have emphasized, the revolutionary era brought both material and ideological tensions and changes to much of America. The war led to increased taxation, inflation, and demands for men to perform military service. John E. Selby's examination of Virginia's wartime experience, John David McBride's analysis of the state's manpower policies, and Norman Risjord's study of political developments from 1780 to 1800 all make it clear that Virginia shared in these material problems.[10] Moreover, throughout the continent, the Revolution's republican ideals not only sanctioned the appeals of established leaders for support from the masses but also legitimized popular protests against entrenched political and economic authorities.[11] These ideals retained much of their subversive power well into the postrevolutionary era in settings as diverse as New York City and the western Pennsylvania frontier.[12] Indeed, much of the debate over the relative importance of material and cultural factors in revolutionary America could be better recast as a discussion of how social and economic circumstances encouraged particular regions, classes, or groups at particular times to incline toward or choose between different ideologies or languages of political discourse.[13]

In the upper valley, both socioeconomic tensions and ideological changes worked to transform the region's political culture. Because of the wartime demand for manpower and tax revenues, public support for the government became both more crucial and more difficult to obtain. Therefore, the region's leaders were compelled to make far greater concessions to popular interests and values than they had done before. Moreover, the Revolution sanctioned political values that placed power more directly in the hands of the entire people and encouraged suspicion of established leaders. These new republican values legitimized both the growing reliance of many officials on popular consent and the increasing exploitation of popular discontent by ambitious men who sought to gain positions of leadership. Thus in the upper valley, as in much of America, it was not simply the transformation of political values or the material stresses of the revolutionary crisis but rather the dynamic interaction of both these factors that produced a movement toward the more fully republican political ethos that would so decisively shape the nation in the coming decades.

Notes

ABBREVIATIONS

Calendar   *Calendar of Virginia State Papers and Other Manuscripts*, ed. William P. Palmer, Sherwin McRae, Raleigh Colston, and H.W. Flournoy, 11 vols. (Richmond: Commonwealth of Virginia, 1875-1893)

DD   Lyman Draper Manuscripts, Kings Mountain Papers, State Historical Society of Wisconsin, Madison; citations include this abbreviation between volume and page number (e.g., 6DD47)

LC   Library of Congress Manuscript Division

QQ   Lyman Draper Manuscripts, Preston Papers, State Historical Society of Wisconsin, Madison; citations include this abbreviation between volume and page number (e.g., 3QQ41)

VHS   Virginia Historical Society, Richmond

VMHB   *Virginia Magazine of History and Biography*

VSL   Virginia State Library, Richmond

WMQ   *William and Mary Quarterly*

ZZ   Lyman Draper Manuscripts, Virginia Papers, State Historical Society of Wisconsin, Madison; citations include this abbreviation between volume and page number (e.g., 2ZZ11)

INTRODUCTION

1. The classic statement of this position was made by Charles S. Sydnor in *Gentlemen Freeholders: Political Practices in Washington's Virginia* (Chapel Hill: University of North Carolina Press for the Institute of Early American History and Culture, Williamsburg, Va., 1952) For a discussion of the gentry's affirmations of devotion to the public good, see Jack P. Greene, " '*Virtus et Libertas*': Political Culture, Social Change, and the Origins of the American Revolution in Virginia, 1763-1766," in *The Southern Experience in the American Revolution*, ed. Jeffrey J. Crow and Larry E. Tise (Chapel Hill: University of North Carolina Press, 1978), 55-108; and Greene, "Society, Ideology, and Politics: An Analysis of the Political Culture of Mid-Eighteenth Century Virginia," in *Society, Free-*

dom, and Conscience: The American Revolution, ed. Richard M. Jellison (New York: Norton, 1976), 14-76. Also see Edmund S. Morgan, *American Slavery, American Freedom: The Ordeal of Colonial Virginia* (New York: Norton, 1975); and Darrett B. Rutman and Anita H. Rutman, *A Place in Time: Middlesex County, Virginia, 1650-1750* (New York: Norton, 1984).

2. Rhys Isaac, *The Transformation of Virginia, 1740-1790* (Chapel Hill: University of North Carolina Press for the Institute of Early American History and Culture, Williamsburg, Va., 1982); Dale Benson, "Wealth and Power in Virginia, 1774-1776: A Study of the Organization of Revolt" (Ph. D. diss, University of Maine, 1970); Richard R. Beeman, *The Evolution of the Southern Backcountry: A Case Study of Lunenburg County, Virginia, 1746-1832* (Philadelphia: University of Pennsylvania Press, 1984). Beeman also asserted that geographic dispersion of the population and the consequent lack of social cohesion inhibited the deferential culture in Lunenburg. In *The Valley of Virginia in the Ameican Revolution, 1763-1789* (Chapel Hill: University of North Carolina Press, 1942), Freeman Hart suggested that despite a predominantly non-English elite class, a deferential culture developed in much of the valley. In "Independence, Improvement, and Authority: Toward a Framework for Understanding the Histories of the Southern Backcountry during the Era of the American Revolution," in *An Uncivil War: The Southern Backcountry during the American Revolution*, ed. Ronald Hoffman, Thad W. Tate, and Peter J. Albert (Charlottesville: University Press of Virginia for the United States Capitol Historical Society, 1985), 3-36, Jack P. Greene argued that respect for the elite was always tenuous and that Virginia leaders retained authority only by continuous recognition of this fact.

3. James Russell Wade Titus, "Soldiers When They Chose to Be So: Virginians at War, 1754-1763" (Ph.D. diss., Rutgers University, 1983).

4. Greene, "Independence, Improvement, and Authority"; see, for example, Beeman, *Evolution of the Southern Backcountry*, chap. 5.

5. Larry G. Bowman, "The Scarcity of Salt in Virginia during the American Revolution," *VMHB* 77 (1969): 464-72.

6. John David McBride, "The Virginia War Effort, 1775-1783: Manpower Policies and Practices" (Ph.D. diss., University of Virginia, 1977); Ronald Hoffman, "The Disaffected in the Revolutionary South," in *The American Revolution: Explorations in the History of American Radicalism*, ed. Alfred Young (DeKalb: Northern Illinois University Press, 1975), 273-316.

7. Issac, *Transformation of Virginia*, esp. chap. 13. Norman K. Risjord, *Chesapeake Politics, 1781-1800* (New York: Columbia University Press, 1978). In *Faithful Magistrates and Republican Lawyers* (Chapel Hill: University of North Carolina Press, 1981), A. G. Roeber argued that the Revolution accelerated the transformation of Virginia from a localistic, tradition-oriented legal culture to a more cosmopolitan and professionalized one.

8. Norman K. Risjord, "How the 'Common Man' Voted in Jefferson's Virginia," in *America: The Middle Period; Essays in Honor of Bernard Mayo*, ed. John B. Boles (Charlottesville: University of Virginia Press, 1973), 36-64. Because of the practice of oral voting, Risjord was able to identify the choices of individual voters and correlate them with wealth, residence, and other factors in fifteen local elections of federal and state officeholders.

9. Richard Beeman, "The Political Response to Social Conflict in the Southern Backcountry: A Comparative View of Virginia and the Carolinas during the Revolution," in *An Uncivil War*, ed. Hoffman, Tate, and Albert, 213-39. Also see Greene, "Independence, Improvement, and Authority," and Gregory H. Nobles, "Republican Resistance or National Integration?: The Backcountry Perspective," paper delivered at the American Society for Eighteenth-Century Studies meeting, Apr. 1988.

10. Rachel N. Klein, "Ordering the Backcountry: The South Carolina Regulation," *WMQ* 3d ser., 38 (1981): 661-80; Thomas P. Slaughter, *The Whiskey Rebellion: Frontier Epilogue to the American Revolution* (New York: Oxford University Press, 1986).

11. See, for example, Rachel N. Klein, "Frontier Planters and the American Revolution: The South Carolina Backcountry, 1755-1782," in *An Uncivil War*, ed. Hoffman, Tate, and Albert, 37-69; A. Roger Ekirch, "Whig Authority and Public Order in Backcountry North Carolina, 1776-1783," ibid., 99-124; and Harvey H. Jackson, "The Rise of the Western Members: Revolutionary Politics and the Georgia Backcountry," ibid., 276-320.

12. See, for example, Jeffrey J. Crow, "Liberty Men and Loyalists: Disorder and Disaffection in the North Carolina Backcountry," ibid., 125-78.

13. See James J.F. Deetz, *In Small Things Forgotten: The Archaeology of Early American Life* (Garden City, N.Y.: Anchor Doubleday, 1977); Herbert G. Gutman, *Work, Culture, and Society in Industrializing America: Essays in American Working Class and Social History* (New York: Knopf, 1976); Philip D. Morgan, "Work and Culture: The Task System and the World of Low Country Blacks," *WMQ* 3d ser., 39 (1982): 563-99; Adam J. Hirsch, "The Collision of Military Cultures in Seventeenth-Century New England," *Journal of American History* 74 (1948): 1187-1212.

14. Bernard Bailyn, *The Ideological Origins of the American Revolution* (Cambridge, Mass.: Harvard University Press, 1967); Gordon S. Wood, *The Creation of the American Republic, 1776-1787* (Chapel Hill: University of North Carolina Press for the Institute of Early American History and Culture, Williamsburg, Va., 1969).

1. LAND, PEOPLE, ECONOMY, AND GOVERNMENT

1. Robert D. Mitchell, *Commercialism and Frontier: Perspectives on the Early Shenandoah Valley* (Charlottesville: University Press of Virginia, 1977), 25.

2. Otis K. Rice, *West Virginia: A History* (Lexington: University Press of Kentucky, 1985), 7-10; Richard K. McMaster, *The History of Hardy County, 1786-1986* (Salem, W.Va.: Printed by Walsworth Press for the Hardy County Public Library, 1986), 1-2; Patricia Givens Johnson, *The New River Settlement* (Pulaski, Va.: Edmunds Printing, 1983), 35-38.

3. See the essays in *Beyond the Covenant Chain: The Iroquois and Their Neighbors in Indian North America, 1600-1800*, ed. Daniel K. Richter and James H. Merrell (Syracuse, N.Y.: Syracuse University Press, 1987).

4. Mitchell, *Commercialism and Frontier*; Hart, *Valley of Virginia*.

5. Evarts B. Greene and Virginia D. Harrington, *American Population before the Federal Census of 1790* (New York: Columbia University Press, 1932), 150. In producing this estimate, Greene and Harrington regarded as adults all individuals above sixteen years of age. They also estimated that this population represented approximately one-third of the total population.

6. Stella Sutherland, *Population Distribution in Colonial America* (New York: Columbia University Press, 1936), 174.

7. Greene and Harrington, *American Population*, 152-53, based on county tithable lists from various years in the period 1782-87; U.S. Bureau of the Census, *Heads of Families at the First Census of the United States Taken in the Year 1790. Records of the State Enumerations. 1782-1785. Virginia* (Washington D.C.: U.S. Government Printing Office, 1908), 9. The apparent discrepancy between the federal census and the earlier tithable counts presumably reflects in part the desire to keep tithables off the tax rolls.

8. The same legislation also created a separate county in Kentucky.

9. Mitchell, *Commercialism and Frontier*, 68, 86, 234; Jackson Turner Main, "The Distribution of Property in Post-Revolutionary Virginia," *Mississippi Valley Historical Review* 41 (1954-55): 255; Risjord, *Chesapeake Politics*, 45.

10. "Moravian Diaries of Travels through Virginia," ed. William J. Hinkle and Charles E. Kemper, *VMHB* 12 (1904-5): 147-53; 11 (1903-4): 122-23.

11. Ibid., 122-230

12. William Cooper, *History of the Shenandoah Valley*, 3 vols. (New York: Lewis Historical Publishing Company, 1952), 1:309; Augusta Order Book 1, 20 Nov. 1746, VSL.

13. Quoted in "Moravian Diaries" 11 (1903-4); 234n.

14. Johnson, *New River Settlement*, 76, 106.

15. Thus, after James Patton's death in 1755, the appraisers of his estate compiled a seven-page list of credits due to his estate (John Logan Anderson, "The Presbyterians and Augusta Parish, 1738-1757: A Political and Social Analysis" [M.A. thesis, University of Virginia, 1985], 26-27, 33-34).

16. Mitchell, *Commercialism and Frontier*, 148-49, 144, 172-76; Hart, *Valley of Virginia*, 12-13.

17. Hart, *Valley of Virginia*, 17-18. Also see Account of Sales of Servants Sold [by William Preston] for Donald, Johnson & Co., undated, but filed under 8 Apr. 1774, Preston Family Papers, 1727-1896, VHS; Edward Johnson and James Donald to William Preston, 30 May 1774, Preston Family of Virginia Papers, reel 4, #836, LC.

18. "Moravian Diaries" 11 (1903-4): 146.

19. *Travels in Virginia in Revolutionary Times* ed. A. J. Morrison (Lynchburg, Va.: J. P. Bell, 1922), 106-9, 120.

20. G. Melvin Herndon, "George Mathews: Frontier Patriot," *VMHB* 77 (1969): 310.

21. Mitchell, *Commercialism and Frontier*, 155-58, 223-28.

22. Robert Gamble to Thomas Jefferson, 10 May 1793, in "Letters to Jefferson from Archibald Cary and Robert Gamble," *WMQ* 2d ser., 6 (1926): 130.

23. Mitchell, *Commercialism and Frontier*, 176.

24. Frank Benton Sarles, "Trade of the Valley of Virginia, 1789-1860" (M.A. thesis, University of Virginia, 1951), 23, 10.

25. Rounded to nearest 0.1 percent; compiled from U.S. Bureau of the Census, *Heads of Families at the First Census of the United States*, 9.

26. Augusta County Quitrent Roll, 1760-62, Preston Family Papers, 1727-1986. Admittedly the nature of the Augusta quitrent roll raises some problems of reliability. First, given the numbers of cases, the extent of the geographic area, and the absence of middle names, it is difficult to distinguish between different individuals bearing the same first and last names. Second, the desire to avoid payment of quitrents led to substantial nonregistration of land, presumably among landowners of all classes. Third, since the quitrent roll gives no indication of the market value of particular tracts of land, it is possible that relatively small landholdings were disproportionately valuable. Yet apparently this was seldom true. According to Robert Mitchell (*Commercialism and Frontier*, 232), good agricultural land remained available at relatively low prices throughout the Shenandoah Valley until the 1770's, so presumably few colonial settlers were being forced onto land of especially low value. Moreover, given the desire of large-scale speculators to sell their lands, the most fertile and best located land was often available more cheaply than less productive land in peripheral areas (ibid., 7, 59-92). Land that was resold by individual settlers also showed relatively little regional variation in price before 1765. According to Mitchell (ibid., 7), land prices remained quite uniform for all of Augusta County between 1755 and 1764. Between 1745 and 1754 there was greater variation, but if the especially remote Calfpasture River lands and the most valuable Beverly Manor lands are excluded, the average price per one hundred acres varied from £ 14.3.4 to £ 18.6.6 Virginia currency among the identifiable subdivisions of the county.

27. It is virtually impossible to separate different individuals bearing the same first and last names. To produce comparable sets of acreage figures for calculating the two sets of statistics given in the table, three categories of entries were excluded: (1) those for which the name was unclear, (2) those which had multiple owners, except when this circumstance clearly resulted from the recent death of an identifiable property holder, and (3) those which listed an individual who was executor, attorney, or otherwise acting in behalf of some other person who was not clearly identified. There were twenty-seven excluded entries, with a mean of 714.481 acres and a median of 380.000. Between 74 and 78 percent of these entries were for less than the mean acreage.

28. Compiled from 1787 land taxes for Augusta, Botetourt, Montgomery, Rockbridge, Russell, and Washington counties, VSL. In this case the number of excluded entries was 103, with a mean of 3,029.476 acres and a median of 250. The biggest excluded entry, however, was for 144,750 acres and the next biggest for 52,992.

29. Mitchell, *Commercialism and Frontier*, 67-70. Turk McCleskey, "Rich Land, Poor Prospects: Real Estate and the Formation of a Social Elite in Augusta County, Virginia, 1738-1770," *VMHB* 98 (1990): 449-86 asserts that landholders were substantially less than half the population.

30. Michael Lee Nicholls, "Origins of the Virginia Southside, 1703-1753: A

168 NOTES TO PAGES 14-16

Social and Economic Study" (Ph.D. diss., College of William and Mary, 1972).
Also see chapter 3 below.

31. For a discussion of such corrections and other aspects of the use of probate records, see Gloria L. Main, "Probate Records as a Source for Early American History," *WMQ* 3d ser., 32 (1975): 89-99.

32. Harold B. Gill, Jr., and George M. Curtis III, "Virginia's Colonial Probate Policies and the Preconditions for Economic History," *VMHB* 87 (1979): 68-73. Debts owed *to* the estate normally were listed.

33. Compiled from Augusta Will Books 1-3 and 5-6. Botetourt Will Book 1, and Washington Will Book 1, VSL. The problems noted above, as well as the relatively small size of the sample, make it very difficult to analyze change over time in the characteristics of the estate inventories. Because county lines changed dramatically over time, it is also difficult to examine changes in smaller parts of the region, and no inventories are available from Montgomery County before 1789. Consequently, no analysis of change over time is attempted here.

34. All percentages in this discussion of the inventories are rounded to the nearest 0.1 percent.

35. More than four pewter or china items were listed in 51.1 percent of the multiple-servant inventories, 35.4 percent of the single-servant inventories, and 27.7 percent of the servantless inventories. The percentage for spices, spice mortars, or pepper boxes were 26.7 percent of the multiple-servant inventories, 20.8 percent of the single-servant inventories, and 9.5 percent of the servantless inventories.

36. See Dorothy McCombs, "Spinning and Weaving in Montgomery County," *Journal of the Roanoke Valley Historical Society* 11 (1980): 1, 86; and Lewis C. Gray, *History of Agriculture in the Southern United States*, 2 vols. (Washington D.C.: Carnegie Institute, 1933), 1:441.

37. Estates that owned more than one wagon or cart wheel or more than one-half of a wagon were counted as owning a wagon.

38. McMaster, *Hardy County*, 131. Of the 157 upper valley inventories from the 1780s that were analyzed, 23.6 percent listed wagons or carts; 16.9 percent of the servantless inventories listed them, 33.3 percent of the one-servant inventories, and 50.0 percent of the multiple-servant inventories. As Robert Mitchell has suggested, it may be that the demand for transportation of military supplies during the Revolutionary War led to a shortage of wagons in the 1780s. (Mitchell, "Agriculture Change and the American Revolution: A Virginia Case Study," *Agriculture History* 47 [1973]: 124-25). Nevertheless, the contest between the two regions is striking.

39. Of servantless estates, 16.5 percent owned cash and 24.6 percent owned debts. The corresponding figures are 15.6 and 40.0 percent for one-servant estates, and 24.4 and 35.6 percent for multiple-servant households. A recent analysis of late eighteenth-century merchant account books in northern New England and western Pennsylvania estimates that 90 percent of the merchants' customers lived within ten miles of them (Michael A. Bellesilles, "A Strict Accounting: The Economical Structure of the American Frontier," paper delivered at the American Historical Association meeting, December 1989).

40. "Moravian Diaries" 11 (1903-4): 125-26.

41. Mitchell, *Commercialism and Frontier*, 144.

42. See, for example, Account of Colonel John Buchanan's estate with Francis Combe, 28 Sept. 1770. Preston Family Papers I, box 1, folder 4, Virginia Polytechnic Institute and State University, Blacksburg; and memorandum signed by Chris Champ, 8 July 1791, Preston Family Papers II, box 3, folder 3, ibid.

43. Looms with or without wheels appeared in 44.4 and 20.8 percent of the multiple-servant and one-servant inventories respectively. In Montgomery County at least, spinning wheels remained much more common than looms well into the nineteenth century (McCombs, "Spinning and Weaving," 99).

44. Warren R. Hofstra, "The Opequon Inventories, Frederick County, Virginia, 1749-1796," *Ulster Folklife* 35 (1989): 42-71; Hofstra, "Land, Ethnicity, and Community at the Opequon Settlement, Virginia, 1730-1800," *VMHB* 98 (1990): 423-48.

45. Although colonial law required that such surveys be registered with the provincial government to obtain full title, many landholders refused to take this last step so as to avoid paying quitrents.

46. In *Surveyors and Statesmen: Land Measuring in Colonial Virginia* (Richmond: Virginia Surveyors Foundation, and the Virginia Association of Surveyors, 1979), Sarah S. Hughes provides a thorough analysis of the colonial Virginia surveyor; for a detailed account of the land acquisition process, see pp. 107-27.

47. Isaac, *Transformation of Virginia*, 84. My description of eastern Virginia culture is drawn chiefly from this source and from Sydnor, *Gentlemen Freeholders*, and Carter L. Hudgins, "Exactly as the Gentry Do in England: Culture, Aspirations, and Material Things in the Eighteenth-Century Chesapeake," paper delivered at the Forty-fifth conference on Early American History, Baltimore, Sept. 1984.

48. Some of these points are discussed by Greene in "'*Virtus et Libertas*'."

2. THE POLITICAL CULTURE OF THE COLONIAL ELITE

1. Augusta Quitrent Roll, 1760-62. As explained in chapter 1, if it is assumed that all entries bearing the same first and last name represent the same individual, the median acreage for all Augusta settlers was 336.000 acres. If it is assumed that each entry is for a different individual, the median is 287.500. The lists of justices are taken from "Justices of the Peace of Colonial Virginia, 1757-1775," *Virginia State Library Bulletin* 14, no. 2/3 (1921): 66-67, 99; Augusta Order Book 2, 19 May 1749, p. 127; and Augusta Order Book 15, 16 Mar. 1773, p. 1.

2. If it is assumed that each justice owned all the tracts listed under his name, the medians are 686, 585, and 395 acres for the Augusta justices in 1749, 1765, and 1773 respectively, and 618 acres for the Botetourt justices in 1770.

3. Several other studies of eastern Virginia counties, however, have noted a decline in wealth among justices of the peace in the late eighteenth century. See Daniel B. Smith, "Changing Patterns of Local Leadership: The

Justices of the Peace of Albemarle County, Virginia, 1760-1820," *Essays in History* 18 (1973-74): 52-84.

4. Robert Douthat Stoner, *A Seed-Bed of the Republic: A Study of the Pioneers in the Upper (Southern) Valley of Virginia* (Kingsport, Tenn.: Kingsport Press for the Roanoke Historical Society, 1962) 285; Mitchell, *Commercialism and Frontier*, 155; Sally A. Eads, "Government by Families in Botetourt County," *Journal of the Roanoke Valley Historical Society* 9, no. 2 (1975): 4.

5. Francis Smith to William Preston, 5 May 1774, Preston Family of Virginia Papers, reel 3, #312.

6. Within the militia hierarchy of the upper valley, the role of kinship relations was also evident, especially in the leadership of the Point Pleasant expedition during Dunmore's War in 1774. Charles Lewis, who commanded the Augusta regiment, was the brother of Andrew Lewis, the expedition's commander, and four of their relatives led companies in the Augusta and Botetourt regiments. In addition, two brothers-in-law, William Fleming and William Christian, commanded the Botetourt regiment and the Fincastle brigade respectively, and William Campbell, Christian's brother-in-law, led a company from Fincastle (Virgil A. Lewis, *History of the Battle of Point Pleasant* [Charleston, W.Va.: Tribune Publishing Co., 1909], 130-31).

7. Preston also sought the assistance of his Williamsburg acquaintance Richard Starke to influence the masters of the College of William and Mary to give him the appointment (Starke to William Preston, 17 Feb. 1768, Preston Family of Virginia Papers, reel 3, #312).

8. See, for example, David Robinson to William Preston, 18 May 1759, 2QQ21-23; Robinson to Preston, 5 Nov. 1761 and 21 Dec. 1770. 2QQ34-36 and 2QQ121.

9. William Preston to Andrew Lewis, 29 Oct. 1757, 1QQ163; notation by Preston on David Robinson to Preston, 13 Aug. 1770, 2QQ118.

10. David Robinson to William Fleming, 16 Feb. 1765, William Fleming Papers, folder 2, Cyrus McCormick Library, Washington and Lee University, Lexington, Va.

11. James Robertson to William Preston, 15 Sept. 1774, 3QQ96. For discussion of Robertson's recruiting problems, see Robertson to Preston, 20 July, 1 Aug., and 1 Sept. 1774, 3QQ66, 3QQ69, and 3QQ88. For another example of seeking appointments for friends, see Andrew Lewis to John Buchanan, 22 Apr. 1758, 2QQ4.

12. Augusta Order Book 3, 27 Aug. 1751, p. 176; list of Augusta justices of the peace dated 12 June 1765, "Justices of the Peace in Colonial Virginia," 66-67.

13. Augusta Order Book 15, 16 Mar. 1773, p. 1; list of Botetourt justices of the peace dated 2 Mar. 1770. "Justices of the Peace in Colonial Virginia," 99.

14. List of Fincastle justices of the peace dated 30 Apr. 1773, "Justices of the Peace in Colonial Virginia," 120.

15. List of Augusta justices of the peace dated 12 June 1765, ibid., 66-67; list of Augusta justices of the peace dated 6 Nov. 1772, ibid., 117-18; list of Botetourt justices of the peace dated 2 Mar. 1770, ibid., 99.

16. List of Fincastle justices of the peace dated 30 Apr. 1773, ibid., 120; list of Botetourt justices of the peace dated 2 Mar. 1770, ibid., 99.

17. Attendance data compiled from court records, Botetourt Order Book, Part I, 1770-71; Augusta Order Books 14-15; List of Augusta justices of the peace dated 12 June 1765, "Justices of the Peace in Colonial Virginia," 66-67. (In 1765 Botetourt was still a part of Augusta County).

18. List of Augusta justices of the peace dated 12 June 1765, "Justices of the Peace in Colonial Virginia," 66-67; Augusta Order Book 3, 27 Aug. 1751, p. 176. Attendance data for 1762 compiled from Augusta Order Book 7.

19. Hughes, *Surveyors and Statesmen*, 89-90. One upper valley leader, Peter Hog, used connections established during his service in the Seven Years' War to elicit support from British military officials for his appointment as a county clerk (Jeffrey Amherst to Francis Fauquier, 24 Jan. 1763, in *The Official Papers of Francis Fauquier, Lieutenant Governor of Virginia, 1758-1768*, ed. George Reese, 3 vols. [Charlottesville: University Press of Virginia, 1980-83], 2:902-3.

20. John Madison to William Preston, 1 Mar. 1767, Preston Family of Virginia Papers, reel 3, #521.

21. The development of this conflict is related in Hughes, *Surveyors and Statesmen*, 100-101, from which much of the remainder of this paragraph is drawn.

22. Edmund Pendleton to William Preston, 6 Feb. 1768, 2QQ102-4.

23. Richard Starke to William Preston, 17 Feb. 1768, Preston Family of Virginia Papers, reel 3, #312; Hughes, *Surveyors and Statesmen*, 101.

24. John Madison to William Preston, 1 Mar. 1767, Preston Family of Virginia Papers, reel 3, #521. Andrew Lewis, who initially sought the new surveyorship for himself, also attempted to exploit eastern contacts. (Andrew Lewis to Preston, 19 Mar. 1767, 2QQ101-2).

25. Hughes, *Surveyors and Statesmen*, 85.

26. Francis Fauuquier to Board of Trade, 13 Feb. 1764, Public Records Office, Colonial Office 5, vol. 1330, #427-32, British Reproductions Collection, LC; Howard McKnight Wilson, *Great Valley Patriots: Western Virginia in the Struggle for Liberty* (Staunton, Va.: McClure Press for the Augusta County Historical Society, 1976), 6-8; F. B. Kegley, *Kegley's Virginia Frontier: The Beginnings of the Southwest, The Roanoke of Colonial Days, 1740-1783* (Roanoke, Va.: Stone Press for the Southwest Virginia Historical Society, 1938), 61.

27. James Patton to unidentified correspondent, Jan. 1753, 1QQ78.

28. Kegley, *Kegley's Virginia Frontier*, 132.

29. See Edmund Pendleton's bill for services to James Patton, 1751-56, Preston Family Papers, 1727-1896; Pendleton to William Preston, 14 Dec. 1762, Breckinridge Family Papers, reel 1, #5, University of Virginia; Pendleton to John Buchanan, 18 June 1764, Preston Family Papers, 1727-1896; George Wythe's receipt of payment from Preston, 14 Dec. 1765, ibid.; Pendleton to Preston, 29 Apr. 1771. Preston Family of Virginia Papers, reel 4, #660.

30. Frank L. Dewey, "The Waterson-Madison Episode: An Incident in Thomas Jefferson's Law Practice," *VMHB* 90 (1982): 165-76. The next two paragraphs are drawn largely from Dewey's article. Dewey, however, focuses on what this episode reveals about Jefferson, the legal profession, and legal and political ethics in eighteenth-century Virginia, whereas my own concern here is with the implications for interregional relationships among the elite.

31. Dewey ("Waterson-Madison Episode," 174n) was uncertain whether Pendleton actually represented Preston but suggested it was unlikely. Two letters from Pendleton to Preston, however, make it clear that Pendleton did in fact defend Preston, Margaret Buchanan, and others against the litigation brought by Madison and his associates (Pendleton to Preston, 29 Apr. 1771 and 23 Apr. 1773, Preston Family of Virginia Papers, reel 4, #660).

32. James Patton and other leaders organized cattle drives to northern markets in the 1750s and 1760s (Mitchell, *Commercialism and Frontier*, 148-49). In "Maryland Border War Refugees Flee to the Roanoke Valley" (*Journal of the Roanoke Valley Historical Society* 9, no. 2 [1975]: 73-76), Patricia Givens Johnson describes a trip by Patton to Lancaster County, Pennsylvania, to recruit settlers for the upper valley. In the 1760s and 1770s, William Preston did business with James Adams, a Wilmington merchant (see, for example, Adams to Preston, 22 Feb. 1760, 2QQ27; Adams to Preston, 11 Feb. 1762 and 16 Oct. 1775, Preston Family Papers, 1727-1896). In 1760 Preston entered into a partnership with William Davies of Philadelphia to provide horses and wagons to an expedition marching against the Cherokees (Memorandum of agreement between Preston and Davies, 19 Aug. 1760, folder of legal papers, 1740-90, William and John Preston Papers, 1740-1960, Duke University, Durham, N.C.).

33. Mitchell, *Commercialism and Frontier*, 162, 223-25.

34. See Edward Johnson to William Preston, Jan. 1774, Preston Family of Virginia Papers, reel 4, #785; Preston to Johnson, 2 Aug. 1774. Preston Family Papers, 1727-1896; Mitchell, *Commercialism and Frontier*, 216-17.

35. Felix Gilbert to Thomas Walker, 16 July 1761, Thomas and Francis Walker Papers, container 162, #0700, LC.

36. Edward Johnson to William Preston, Jan. 1774, Preston Family of Virginia Papers, reel 4, #785; Johnson to Preston 12 July 1775, Preston Family Papers, 1746-1938, section 31, VHS; Johnson to Preston, 14 Oct. 1775 and 10 Sept. 1771, Preston Family Papers, 1727-1896; Johnson to Preston, 23 Jan. 1773, Preston Family Papers, 1727-1896.

37. See Edward Johnson to William Preston, 8 Apr., 2 July 1774, Preston Family Papers, 1727-1896; Account of Sales of Servants, 8 Apr. 1774. ibid.; Johnson and James Donald to Preston, 30 May 1774, Preston Family of Virginia Papers, reel 4, #819; Preston to Johnson, 2 Aug. 1774, ibid., #836; Johnson to Preston, 8 Sept. 1775, ibid., reel 5, #834.

38. Edmund Pendleton to William Preston, 29 Apr. 1771, 30 Mar. 1775; Preston Family Papers, 1727-1896; Preston to Robert Doack, 1 Oct. 1771, Campbell-Preston Papers, LC; Pendleton to Preston, 4 June 1774, 3QQ36.

39. Edmund Pendleton to William Preston, 8 Sept. 1775, Preston Family of Virginia Papers, reel 5, #897; William Byrd to Preston, 16 Nov. 1772, 2QQ138-39; Nicholas Davies to Preston, 2 Feb. 1771, Preston Family of Virginia Papers, reel 4, #647; William Cabell, Jr. to Preston, 27 Dec. 1769, ibid., #609; John Aylett to Preston, 10 Jan. 1770, Preston Family Papers, 1727-1896; Thomas Lewis to Preston, 28, Aug. 1770, Preston Family of Virginia Papers, reel 4, #635; William Rind to Preston, 15 Mar. 1768, ibid., reel 3, #554; Pendleton to Preston, 14 Dec. 1762, Breckinridge Family Papers, reel 1, #5, University of Virginia;

John Randolph to Preston, 1 July 1767, and John Talbot to Preston, 7 June 1773, Preston Family Papers, 1727-1896.

In relationships with eastern leaders, however, the valley elite was far from servile. As Sarah Hughes has pointed out (*Surveyors and Statesmen*, 101-5), Thomas Lewis and William Preston successfully defended their interests as county surveyors against the efforts of eastern land speculators to have independent surveyors appointed for the territories beyond the Appalachians. Throughout the 1770s Lewis and Preston opposed such appointments, which reduced the fees and influence of their assistants and themselves, and in 1779 the revolutionary government of Virginia passed legislation confirming much of their position.

40. John Craig, Autobiography, in Lillian Kennerly Craig, *Reverend John Craig. 1709-1774, His Descendants and Allied Families* (New Orleans: Accurate Letter Press, 1963), 54-55; John Stuart, "Transcript of the Memoir of Indian Wars and Other Occurrences, 1749-1780," copy made by Samuel Lewis from the original manuscript, ca. 1800, VHS.

41. Francis Smith to William Preston, 5 May 1774, Preston Family of Virginia Papers, reel 4, #812. For other expressions of deference toward superiors by lesser leaders, see James Robertson to Preston, 21 Mar. 1774, 3QQ14; Robert Doack to Preston, 12 July 1774, 3QQ61. Green's petition of 30 Jan. 1761 appears in Augusta Parish Vestry Book, p. 344, VSL. For other examples of such deferential petitions, see ibid., 28 Mar. 1758, 30 Jan., 18 Nov. 1761, Oct. and 22 Nov. 1766, pp. 232, 345, 418, and 420.

42. Augusta Order Book 1, 16 Sept. 1747, p. 286; Adam Breckinridge to Robert Breckinridge, 7 Apr. 176_, Breckinridge Family Papers, vol. 1, LC; *Virginia Gazette* (Purdle and Dixon), 30 June 1774. Jones's advertisement was dated Augusta, 18 June 1774.

43. For a brief description of housing in eastern Virginia, see Hughes, *Surveyors and Statesmen*, 161. For a useful survey of scholarship on the architectural history of Virginia, see Dell Upton, "New View of the Virginia Landscape," *VMHB* 96 (1988): 403-70.

44. Francis J. Niederer, *The Town of Fincastle, Virginia* (Charlottesville: University Press of Virginia, 1965), 4.

45. Augusta Vestry Book, 22 Aug. 1748, p. 136. Also see ibid., 20 July 1747, p. 3.

46. Hughes, *Surveyors and Statesmen*, 161; Patricia Givens Johnson, *William Preston and the Allegheny Pioneers* (Pulaski, Va.: B.D. Smith, 1976), 199.

47. Samuel Houston to Sidney Smith Baxter, Jan. 1837, VHS.

48. John Brown to William Preston, 13 Jan. 1773, 28 May 1774, 23 Mar., June, 25 July 1775, 2QQ141, 3QQ29, 4QQ12, 4QQ22, 4QQ26. David Robinson to Preston, 18 May 1759 and 21 Dec. 1770, 2QQ21-23 and 2QQ121; Thomas Lewis to Preston, 4 Jan. 1774, Preston Family of Virginia Papers, reel 4, #780; Preston to Lettice Breckinridge, 9 Oct. 1774, Breckinridge Family Papers, vol. 1, #42, LC. Social visits were particularly important for women and children of elite families. See for example Edward Johnson to Preston, 10 Sept. 1771, Preston Family Papers, 1727-1896. Anne Christian to Anne Fleming, 12 June 1772, William Fleming Papers, folder 2; Stephen

Trigg to Anne Fleming, 28 July 1773, and Christian to Anne Fleming, 4 Apr. 1774, ibid., folder 3.

49. David Robinson to William Preston, 18 May 1759, 2QQ21-23; Stephen Trigg to Anne Fleming, 28 July 1773, William Fleming Papers, folder 3; Robinson to William Fleming, 22 Oct. 1764, ibid., folder 2; John Madison to Preston, 6 May 1770, William and John Preston Papers, 1740-1960.

50. Augusta Order Book 1, 12 Feb. 1746. The next year the court also ordered that Samuel Wilkins not retail liquor at the courthouse "until he Provide Lodging and Diet for men & Provender &c for horses" (ibid., 19 Feb. 1747).

51. Ibid., Sept. 1747, p. 248. In November 1747 James Brown received a license to keep an ordinary at the court house (ibid., 19 Nov. 1747, p. 321).

52. Botetourt Order Book, Part 1, 1770-71, 10 May, 16 Aug. 1770, pp. 83, 143.

53. David Robinson to William Fleming, 16 Feb. 1765, William Fleming Papers, folder 2; Arthur Campbell to William Preston, 28 Oct. 1774 3QQ126; William Campbell to Preston, 1 May 1773, Preston Family of Virginia Papers, reel 4, #742; William Christian to Anne Fleming, 16 Jan. 1772, Hugh Blair Grigsby Papers, 1745-1949, section 133, VHS.

54. John Hook to John Todd, 30 July 1774, John Hook Papers, Letterbook 1774-87, VSL; Thomas Lewis to William Preston, 26 Dec. 1767, Preston Family Papers, 1727-1896; George Johnston to brother, 9 June 1798, Zachariah Johnston Papers, VSL. Not all leaders attended court consistently, however. In March 1774 William Preston recorded his disappointment that John Wood did not meet him at Fincastle court after he had gone there for that express purpose, implying that otherwise he would not have attended the session (Wood to Preston, 21 Jan. 1774, 3QQ4; Preston's notation dated March 1774). Yet in a letter dated ten days after Wood's, Daniel Smith, a Clinch River leader, promised to see Preston "at Court (at which I hear you'll be)" (Smith to Preston, 31 Jan. 1774, 3QQ2). Apparently, although Preston and other leaders did not always attend court, the sessions were so significant as a gathering point that reports of their plans to attend often circulated among their peers, even those who, like Smith, lived in diferent parts of their counties.

55. See for example Augusta Order Book 1, 20 Aug. 1747, pp. 253, 254; Augusta Order Book 2, 27 Aug. 1750, p. 424; Augusta Order Book 7, 19 Aug. 1762, pp. 293-94; Botetourt Order Book, Part I, 1770-71, 12 June 1770, p. 90; Botetourt Minutes, 14 Sept. 1773, 10 Aug. 1774 in Lewis Preston Summers, *Annals of Southwestern Virginia, 1769-1800* (Abingdon, Va.: L.P. Sumners, 1929), 203 233; Augusta Order Book 7, 24 May 1762, p. 224, 253.

56. Augusta Order Book 7, 19 Feb. 1762, p. 166.

57. See Augusta Order Book 1, 10 Mar. 1746; Augusta Order Book 2, 18 May 1749, p. 119.

58. See Augusta Order Book 2, 18 May 1749, p. 113; 24 May 1750, p. 376.

59. Ibid., 20 Aug. 1748, pp. 60-61.

60. Augusta Order Book 1, 21 Aug. 1747, p. 257.

61. See ibid., 18 June 1746; 16 Sept. 1747, pp. 286-88; Augusta Order Book 2, 19 May 1748, pp. 10-11; 15 Aug. 1748, pp. 47, 49; 18 May 1749, p. 112; 22 Aug.

NOTES TO PAGES 32-33

1749, pp. 152-54; 27 Feb. 1750, p. 313; Augusta Order Book 15, 16 Mar. 1773, p. 10; 25 Aug. 1773, p. 219; 17 Nov. 1773, p. 225; Botetourt Minutes, 9 Sept. 1772, 9 Mar. 1773, in Summers, *Annals*, 151, 176.

62. Augusta Order Book 2, 19 Aug. 1748, p. 59; 18 Feb. 1749, p. 102; 18 May 1749, p. 122.

63. Augusta Order Book 7, 23 Feb. 1762, p. 196. This policy of leniency to penitent offenders was also applied to other delinquencies. See Augusta Order Book 1, 21 Aug. 1747, p. 257; Augusta Order Book 2, 19 May 1749, p. 128; Augusta Order Book 7, 18 Feb. 1763, p. 477.

64. See Augusta Order Book 2, 22 May 1749, p. 148; 2 Dec. 1749, p. 311; Augusta Order Book 15, 19 May 1773, p. 102; 22 May 1773, p. 129; 19 May 1774, p. 481. The county also required these men to return any law books that had been issued to them.

65. Augusta Order Book 1, 21 Aug. 1747, p. 257. Also see ibid., 18 Feb. 1748, pp. 315, 364, for charges that Gay had been overly lenient with an imprisoned horse thief.

66. Augusta Order Book 2, 21 May 1748, p. 32. For further examples of punishment of insolence and misbehavior at court, see ibid., 2 Dec. 1749, p. 306; 1 Mar. 1750, p. 327; Botetourt Minutes, 14 Sept. 1773, in Summers, *Annals*, 203.

67. For an example of proceedings against justices, see Augusta Order Book 1, 20 Nov. 1746. For an example of punishment of attorneys, see ibid., 21 Feb. 1746, for charges against Gabriel Jones and Thomas Chew.

68. Ibid., 12 Feb. 1746.

69. For the court's dealing with Sevier, see Augusta Order Book 2, 20 Apr. 1748, p. 2; 18 May 1749, p. 119. For examples of treatment of other masters of indentured servants, see Augusta Order Book 1, 20 Sept. 1746; Augusta Order Book 2, 19 Oct. 1748, p. 65; Augusta Order Book 8, 18 Feb. 1764, pp. 122-23; Botetourt Order Book, Part I, 1770-71, 8 May 1770, p. 47; Botetourt Minutes, 14 Mar. 1775, in Summers, *Annals*, 242.

70. Richard R. Beeman, "Social Change and Cultural Conflict in Lunenburg County, 1746-1774," *WMQ* 3d ser., 35 (1978): 459-60. Also see Beeman, *Evolution of the Southern Backcountry*.

71. See Augusta Order Book 1, 10 Feb. 1746; 20 June 1746; 18 Feb. 1747; 21 May 1747; 18 June 1747; 19 June 1747; 21 Nov. 1747, p. 334; Augusta Order Book 7, 15 Feb. 1763, p. 452; Augusta Order Book 15, 23 Mar. 1773, p. 94; 15 Mar. 1774, p. 310; Botetourt Order Book, Part I, 1770-71, 8 May 1770, p. 47; 12 June 1770, p. 92; 13 Nov. 1770, p. 188; Botetourt Minutes, 9 Sept. 1772, in Summers, *Annals*, 151-52.

72. Augusta Order Book 15, 23 Aug. 1773, p. 197. Also see ibid., 19 Mar. 1773, p. 32; Augusta Order book 2, 27 Nov. 1750, p. 490.

73. See Augusta Order Book 1, 27 May 1747; Augusta Order Book 2, 21 May 1748, pp. 33-34; 18 May 1749, pp. 118-19; 29 Nov. 1749, p. 193; 22 May 1750, p. 490.

74. See Augusta Order Book 1, 20 Nov. 1747, p. 325; Augusta Order Book 2, 21 May 1748, p. 30; Augusta Order Book 7, 18 May 1763, p. 477; 17 Mar. 1774, p. 329; Botetourt Minutes, 11 Sept. 1772, in Summers, *Annals*, 156.

75. See Augusta Order Book 1, 18 Mar. 1747; 21 May 1748, p. 30; 1 June 1748, p. 44; 15 Aug. 1748, p. 45.

76. See ibid., 18 Sept. 1746; Augusta Order Book 2, 19 May 1748, pp. 10-11; 25 May 1750, pp. 380-81; Augusta Order Book 7, 22 May 1762, p. 230; Augusta Order Book 15, 22 May 1773, pp. 126-27; 2 May 1774, p. 528; Botetourt Order Book, Part I, 1770-71, 10 May 1770, p. 84.

77. See Augusta Order Book 7, 21 May 1762, p. 229; 22 May 1762, p. 236; Augusta Order Book 15, 16 Mar. 1773, p. 10; 17 Mar. 1773, pp. 18-19; Botetourt Order Book, Part I, 1770-71, 14 Feb. 1770, pp. 8-9; 14 Mar. 1770, p. 26; 8 May 1770, p. 62.

78. See, for example, the appointment of twenty-six constables for different Botetourt County neighborhoods (Botetourt Order Book, Part I, 1770-71, 14 Feb. 1770, p. 7).

79. Augusta Order Book 2, 20 Apr. 1748, p. 2; 19 Oct. 1748, p. 65.

80. Augusta Order Book 1, 15 Apr. 1746.

81. Ibid., 19 Nov. 1746.

82. Augusta Order Book 2, 28 Aug. 1750, p. 436.

83. See Augusta Order Book 1, 20 Nov. 1747, pp. 331-32; Augusta Order Book 2, 21 May 1748, pp. 33-34; 15 Aug. 1748, p. 51; Augusta Order Book 15, 18 Nov. 1773, p. 241; Botetourt Order Book, Part I, 1770-71, 13 Nov. 1770, p. 188. D. Alan Williams suggested that in much of eighteenth-century Virginia, the fees and salaries derived from these positions made them attractive to smaller planters and minimized turnover rates ("The Small Farmer in Eighteenth-Century Virginia Politics," *Agricultural History* 43 [1969]: 96-98).

84. Mitchell, *Commercialism and Frontier*, 44-45.

85. Hart, *Valley of Virginia*; Eads, "Government by Families," 3.

86. Lucille Griffith, *The Virginia House of Burgesses, 1750-1774* (University, Ala.: University of Alabama Press, 1963), 102-3. Among the burgesses Griffith identified James Patton, William Preston, Israel Christian, Samuel McDowell, and Charles Lewis as Presbyterians. In addition, Charles Kemper asserted that John Wilson acquired land in Chester County, Pennsylvania, before coming to the Valley ("Early Settlers in the Valley of Virginia," *WMQ* 2d ser., 6 [1926]: 60). If this is correct, Wilson may well have been Scotch-Irish and Presbyterian.

87. Patricia Barton, "The Pattons of Donegal," reprint from *Derry People* (Donegal, Ireland), 11 May 1974, VHS.

88. Eads, "Government by Families," 3.

89. Copy of James Preston to William Preston, 22 Feb. 1770, Preston Family Papers, University of Virginia; Thomas Preston to William Preston, 10 Apr. 1770 and 23 May 1773, Preston Family of Virginia Papers, reel 4, #622. James Preston mentioned having written two other letters since 1765. In their letters of 1769 and 1770, James and Thomas Preston both mentioned receiving a letter from William Preston. It is likely that many of the letters, both from Ulster and from America, failed to reach their destination.

90. Hughes, *Surveyors and Statesmen*, 91-92.

91. John Brown to William Preston, 26 Nov. 1771, 2QQ129.

92. Tinkling Spring Commissioners Book, 14 Aug. 1771, p. 2, Tinkling

Spring Church Records, Union Theological Seminary, Richmond, Va. The other two commissioners were George Finly and George Hutchison.

93. James Latta to William Preston, 9 Sept. 1769, Preston Family of Virginia Papers, reel 4, #605; John Brown to Preston, 26 Nov. 1771, 6 Mar. 1773, 23, 10 Mar. 1775, 2QQ129, 2QQ144, 4QQ12, 4QQ34.

94. Tinkling Spring Commissioners Book, 14 Aug. 1741, pp. 2-3.

95. These frictions were discussed by John Craig in his Autobiography, 54-55. Patton was a commissioner, but Lewis was not. This conflict is also discussed elsewhere in this chapter.

96. Tinkling Spring Commissioners Book, 6 Nov. 1770, p. 35. For at least brief periods of time, the conflict between advocates and opponents of the Great Awakening disrupted some Presbyterian churches. See for example Craig, Autobiography, 55-56; John Brown to William Preston, 3 Mar. 1775, 4QQ12.

97. Leonard J. Trinterud, The Forming of an American Tradition: A Re-examination of Colonial Presbyterianism (Philadelphia: Westminster Press, 1949), 16-19; Howard Miller, The Revolutionary College: American Presbyterian Higher Education, 1707-1818 (New York: New York University Press, 1976).

98. Legal Papers: Charles Cummings and Sinking Springs, 1772-1889, 5 Jan. 1773, Campbell Family Papers, 1773-1908, Duke University. Essentially the same petition was addressed to Cummings by Brown's Meeting House in Augusta County. This petition, however, was undated (ibid.).

99. Tinkling Spring Commissioners Book, p. 56. The entry is undated, but the dates of surrounding entries place it clearly within the colonial period.

100. See, for example, ibid., undated entry, p. 26.

101. James G. Leyburn, The Scotch-Irish: A Social History (Chapel Hill: University of North Carolina Press, 1962), 286; Tinkling Spring Commissioners Book, 4 Feb. 1766, p. 35; Copy of [Tinkling Spring] session meeting notes, 25 Jan. 1755, Zachariah and Thomas Johnston Papers, 1717-1858, "Papers, Account Books, etc. Ca 1751-1800," Duke University.

102. Tinkling Spring Commissioners Book, 23 Mar. 1746, p. 24.

103. Hart, Valley of Virginia, 47-48. A petition to remove the dissenters from the vestry was sent to the legislature in 1748 (Augusta Order Book 2, 20 Aug. 1748, p. 60).

104. Augusta Vestry Book, 6 Apr. 1747.

105. Katherine L. Brown. Hills of the Lord: Background of the Episcopal Church in Southwestern Virginia, 1738-1938 (Roanoke, Va.: Diocese of Southwestern Virginia, 1979), 142; Augusta Vestry Book, 21 Nov. 1758 and 27 Nov. 1759, pp. 236, 267.

106. Augusta Vestry Book, 20 July 1747.

107. Ibid. 27 Nov. 1755, 20 May and 24 Nov. 1760, pp. 167, 318, 323-25. In 1773 the vestry stated its intention to build a second church in northern Augusta County if the people there wanted one (Ibid., 10 Mar. 1773, p. 494).

108. Tinkling Spring Commissioners Book, 27 May 1766.

109. For completion of the Anglican church, see Augusta Vestry Book, 25 June 1763, p. 393. Howard McKnight Wilson, The Lexington Presbytery Heritage:

The Presbytery of Lexington and Its Churches in the Synod of Virginia, Presbyterian Church in the United States (Verona, Va: McClure Press, 1971), 227, makes it clear that there was no Presbyterian church in Staunton at this time.

110. Craig, Autobiography, 54-55. Although Patton's excuse for this action was to question Craig about a runaway servant, Craig felt that the real reasons were to discredit him in the eyes of his congregation and to provoke him into saying something in anger that could be used to bring legal charges against him.

111. Thomas Lewis to William Preston, 11 Aug. 1781, 5QQ97; Edmund Pendleton to Preston, 1 Nov. 1781, 5QQ99; Hughes, *Surveyors and Statesmen*, 96-98.

112. Patton had purchased a claim to 1,035 acres which the settler had obtained from the Governor's Council through a caveat action (Copy of undated bill of complaint of John Madison, Jr., against William Preston and David Smith [apparently written sometime after 30 Oct. 1772], Preston Family Papers, 1727-1896). For the action of the Augusta court against Patton, see Augusta Order Book 1, 16 Apr. and 12 May 1746.

113. Augusta Order Book 1; 21 Aug. 1747, p. 257; 7 Mar. 1748, p. 361, abstracted in Lyman Chalkley, *Chronicles of the Scotch-Irish Settlement in Virginia. Abstracted from the Original Court Records of Augusta County. 1745-1800*, 3 vols. (Rosslyn, Va.: Commonwealth Printing Co., 1912), 1:31, 34.

114. Augusta Order Book 2, 18 May 1749, p. 110.

115. Bell vs. Borden's Executor, Augusta County Court Judgments at Rules, 1751, and Augusta County Court Judgments, May 1753, abstracted in Chalkley, *Chronicles of the Scotch Irish Settlement* 1:307.

116. Mitchell, *Commercialism and Frontier*, 81.

117. Warrant for arrest of John Connoly, issued by James Patton, 30 Jan. 1753, 1QQ70; Deposition of John Watts, 20 Jan. 1753, 1QQ71; Patton to Robert Dinwiddie, Jan. 1753, 1QQ73-74. See also Augusta Order Book 2, 21 May 1748, p. 32.

118. The riot is discussed in Griffith, *Virginia House of Burgesses*, 84-86, using the records contained in *Journals of the House of Burgesses, 1752-1755, 1756-1758*, ed. H.R. McIlwaine (Richmond: Virginia State Library, 1909), 347, 381-83, 390, 422, 446-47. The following discussion draws on all these sources.

119. Augusta Quitrent Roll, 1760-62.

120. *Journals of the House of Burgesses, 1752-1755*, 447.

121. Craig, Autobiography, 54.

122. Robert Dinwiddie to John Buchanan, 14 Aug. 1755, 1QQ87.

123. Certificate signed by John Blair, 23 Aug. 1756, 1QQ136. Governor Dinwiddie may have exacerbated this quarrel by refusing immediately to name a replacement for Patton as county lieutenant and by expressing some initial doubt as to whether Lewis or Buchanan was the senior officer (Robert Dinwiddie to John Buchanan, 11 Aug. 1755, in *The Official Papers of Robert Dinwiddie*, ed. R.A. Brock, 2 vols. [Richmond: Virginia Historical Society, 1883-84], 2:155; Dinwiddie to Andrew Lewis, 15 Sept. 1755, ibid., 199; Dinwiddie to William Preston, 15 Aug. 1755, ibid., 200).

124. William Fleming to Francis Fauquier, 26 July 1763, *Papers of Francis Fauquier*, 2:997-99.

125. Recommendation of the Botetourt County Court for the office of sheriff, 16 Aug. 1770, Colonial Papers, folder 48, #18 (2), VSL; Deposition of John May, Clerk of Botetourt County Court, 16 Oct. 1770, ibid. (3). Preston and the other four judges dissented from the decision to recommend Christian and two other men for the office of sheriff. Normally Virginia country courts nominated three men, and the first named (in this case Christian) was expected to get the appointment. At Christian's request, however, the county clerk, John May, formally stated that only two of the dissenting justices objected specifically to him.

126. Francis Fauquier to Henry Bouquet, ca. Sept. 1764, *Papers of Francis Fauquier,* 2:1156.

127. Arthur Campbell to William Preston, 9, 12 Aug. 1774, 3QQ72 and 3QQ75; Preston to Campbell, 13 Aug. 1774, 3QQ76.

128. Eads, "Government by Families," 2; Boetourt Order Book, Part I, 1770-71, 15 Feb. 1770, p. 10. For the earlier rivalry between Bowyer and Christian, see Eads, "Government by Families," 2; Augusta Order Book 7, 19 Aug. 1762; 18 Feb. 1763, p. 477.

129. Botetourt Order Book, Part I, 1770-71, 1770 passim.

130. *Statutes at Large, Being a Collection of All the Laws of Virginia,* ed. William W. Hening, 13 vols. (Richmond: J.W. Randolph, 1823-35), Feb. 1772, 8:616.

131. Eads, "Government by Families," 2; Hughes, *Surveyors and Statesmen,* 100-101; John Madison to William Preston, 1 Mar. 1767, Preston Family of Virginia Papers, reel 3, #521; Thomas Lewis to Preston, 26 Dec. 1767, ibid., reel 3, #540; Richard Starke to Preston, 17 Feb. 1768, ibid., reel 3, #312; Andrew Lewis to Preston, 19 Mar. 1767, 2QQ101-2; Thomas Lewis to (apparently) Preston, 20 Mar. 1767, Brenckinridge Family Papers, reel 1, #10, University of Virginia; Preston to Robert Breckinridge, 1 Apr. 1767, Breckinridge Family Papers, vol. 1, LC.

132. Thomas Lewis to William Preston, 24 Feb. 1767, 2QQ100; Unidentified correspondent to (apparently) Preston, 4 Apr. 1770, Preston Family Papers, 1727-1896.

133. William Preston to William Byrd, 14 May 1774, 3QQ24; Preston to Edmund Pendleton, 14 May 1774, 3QQ25; Pendleton to Preston, 4 June 1774, 3QQ36. Opponents of new counties often charged that the proponents were motivated chiefly by the desire for public offices in the new counties (see, for example, John Madison to Preston, 1 Mar. 1767, Preston Family of Virginia Papers, reel 3, #521; Unidentified correspondent to [apparently] Preston, 4 Apr. 1770, Preston Family Papers, 1727-1896; Preston to Pendleton, 14 May 1774, 3QQ25).

134. Augusta Vestry Book, 16 May 1753, p. 120.

135. Thomas Lewis to William Preston, 4 Jan. 1774, Preston Family of Virginia Papers, reel 4, #780. Also see Lewis to Preston, 15 Mar. 1774, 3QQ13.

136. Alexander Ingram to William Preston, 3 Jan. 1770, Preston Family of Virginia Papers, reel 4, #613; Thomas Lewis to Preston, 1767, ibid., reel 3, #541. In view of the analysis made in Dewey, "Waterson-Madison Episode," John Madison, Jr., and his associates may well have been the culprits in 1767.

If so, they began their efforts several years earlier than Dewey was able to determine from his material.

137. Eads, "Government by Families," 2.

138. Richard Starke to William Preston, 17 Feb. 1768, Preston Family of Virginia Papers, reel 3, #312.

139. Augusta Vestry Book, 21 Nov. 1767, p. 427; 21 Nov. 1769.

140. Augusta Order Book 7, 19 Aug. 1762, p. 292; 18 Feb. 1763, p. 477.

141. For another instance of this play on the surname Christian, see Alexander Ingram to William Preston, 3 Jan. 1770, Preston Family of Virginia Papers, reel 4, #613.

142. John Madison to William Preston, 1 Mar. 1767, ibid., reel 3, #521.

143. Hughes, *Surveyors and Statesmen*, 100-101.

3. THE MILITIA AND POPULAR LOCALISM

1. Compiled from Augusta Order Book 2 (1749), pp. 68-311; Augusta Order Book 7 (1762), pp. 151-448; Augusta Order Book 14 (1773), pp. 469-70; Augusta Order Book 15 (1773), pp. 1-301; Botetourt County Order Book, Part I, 1770-71, pp. 1-187.

2. William Preston to Edmund Pendleton, 14 May 1774, 3QQ25. In explaining to the Board of Trade an act of the House of Burgesses reducing the frequency of court sessions in frontier counties, Governor William Gooch noted that monthly sessions were injurious to both the justices and the people as a whole (Gooch to Board of Trade, ca. 1749, Colonial Office 5, vol. 1327, #90-91, British Reproductions Collection).

3. William Christian to Arthur Campbell, 19 Feb. 1782, 9DD32.

4. Augusta Vestry Book, 12 Mar. 1768, p. 446.

5. Frederick Stokes Aldridge, "Organization and Administration of the Militia System of Colonial Virginia" (Ph.D. diss., American University, 1964), 197.

6. See, for example, William Cocke to William Preston, Aug. or Sept. 1774, 3QQ87; Arthur Campbell to Preston, 12 Aug. 1774, 3QQ75; William Russell to Preston, 28 Aug. 1774, 3QQ84.

7. See, for example, William Preston to Arthur Campbell, 25 Aug. 1774, 3QQ82; William Christian to Joseph Cloyd, 29 June 1774, 3QQ49; Campbell to Preston, 17, 29 Sept., and 10 Oct. 1774, 3QQ98, 3QQ106, and 3QQ109.

8. In September 1774, for example, Arthur Campbell ordered a group of men from his training company to perform active duty under his cousin William Campbell. When he made the draft, he also requested that William Campbell judge which of the men then on duty from that training company had the greatest need to return home, clearly assuming that William Campbell had some knowledge of that community (Arthur Campbell to William Campbell, 6 July 1774, Campbell-Preston Papers, reel 1, #44). Several days later, another Fincastle field officer, William Christian, suggested to county lieutenant William Preston which training companies could best spare men for active duty (Christian to Preston, 9 July 1774, 3QQ60).

9. See Arthur Campbell to William Campbell, 6 July 1774, Campbell-Preston Papers, reel 1, #44; James Robertson to William Preston, 26 July, 6, 12 Aug. 1774, 3QQ67, 3QQ71, and 3QQ74.

10. On fort construction, see William Russell to William Preston, 26 Feb. 1774, 3QQ46; and William Cocke, Circular Letter to Inhabitants on the Frontier of Holston, 25 Sept. 1774, 3QQ103. On dispatching of scouts, see Russell to Preston, 7 May 1774, 3QQ23; and Daniel Smith to Preston, 8 July 1774, 3QQ57. On mobilization of men, see James Patton to William Gooch, 23 Oct. 1742, Colonial Office 5, vol. 1325, #237-39, British Reproductions Collection; William Cocke, Circular Letter to Inhabitants on the Frontier of Holston, 25 Sept. 1774, 3QQ103; Arthur Campbell to Preston, 4 Oct. 1774, 3QQ112.

11. William Doack to William Preston, 22 Sept. 1774, 3QQ101; Arthur Campbell to Preston, 17 Sept. 1774, 3QQ98; Preston to James Robertson, 22 July 1774, 3QQ138; Preston, Instructions to the Scouts that go down New River, July 1774, Preston Family of Virginia Papers, reel 4, #835 (a typed copy from Auditor's Papers, VSL); Andrew Lewis to Preston, 23 Nov. 1756, 1QQ137; Robert Dinwiddie to James Buchanan, 14 Aug. 1755, 1QQ86. For other expressions of Dinwiddie's concern with indiscipline in the Augusta militia, see Dinwiddie to William Wright, 8 July 1755, *Official Papers of Robert Dinwiddie*, 2:92; Dinwiddie to Buchanan, 8 Aug. 1757, ibid., 681-82, and passim.

12. Kegley, *Kegley's Virginia Frontier*, 206-8; William Preston to Andrew Lewis, 4 Apr. 1757, 1QQ152-53. In 1755 Augusta County lieutenant James Patton predicted that he would be unable to raise a company of men for frontier defense (Dinwiddie to [Peter] Jefferson, 9 July [1755], *Official Papers of Robert Dinwiddie*, 2:95).

13. Arthur Campbell to William Preston, 17 Oct. 1774, 3QQ125; James Robertson to Preston, 1, 11 Aug. 1774, 3QQ69 and 3QQ73.

14. John Brown to William Preston, 22 Aug. 1774, 3QQ81; Andrew Lewis to Preston, 14 Aug. 1774, 3QQ77; Arthur Campbell to Preston, 12 Aug. 1774, 3QQ75; James Roberton to Preston, 1, 4 Sept. 1774, 3QQ88 and 3QQ91; Michael Woods to Preston, 16 Sept. 1774, 3QQ97.

15. James Patton to William Gooch, 23 Oct. 1742, Colonial Office 5, vol. 1325, #237-39, British Reproductions Collection; Kegley, *Kegley's Virginia Frontier*, 154; Oren F. Morton, *A History of Rockbridge County, Virginia* (Staunton, Va.: McClure Co., 1920), 64-65.

16. Proclamation of Francis Fauquier, 13 May 1765, Broadside Collection, VSL (#2990 in *Southeastern Broadsides before 1877: A Bibliography*, ed. Ray O. Hummel [Richmond: Virginia State Library, 1971]); Andrew Lewis to Fauquier, 9 May, 3 June 1765, *Journal of the House of Burgesses, 1761-1765*, ed J.P. Kennedy and H.B. McIlwaine (Richmond: Virginia State Library, 1907), xx, xxiii; Proclamation of the Augusta Boys, 4 June 1765, ibid., xxiv.

17. Francis Fauquier to the Board of Trade, 1 Aug. 1765, *Papers of Francis Fauquier*, 3:1265-69; Fauquier to John Stuart, 21 Nov. 1767, ibid., 1516. In 1765 a Cherokee party wishing to communicate with Virginia authorities informed a British official on the frontier that they were reluctant to travel through the upper valley because they feared violence from local settlers (George Price to John Stuart, 8 Dec. 1765, ibid., 1336-37).

18. Arthur Campbell to William Preston, June 1774, 22 June 1774, 3QQ40, 3QQ41; William Christian to Preston, 9 July 1774, 3QQ60.

19. In "'A dastardly set of people': Scotch-Irish Society in the Valley of Virginia, 1736-1774" (paper presented at Southern Historical Society, 1986), Turk McCleskey argued that racism and the stereotypical refusal of frontiersmen to distinguish between Indian tribes played no role in the Augusta Boys incident in 1765. He asserted that no other Cherokees were murdered in Augusta before 1774 and that in 1765 the murderers believed that their victims were Shawnees rather than Cherokees. There were, however, other incidents of violence against friendly Cherokees during the colonial years in the upper valley. The murder at Watauga in 1774 is discussed in this chapter, and the violent abuse of a Cherokee leader in 1753 is noted in chapter 2. In 1765 Andrew Lewis tried to warn the group attacked by the Augusta Boys that even the pass might not protect them. (Andrew Lewis to Francis Fauquier, 9 May 1765, *Papers of Francis Fauquier*, 3:1234).

The Augusta Boys' claim that their victims were Shawnees may have been insincere posturing. When the charge was first made as the Indians arrived in Staunton, Lewis found that the accusers "could not make out anything like a proof that they were other than Cherokees" (Lewis to Fauquier, 5 June 1765, ibid., 1254). A later proclamation also included the preposterous allegation that Lewis was secretly assisting the French (Proclamation of the Augusta Boys [ca. 4 June 1765, ibid., 1255-56). According to Lewis, the mob that attacked the Augusta jail declared "that they would never suffer a man to be Confined or brought to Justice for killing of Savages" (Lewis to Fauquier, 3 June 1765, ibid., 1248). Popular cynicism regarding tribal identities may have been increased by the memory of a series of Indian attacks in the counties east of the Blue Ridge in 1758, when transient Cherokee parties attacked local settlers, stole property, and on several occasions claimed that they were really Shawnees (William Callaway to George Washington, 15 May 1758, in *Letters to Washington and Accompanying Papers*, ed. Stanislaus M. Hamilton, 5 vols. [Boston: Houghton, Mifflin, 1898-1902], 2:296-98; also see President Blair to Washington, 24 May 1758 and enclosed documents, ibid., 304-16). Other episodes of violence against friendly Indians occurred elsewhere along the backcountry frontier. See Harry M. Ward, *Major General Adam Stephen and the Cause of American Liberty* (Charlottesville: University Press of Virginia, 1989), 99-100; Edward J. Cashin, "Sowing the Wind: Governor Wright and the Georgia Backcountry on the Eve of the Revolution," in *Forty Years of Diversity: Essays on Colonial Georgia*, ed. Harvey H. Jackson and Phinizy Spalding (Athens: University of Georgia Press, 1984), 237-39, 241-42. Whatever role racism played in these events, it obviously interacted with a variety of other social, cultural, and economic factors, which is the point argued in the text.

20. Craig, Autobiography, 54; James Patton to Robert Dinwiddie, Jan. 1753, 1QQ73-74.

21. James Robertson to William Preston, 20 July 1774, 3QQ66; Arthur Campbell to Preston, 17 Oct. 1774, 3QQ125; Campbell to William Campbell, 6 July 1774, Campbell-Preston Papers, reel 1, #44; William Russell to Preston, 7 May 1774, 3QQ23.

183

22. John Stuart, "Transcript of the Memoir of Indian Wars and Other Occurrences, 1749-1780," copy made by Samuel Lewis.

23. William Preston, Diary of the Sandy Creek expedition, 9 Feb.-13 Mar. 1756, pp. 12-16 of typescript, 1QQ96-123.

24. Stuart, "Transcript of the Memoir," 12-13.

25. *Documentary History of Dunmore's War, 1774*, ed. Reuben Gold Thwaites and Louise Phelps Kellogg (Madison: Wisconsin Historical Society, 1905), 435.

26. Stuart, "Transcript of the Memoir," 18-19.

27. Ibid., 9.

28. William Christian to William Preston, 15 Oct. 1774, *Documentary History of Dunmore's War*, 261-66; ballad, ibid., 434-35.

29. William Cocke's Circular Letter to Inhabitants on the Frontier of Holston, 25 Sept. 1774, 3QQ103; Arthur Campbell to William Preston, 29 Sept., 9, 13, 17 Oct. 1774, 3QQ106, 3QQ117, 3QQ120, and 3QQ125; Cocke to Preston, 27 Oct. 1774, 3QQ126. At one point during the Seven Years' War, Augusta militiamen may have pushed for the right to elect their own officers, for Governor Dinwiddie insisted in a letter to Andrew Lewis that they not be allowed to do so. (Robert Dinwiddie to Andrew Lewis, 23 Dec. 1756, *Official Papers of Robert Dinwiddie*, 2:569).

In *Albion's Seed: Four British Folkways in America* (New York: Oxford University Press, 1989), David Hackett Fischer suggested that the entire southern backcountry was shaped by a culture that emphasized a politics of personal loyalty to charismatic leaders who won support by bold and decisive actions. Backcountry settlers, he asserted, brought this culture to America from northern Ireland and the border between England and Scotland. Whatever the merits of Fischer's argument, as the chapter demonstrates, other factors also shaped the values of common folk in the upper valley. Moreover, chapter 2 makes clear that despite their Scotch-Irish heritage, the region's leaders accepted much of the English culture of eastern Virginia.

30. In "Soldiers When They Chose to Be So," James R.W. Titus makes some of the same points about localist orientations among lower-class Virginians. Unfortunately, the statewide scope of his analysis, and its primary focus on provincial troops performing active duty rather than the militia, prevents him from going substantially beyond a statement of the hypothesis to illustrations of specific instances of popular attitudes and actions set in particular local communities. The more valuable aspects of Titus's study are its explanation of the changing attitudes of Virginia leaders and its suggestions regarding the impact of slavery on lower-class Virginians' conception of liberty.

31. Report of council of Botetourt militia officers, 12 Aug. 1774, Auditor's Papers, William Preston section; Arthur Campbell to William Preston, 29 Sept. 1774, 3QQ106; John Montgomery to Preston, 2 Oct. 1774, 3QQ110. See also James Robertson to Preston, 12 Aug. 1774, 3QQ74; Andrew Lewis to Robert Dinwiddie, June 1756, 1QQ152-53.

32. Andrew Lewis to William Preston, 26 Feb. 1757, 1QQ150-51; Preston to Lewis, 4 Apr. 1757, 1QQ152-53; William Russell to Preston, 26 June 1774, 3QQ46.

33. William Christian to Preston, 4 July 1774, 3QQ54. See also Bryce Russell to Preston, 2 July 1774, 3QQ52; Preston to unidentified correspondent, 28 Sept. 1774, in *American Archives* . . . , ed. Peter Force, 9 vols. (1837-53; rpt. New York: Johnson Reprint Corporation, 1972), 4th ser. vol. 1, col. 808.

34. Arthur Campbell to William Preston, 6 Oct. 1774, 3QQ115.

35. Kegley, *Kegley's Virginia Frontier*, 139-40.

36. Joseph Cloyd to William Preston, 4 Apr. 1774, 3QQ17.

37. William Russell to William Preston, 26 June 1774, 3QQ46.

38. Daniel Smith to William Preston, 13 Oct. 1774, 3QQ119; Arthur Campbell to Preston, 13 Oct. 1774, 3QQ119.

39. Arthur Campbell to William Preston, 12, 19, 28 Aug. 1774, 3QQ75, 3QQ80, and 3QQ85; Campbell to William Campbell, 29 Aug. 1774, Campbell-Preston Papers, reel 1, #45; James Thompson to Preston, 19 Aug. 177[4], Ellet Papers, Virginia Polytechnic Institute and State University; James Robertson to Preston, 1 Sept. 1774, 3QQ88.

40. Arthur Campbell to William Preston, 12, 19 Aug. 1774, 3QQ79 and 3QQ80.

41. Craig, Autobiography, 57.

42. Hugh McAden Journal, 22 Sept. 1755, quoted in William Henry Foote, *Sketches of North Carolina, Historical and Biographical, Illustrative of the Principles of a Portion of Her Early Settlers* (New York: Robert Carter, 1846), 168.

43. Andrew Lewis to William Preston, 26 Feb. 1757, 1QQ150-51; Preston to Lewis, 4 Apr. 1757, 1QQ151-53; Bryce Russell to Preston, 2 July 1774, 3QQ52. For other such references see Lewis to Robert Dinwiddie, June 1756, 1QQ131; Preston to Edward Johnson, 2 Aug. 1774, Preston Family of Virginia Papers, reel 4, #836. For a discussion of apparently similar behavior in the northern valley, see Warren R. Hofstra, "'A Parcel of Barbarians and an Uncooth Set of People': Settlers and Settlements of the Shenandoah Valley," paper delivered at the conference "George Washington and the Virginia Backcountry," 21-22 Apr. 1989, Shenandoah College, Winchester, Va.

44. Daniel Smith to William Preston, 8 July 1774, 3QQ57; George Adams to Preston, 4 Oct. 1774, 3QQ113; William Christian to Preston, 4 July 1774, 3QQ54; Francis Fauquier to Preston, 24 July 1763, 2QQ42.

45. See, for example, William Fleming to Francis Fauquier, 26 July 1763, *Papers of Francis Fauquier*, 2:998; William Preston to Samuel McDowell, 27 May 1774, 3QQ27; William Russell to Preston, 26 June 1774 3QQ46; William Christian to Joseph Cloyd, 29 June 1774, 3QQ49; Arthur Campbell to Preston, 1 July 1774, 3QQ50; William Cocke to Preston, 19 Sept. 1774, 3QQ99.

46. Arthur Campbell to William Preston, 23 June, 9 July 1774, 3QQ44 and 3QQ58; William Christian to Preston, 9 July 1774, 3QQ60.

47. William Preston, Address to the Cherokees, 11 June 1774, Preston Family of Virginia Papers, reel 4, #823.

48. Report of council of Botetourt militia officers, 12 Aug. 1774, Auditor's Papers, William Preston section, #230; Arthur Campbell to Preston, 6 Oct. 1774, 3QQ115; see also William Christian to Preston 12 July 1774, 3QQ63.

49. Augusta County Court Judgments, Feb. 1763, Israel Christian vs. George Wilson, in Chalkley, *Chronicles of the Scotch Irish Settlement*, 1:500-501;

Deposition of Adam Wallace concerning the case of John Bowyer, 10 Sept. 1774, Colonial Papers, folder 50, #21. For another reference to Bowyer's efforts to retard the Point Pleasant expedition, see Proceedings of Virginia convention, 8 Jan. 1776 in *American Archives*, ed. Force, 4th ser., vol. 4, cols. 114-115.

50. William Preston, Diary of the Sandy Creek expedition, 9 Feb.-13 Mar. 1756, pp. 13-14 of typescript, 1QQ96-123.

51. Arthur Campbell to William Preston 19 Aug. 1774, 3QQ80. For another instance of popular mistrust regarding militia pay, see Preston to [Robert Dinwiddie], 8 Apr. 1756, 1QQ124.

52. Augusta Order Book 7, 18 Feb. 1762, p. 161; Morton, *History of Rockbridge County*, 49.

53. For examples of concern with negligence of minor officials, see the undated and unsigned grand jury instructions in Preston Family of Virginia Papers, reel 13, #3497. The guide suggests they were written by either William Preston or John Buchanan. Also see Augusta Order Book 1, 20 Nov. 1746; Augusta Order Book 7, 24 Feb. 1762, p. 203; Augusta Order Book 15, 24 May 1773, p. 138; 17 Mar. 1774, p. 329; 18 May 1774, p. 466.

54. For examples of turnover among road overseers, see Augusta Order Book 1, 13 May 1746; 17 Mar. 1748, p. 360; Augusta Order Book 2, 18 May 1748, pp. 5-8; 22 Aug. 1749, p. 151; 1 Dec. 1749, p. 197; 22 May 1750, pp. 356, 359, 363; 1 Sept. 1750, p. 458; Augusta Order Book 7, 18 May 1762, pp. 208, 211-12; Augusta Order Book 15, 16 Mar. 1773, pp. 10-11; 18 May 1773, pp. 98-99; 17 Aug. 1773, pp. 148-49; 22 Mar. 1774, p. 442; 17 May 1774, pp. 451, 455-57; Botetourt Order Book Part I, 1770-71, 8 May 1770, p. 48; 13 Nov. 1770, p. 187.

For examples of turnover among constables, see Augusta Order Book 1, 10 Mar. 1746; 21 May 1747; Augusta Order Book 2, 18 May 1748, pp. 4-5; 15 Aug. 1748, pp. 47, 49-50; Augusta Order Book 7, 18 May 1762, pp. 208-9; 16 Nov. 1762, p. 355; Augusta Order Book 15, 18 May 1773, p. 97; 17 Aug. 1773, pp. 144, 149, 151; 16 Mar. 1774, pp. 317, 319, 322A; 18 May 1774, p. 475.

For examples of constables petitioning for their own removal, see Augusta Order Book 2, 20 May 1748, p. 17; 22 May 1750, pp. 354-56; 23 May 1750, pp. 363-67. In many other cases, appointment orders specified that the incumbent official would be discharged as soon as the new constable was sworn in. See, for example, ibid., 18 May 1749, pp. 111-12, 115-17; 22 Aug. 1749, p. 150; 29 Nov. 1750, p. 502; Botetourt Order Book, Part I, 1770-71, 14 Mar. 1770, p. 26; 10 May 1770, p. 83; 12 June 1770, p. 91; 14 Aug. 1770, p. 117.

55. William Christian to Margaret Christian, 1 May 1772, Campbell-Preston Papers. Also see memorandum of Evan Shelby, 17 June 1775, Shelby Family Papers, vol. 1, #418. LC, for a description of Shelby's problems with a recalcitrant squatter.

56. Thomas Walker to William Preston, 27 May 1771, 2QQ125. For an example of a lease contract see the agreement between William Campbell and William Crabtree, 18 Mar. 1773, Campbell-Preston papers, reel 1.

57. Thomas Lewis to William Preston, 2 Apr. 1770, Preston Family of Virginia Papers, reel 4, #620. See also Hughes, *Surveyors and Statesmen*, 108-159. For an apparent example of such favoritism in the upper valley, see William

Vause to Preston, 14 Aug. 1770, Preston Family Papers, 1727-1896. Preston had informed Vause of a desirable piece of land and secured it for him.

58. When preparing to resell some land in 1773, Arthur Campbell discovered a mistake in the patent, which he feared might endanger the title (Arthur Campbell to William Campbell, 27 Mar. 1773, Campbell-Preston Papers, reel 1). Similarly, Benjamin Estill, who was living on land purchased from James Patton, discovered in 1775 that through some mistake Patton had not patented that tract (Statement dated 2 Aug. 1775, Preston Family Papers, 1727-1896). Both Campbell and Estill were prominent upper valley leaders. The purchasers of Campbell's land, the Bowens, apparently were not, and problems arising from surveyors' errors presumably threatened land sellers and purchasers of all social statuses.

59. Thomas Lewis to William Preston, 4 Jan. 1774, Preston Family of Virginia Papers, reel 4, #780; Lewis to Preston, 15 Mar. 1774, 3QQ13. From Lewis's language, however, it is unclear whether he feared Preston would be attacked only in court or also by the inciting of popular discontent. Also see Hughes, *Surveyors and Statesmen*, 109-10, 114; William Gooch to Board of Trade, 11 Mar. 1746, Colonial Office 5, vol. 1326, #121, British Reproductions Collection.

60. Hughes, *Surveyors and Statesmen*, 112.

61. Francis Smith to William Preston, 5 May 1774, Preston Family of Virginia Papers, reel 4, #812.

62. Peter Hog to William Preston, undated but apparently ca. 3 June 1774, ibid., #822. In 1744 a similar resentment of nonresident surveyors who failed to provide services may well have shaped the Virginia legislature's "Act to oblige the Surveyors of the Counties of Albemarle and Augusta to reside in the respective counties of which they are surveyors" (*Legislative Journals of the Council of Colonial Virginia*, ed. H.R. McIlwaine, 3 vols. [Richmond: Colonial Press, Everett Waddey Co., 1918-19], 2:953-54, 956-58).

63. Lyman Chalkley, "Before the Gates of the Wilderness Road," *VMHB* 30 (1922): 194. For a possible earlier instance of such practices by Calhoun, see Augusta Order Book 1, 19 Sept. 1746.

64. Robert Doack to William Preston, 20 Nov. 1771, 2QQ128.

65. See Edmund Pendleton's instructions to William Preston, 29 Apr. 1771, Preston Family Papers, 1727-1896. In at least one case, this practice clearly angered a settler who sought to maximize the value of his purchase (John Buchanan, Surveying Journal, Oct. 1745, in Goodridge Wilson, *Smyth County History and Traditions* [Kingsport, Tenn.: Kingsport Press, 1932], 10-15).

66. McCleskey, "Rich Land, Poor Prospects."

67. James Patton to unidentified correspondent, Jan. 1753, 1QQ78; Thomas Lewis to William Preston, 1767, Preston Family of Virginia Papers, reel 3, #542. Also see Alexander Ingram to Preston, 3 Jan. 1770, ibid., reel 4, #613.

68. Thomas Lewis to William Preston, 2 Jan. 1771, ibid., #646. Frank Dewey identifies Andrew Johnston as an associate of John Madison, Jr., in the caveating scheme and provides a general description of the affair ("Waterson-Madison Episode," 165-76).

69. Everett Dick, *The Dixie Frontier: A Social History of the Southern Frontier from the First Transmontane Beginnings to the Civil War* (New York: Knopf, 1948), 8;

Wayland F. Dunaway, *The Scotch-Irish of Colonial Pennsylvania* (Chapel Hill: University of North Carolina Press, 1944), 166; Stevenson Whitcomb Fletcher, *Pennsylvania Agriculture and Country Life, 1640-1840*, 2 vols. (Harrisburg: Historical and Museum Commission, 1950-55), 1:21-23.

70. Deposition of Mrs. James Greenlee, taken 10 Nov. 1806 in the suit of Joseph Burden, Plaintiff vs. Alexander Caeton and others, Defendants, in Cooper, *History of the Shenandoah Valley*, 274-79. The point here, of course, is not that Borden enthusiastically embraced such attitudes; the terms of his land grant required him to find settlers.

71. Walter Crockett to William Preston, 7 Apr. 1779, Auditor's Papers, William Preston section; Preston memorandum, 20 July 1780, 5QQ41; Thomas Dugglis confession, 19 Aug. 1780, 5QQ60.

72. Samuel Houston to Sidney Smith Baxter, Jan. 1837, Virginia Historical Society. For other examples of kinship clustering, see Augusta Vestry Book, Mar. 1765, p. 383; Emory Hamilton, "Blackmore's Fort," *Southwest Virginian*, Feb. 1981, pp. 29-30; Joseph L. Miller, "Carter Genealogy," *WMQ* 1st ser., 19 (1910-11): 121. As Sally Eads has noted, upper valley leaders also frequently settled in extended family groups ("Government by Families," 3-4).

73. James W. Alexander, *The Life of Archibald Alexander* (New York: Charles Scribner, 1854), 6.

74. James Geddes Craighead, *The Craighead Family: A Genealogical Memoir of the Descendants of Reverend Thomas and Margaret Craighead. 1658-1876* (Philadelphia: Printed for the descendants by Sherman and Co., printers, 1876), 10.

75. Paula Hathaway Anderson-Green, "The New River Frontier Settlement on the Virginia-North Carolina Border, 1760-1820." *VMHB* 86 (1978): 413-31; Glenn C. Trewartha, "Types of Rural Settlement in Colonial America," *Geographical Review* 36 (1946): 595. Also see Charles Augustus Hanna, *The Scotch Irish: Or the Scot in North Ireland, and North America*, 2 vols. (New York: G.P. Putnam's Sons, 1902), 2:46.

76. See, for example, McMaster, *History of Hardy County*, 23-25.

77. Hofstra, "Land, Ethnicity, and Community." According to David Hackett Fisher, many backcountry communities possessed such strong internal cohesion that they were able to force out undesired neighbors by the informal but effective social and physical pressures that they called "hating out" (*Albion's Seed*, 292).

4. THE ROOTS OF BACKCOUNTRY ORDER

1. Klein, "Ordering the Backcountry"; Richard Maxwell Brown, *The South Carolina Regulators* (Cambridge; Mass.: Harvard University Press, 1963). As Klein points out, however, despite their initial indifference, provincial leaders began to respond to frontier grievances by the late 1760s, and they made more substantial concessions during the revolutionary era ("Frontier Planters and the American Revolution").

2. George William Franz, "Paxton: A Study of Community Structure and

Mobility in the Colonial Pennsylvania Backcountry" (Ph.D. diss., Rutgers University, 1974).

3. A. Roger Ekirch, *"Poor Carolina"*: Politics and Society in Colonial North Carolina, 1729-1776 (Chapel Hill: University of North Carolina Press, 1981). In *Evolution of the Southern Backcountry*, Richard R. Beeman asserted that in Lunenburg County, Virginia, the low economic status of early leaders reduced their ability to command respect and deference from fellow settlers.

4. As Antonio Gramsci noted, elite groups in peripheral areas often accept the power and values of their cosmopolitan counterparts without fully imposing those values upon the populace ("The Function of Piedmont," *Selections from the Prison Notebooks of Antonio Gramsci*, ed. and trans. Quintin Hoare and Geoffrey Nowell Smith [New York: International Publishers, 1971], 104-6).

5. To some degree these questions are considered by Rachel Klein and Richard Beeman in their respective analyses of the South Carolina backcountry and Lunenburg County, Virginia. They receive much fuller consideration in Gregory H. Noble's *Divisions throughout the Whole: Politics and Society in Hampshire County, Massachusetts, 1740-1775* (Cambridge, Eng.: Cambridge University Press, 1983).

6. For examples of cooperative agricultural labor, see David P. Szatsmary, *Shay's Rebellion: The Making of an Agrarian Insurrection* (Amherst: University of Massachusetts Press, 1980).

7. See, for example, Arthur Campbell to William Campbell, 6 July 1774, Campbell-Preston Papers, reel 1, #44; William Russell to William Preston, 7 May 1774, 3QQ23. This is not meant to assert that cooperative labor and local labor exchanges did not occur in the upper valley. For example, Samuel Houston later recollected that colonial settlers did practice collective labor (Samuel Houston to Sidney Smith Baxter, Jan. 1837 [?], VHS). Various other sources describe small groups of neighbors working together in their fields. Moreover, many families apparently depended on their neighbors to convert thread spun on their wheels into usable cloth. Nevertheless, upper valley neighborhoods often failed to employ such cooperative practices at times when they were especially needed.

8. Arthur Campbell to William Campbell, 17 Oct. 1774, 3QQ125. For another apparent occurrence of such popular attitudes, see George Adams to William Preston, 4 Oct. 1774, 3QQ113. Similarly, although neighborhood groups often pressed for the construction of local forts, they were not always able to reach a community consensus on their location. Thus Arthur Campbell reported in October 1774 that two settlers on the southern frontier had removed their families, "disagreeing with the Majority of the local Inhabitants as to the place to build a Fort" (Arthur Campbell to Preston, 6 Oct. 1774, 3QQ115).

9. Thomas Walker to William Preston, 15 Dec. 1773, 2QQ157. In an undated affadavit, Preston confirmed that this policy was followed (Preston Family of Virginia Papers, reel 13, #3501).

10. Mitchell, *Commercialism and Frontier*, 45-47, 52-53. For discussion of these and other aspects of community, see C.J. Calhoun, "Community: Toward a Variable Conceptualization for Comparative Research," *Social History* 5 (1980): 105-29.

11. Proceedings of the Augusta Court Martial, 2 Sept 1747, 1QQ36.

12. See, for example, William Fleming to William Preston, 19 Nov. 1773, Preston Family Papers, 1727-1896; Memorandum by Preston regarding Captain Meredith's warrants lodged 12 May 1774, Preston Family of Virginia Papers, reel 4, #814. When acting on behalf of his eastern Virginia friend Edmund Pendleton, Preston promised such settlers that if they entered into contracts for future purchase of their land, he would relinquish the right to sell those lands to other persons in the meantime. Preston also offered credit to those who wished to enter into immediate contracts to purchase (Preston to Robert Doack, 1 Oct. 1771, Campbell-Preston Papers, reel 1, #24).

13. Both these perceptions were explicitly stated by Thomas Walker in a letter to William Preston, 27 May 1771, 2QQ125.

14. William Preston to Robert Dinwiddie (?), 8 Apr. 1756, 1QQ124. See Preston Family of Virginia Papers, reels 2-3, passim, for other examples of such extensions of credit. James Robertson's letter of 4 April 1793 to John Preston suggests that such practices were normal throughout the colonial period. The letter also suggests, however, that some officers may have extended credit on terms that exploited their men (Robertson to Preston, 4 Apr. 1793, ibid., reel 7, #1794).

15. See Arthur Campbell to William Preston, 19, 28 Aug. 1774, 3QQ80 and 3QQ85; William Christian to Preston, 3 Sept. 1774, 3QQ89; Campbell to Preston, 9 Oct. 1774, 3QQ117.

16. Minutes of council of militia officers at Botetourt, 12 Aug. 1774, Auditor's Papers, William Preston section.

17. For examples of persuasion of settlers, see James Patton to Robert Dinwiddie (?), 26 July 1754, Preston Family of Virginia Papers, reel 2, #135; Daniel Smith to William Preston, 8 July 1774, 3QQ57; William Cocke to Preston, 19 Sept. 1774, 3QQ99. For Preston's dealings with the Bullpasture settlers, see Andrew Lewis to Preston, 26 Feb. 1757, 1QQ150-51; Preston to Lewis, 4 Apr. 1757, 1QQ152-54. For other examples of promising assistance in defending local communities, see William Russell to Preston, 26 June 1774, 3QQ46; William Christian to Joseph Cloyd, 29 June 1774, 3QQ49.

18. William Christian to William Preston, 4 July 1774, 3QQ54.

19. See, for example, Andrew (?) Lewis to Robert Dinwiddie (?), June 1756, 1QQ133; William Cocke's Circular Letter to Inhabitants on the Frontier of Holston, 25 Sept. 1774, 3QQ103.

20. Robert Dinwiddie to Andrew Lewis, 17 Dec. 1756, *Official Papers of Robert Dinwiddie*, 2:567.

21. See, for example, Andrew (?) Lewis to Robert Dinwiddie (?), June 1756, 1QQ133; Robert Doack to William Preston, 12 July 1774, 3QQ61. George Adams also requested that men be stationed in his Holston River neighborhood to encourage settlers to remain in the area and harvest their crops (Adams to Preston, 4 Oct. 1774, 3QQ113).

22. Bryce Russell to William Preston, 2 July 1774, 3QQ52. Also see Daniel Smith to Preston, 30 May 1774, 3QQ149; Robert Doack to Preston, 12 July 1774, 3QQ61.

23. John Montgomery to William Preston, 2 Oct. 1774, 3QQ110.

24. Andrew Lewis to William Preston, 26 Feb. 1757, 1QQ150-51; Preston to Lewis, 4 Apr. 1757, 1QQ152-54; William Russell to Preston, 26 June 1774, 3QQ46.

25. Joseph Cloyd to William Preston, 4 Apr. 1774, 3QQ17; Preston, Diary of the Sandy Creek expedition, 9 Feb.-13 Mar. 1756, pp. 12-13 of typescript, 1QQ96- 123; Robert Dinwiddie to John Buchanan, 11 Aug. 1755, *Official Papers of Robert Dinwiddie*, 2:154-55; Dinwiddie to [Andrew] Lewis, 23 Dec. 1756, p. 569; Dinwiddie to Buchanan, 8 Aug. 1757, pp. 681-82. For further complaints see Lewis to Preston, 11 Nov. 1756, 1QQ137; Preston to James Robertson, 22 July 1774, 3QQ138.

26. William Cocke's Circular letter to Inhabitants on the Frontier of the Holston, 25 Sept. 1774, 3QQ103; Arthur Campbell to William Preston, 17, 9 Oct. 1774, 3QQ125, 3QQ127; Joshua Caldwell, *Sketches of the Bench and Bar of Tennessee* (Knoxville: Ogden Brothers and Co., printers, 1898), 24-25.

27. William Goodrich, "William Cocke—Born 1748, Died 1828," *American Historical Magazine* 1 (1896): 224-29.

28. Wilson, *Great Valley Patriots*, p. 17.

29. Arthur Campbell to William Campbell, 29 Aug. 1774, Campbell-Preston Papers, reel 1, #45; Arthur Campbell to Preston, 28 Aug. 1774, 3QQ85. Apparently Drake had used the same tactics in an earlier meeting to defeat Campbell (Arthur Campbell to Preston, 12 Aug. 1774, 3QQ75).

30. William Cocke to Preston, Aug. or Sept. and 27 Oct. 1774, 3QQ87, 3QQ126; Arthur Campbell to Preston, 27 Jan. 1775 (?), 4QQ4.

31. Andrew Lewis to Francis Fauquier, 15 June 1765, *Papers of Francis Fauquier*, 3:1253-55. Lewis also suggested that Hog had played some role in getting a justice of the peace to take depositions regarding the tribal identity of the murdered Indians.

32. William Preston, Diary of the Sandy Creek expedition, 9 Feb.-13 Mar. 1756, pp. 15-16 of typescript, 1QQ96-123; Gordon Aronhime, "Colonel John Smith (1701-1783): Unsung Hero of Virginia Colonial Frontier," *Augusta Historical Bulletin* 14 (Spring 1978): 5-32; Cooper, *History of the Shenandoah Valley*, 1:492; Robert Dinwiddie to John Smith, 15 Jan. 1756, *Official Papers of Robert Dinwiddie*, 2:322-23. Dinwiddie may have been partially responsible for this friction, for he sent instructions for other officers to Captain Woodson and implied several times that Peter Hog might be given the command (Dinwiddie to [Peter] Hog, 15 Dec. 1755; Dinwiddie to [William] Preston and [John] Smith, 15 Dec. 1755; Dinwiddie to Richard Pearls, 15 Dec. 1755; Dinwiddie to Captain Woodson, 15 Dec. 1755, ibid. 294-98).

33. Daniel Smith to William Preston, 30 May, 8 July, 13 Oct., 22 Mar., 4 Oct., 13 Oct. 1774, 3QQ149, 3QQ57, 3QQ119, 3QQ15, and 3QQ114.

34. Daniel Smith to William Preston, 31 Jan., 22 Mar. 1774, 3QQ2 and 3QQ15; Walter T. Durham, *Daniel Smith: Frontier Statesman* (Nashville: Parthenon Press, 1976); Mary Kegley, "Who the Fifteen Signers Were," *Journal of the Roanoke Valley Historical Society* 9, 2 (1975): 36.

35. William Russell to William Preston, 26 June, 13 July, 16 Aug. 1774, 3QQ46, 3QQ64, and 3QQ78. Emphasis added.

36. William Russell, Instructions to Richard Stanton, Edward Sharpe,

Ephraim Drake, and William Harrel, scouts, 15 Apr. 1774, 3QQ18; Russell to William Preston, 7 May 1774, 3QQ23. In the instructions Russell gave first mention to the threat that such a war would present to expansion into the Ohio Valley rather than its threat to local settlements.

37. William Russell to William Preston, 13 July 1774, 3QQ64. Russell presumably referred to Arthur Campbell on the Holston River and William Christian on the New. His rivalry with Campbell would intensify in the revolutionary and postrevolutionary years.

38. See, for example, Bryce Russell to William Preston, 2 July 1774, 3QQ52; Robert Doack to Preston, 12 July 1774, 3QQ61; George Adams to Preston, 4 Oct. 1774, 3QQ113; Augusta County Court Material Records, Sept. 1759, VSL.

39. Arthur Campbell to Daniel Smith, 3 Oct. 1774, 9DD3; William Preston to Andrew Lewis, 4 Apr. 1757, 1QQ152-53; Lewis to Preston, 26 Feb. 1757, 1QQ150-51. For other examples, see Preston to Campbell, 13 Aug. 1774, 3QQ76; Preston to David Long, 13 Aug. 1774, 3QQ140.

40. Robert Doack to William Preston, 20 Nov. 1771, 2QQ128; Francis Smith to Preston, 5 May 1774, Preston Family of Virginia Papers, reel 4, #812.

41. Chalkley, "Before the Gates of the Wilderness Road," 194; Johnson, *New River Settlement*, 77-78; Augusta Order Book 1, 19 Sept. 1746; Augusta Order Book 2, 29 Nov. 1750, pp. 501-2; 30 Nov. 1750, p. 514.

42. Chalkley, "Before the Gates of the Wilderness Road," 196.

43. *Sevier Family History with the Collected Letters of General John Sevier First Governor of Tennessee and Twenty-eight Collateral Family Lineages*, ed. Cora Bales Sevier and Nancy S. Madden (Washington D.C.: N.p., 1961), 2, 6.

5. TOWARD THE REPUBLIC

1. Upper valley burgesses signed several nonimportation resolutions in Willamsburg in 1769 and 1770 (*The Papers of Thomas Jefferson*, ed. Julian P. Boyd et al., 21 vols. [Princeton: Princeton University Press, 1950-83], 1:30, 46). These actions, however, had little effect within the region.

2. For examples or correspondence from eastern Virginia regarding the imperial crisis, see Edmund Pendleton to William Preston, 4 June 1774, 3QQ36; Edward Johnson to Preston, 2 July 1774, Preston Family of Virginia Papers, reel 4, #826; Hugh Mercer to Preston, 20 Sept. 1774, 3QQ100.

3. Thomas Lewis to William Preston, 8 June 1774, 3QQ68; John Brown to Preston, 28 May 1774, 3QQ29.

4. Petition of William Christian, 3 Jan. 1776, Preston Family of Virginia Papers, reel 5, #912. Also see Dunmore's criticism of the assembly in his letter to the county lieutenants, 10 June 1774, 3QQ39.

5. Fincastle County address, 20 Jan. 1775, *Virginia Gazette* (Purdie), 18 Feb. 1775, in *Revolutionary Virginia: The Road to Independence*, ed. and comp. William James Van Schreeven, Robert L. Scribner, and Brent Tarter, 7 vols. (Charlottesville: University Press of Virginia for the Virginia Independence Bicentennial Commission, 1973-83), 2:254-56.

6. Address of the Freeholders and Inhabitants of the County of Botetourt, Feb. 1775, in *American Archives*, ed. Force, 4th ser., vol. 1, cols. 1255-56.

7. George Bancroft, *A History of the United States from the Discovery of the American Continent*, 5th ed., 10 vols. (Boston: Little, Brown, 1839-75), 7:75.

8. Fincastle County address, 20 Jan. 1775, in *Revolutionary Virginia*, ed. Van Schreeven et al., 2:254-56; Election and instructions to Augusta County delegates, 22 Feb. 1775, *Virginia Gazette* (Pinkney), 16 Mar. 1775, ibid., 298-300.

9. Thad Tate, "The Fincastle Resolutions: Southwest Virginia's Commitment," *Journal of the Roanoke Valley Historical Society* 9, no. 2 (1975): 22-23; announcement by William Christian and Stephen Trigg, 18 Feb. 1775, in *Revolutionary Virginia*, ed. Van Schreeven et al., 2:293; Election of and instructions to Augusta County delegates, 22 Feb. 1775, ibid., 298-300; Address of Botetourt freeholders, *Virginia Gazette* (Dixon and Hunter), 11 Mar. 1775, ibid., 324-25.

10. Fincastle County address, 20 Jan. 1775, in *Revolutionary Virginia*; ed. Van Schreeven et al., 2:254-56; Tate, "Fincastle Resolutions," 28-29.

11. Election of and instructions to Augusta County delegates, 22 Feb. 1775, in *Revolutionary Virginia*, ed. Van Schreeven et al., 2:298-300; Address of Botetourt freeholders, 11 Mar. 1775, ibid., 324-25.

12. Thad Tate made this point in "Fincastle Resolutions," 28-29.

13. Andrew Lewis to William Fleming, 18 Apr. 1775, 15DD9; William Preston's circular letter, 20 Apr. 1775, 16DD5.

14. *Virginia Gazette* (Purdie), 22 July 1775, supplement.

15. Philip Fithian Journal, 6 June 1775, quoted in Hart, *Valley of Virginia*, 87.

16. See, for example, the membership of the Fincastle County committee elected in January 1775 (Fincastle County address, 20 Jan. 1775, in *Revolutionary Virginia*, ed. Van Schreeven et al., 2:254-56).

17. Election of and instructions to Augusta County delegates, 22 Feb. 1775, ibid., 298-300; Address of Botetourt freeholders, 11 Mar. 1775, ibid., 324-25; Address of Freeholders of Fincastle County to Governor Dunmore, 8 Apr. 1775, quoted in Lewis, *Battle of Point Pleasant*, 92-93. During the preceding months, various eastern Virginia leaders also thanked the governor for his actions in Dunmore's War. See, for example, the address in December 1774 of Williamsburg and Norfolk leaders and of the president and faculty of the College of William and Mary (*American Archives*, ed. Force, 4th ser., vol. 1, cols. 1018-20) and the resolutions of the Virginia Convention, 25 Mar. 1775, ibid., vol. 2, col. 170. For a northern valley leader's earlier expression of greater militance and willingness to undertake armed resistance to Britain, see Adam Stephen to R.H. Lee, 27 Aug 1774, ibid., vol. 1, cols. 739-40.

18. Bailyn, *Ideological Origins*, chap. 6, "The Contagion of Liberty."

19. Petition of the committee of Pendleton district, West Fincastle County, to the Convention of the Colony of Virginia, ca. Feb. 1776, printed in *Revolutionary Virginia*, ed. Van Schreeven et. al., 6:42-43.

20. Anthony Bledsoe to William Preston, 14 May 1776, 4QQ39; William Christian to Preston, 8 June 1776, 4QQ49; William Cocke to Bledsoe, 27 May 1776, 4QQ44.

21. *Virginia Gazette* (Purdie), 18 Oct. 1776; *Virginia Gazette* (Dixon and Hunter), 20 Dec. 1776.

22. Thomas Perkins Abernethy, *Western Lands and the American Revolution* (New York: D. Appleton-Century Company, for the Institute for Research in the Social Sciences, Unviersity of Virginia, 1937), 123-35.

23. William Preston to Lord Dunmore, 23 Jan. 1775, Preston Family of Virginia Papers, reel 4, #862; Preston to Dunmore, 10 Mar. 1775, 4QQ7.

24. Unidentified correspondent to William Preston, 29 Mar. 1775, Preston Family Papers, 1727-1896.

25. Thomas Lewis to William Preston, 8 June 1774, 3QQ38. A letter from Lewis implies that Preston intended to delay returning the surveys (Lewis to Preston, 19 June 1775, 4QQ20). Preston later claimed that he had made such promises (Petition of Preston to the Virginia convention, 10 July 1775, in *Revolutionary Virginia*, ed. Van Schreeven et al., 3:275-76.

26. Abernethy, *Western Lands*, 128-29.

27. William Preston to Oconastota, Little Carpenter, Judge Friend, et al., June 1775, 4QQ17.

28. William Madison to William Preston, July 1775, 4QQ30: Preston to William Christian, Aug. 1775, 4QQ32; Abernethy, *Western Lands*, 129-30; Petition of the Fincastle County Committee to the Virginia Convention, July 1775, in *Revolutionary Virginia*, ed. Van Schreeven et al., 3:280-81. The convention had already begun an investigation into the legitimacy of Dunmore's new policy and had recommended that no persons make purchases of land under those conditions (Proceedings of the Virginia convention, 27 Mar. 1775, in *American Archives*, ed. Force, 4th ser., vol. 2, cols. 171-72).

29. William Christian to William Preston, 4, 12 July 1775, 4QQ23 and 4QQ25; Preston to Christian, Aug. 1775, 4QQ32.

30. John Brown to William Preston, 10, 24 Aug. 1775, 4QQ28 and 4QQ31.

31. Thomas Lewis to William Preston, 19 Aug. 1775, 4QQ29; William Christian to Preston, 27 Aug. 1775, William and John Preston Papers, 1740-1960.

32. John Brown to William Preston, 10, 24 Aug. 1775, 4QQ28 and 4QQ31.

33. John Dickerson to William Preston, 16 Dec. 1775, 4QQ35; Committee resolutions, 6 Sept. 1775, Breckinridge Family Papers, reel 1, #27, University of Virginia. The latter document fails to identify the county in which these proceedings took place.

34. James McGavock to William Preston 14 Aug. 1776, 4QQ69; Johnson, *William Preston*, 181-82; Edward Johnson to Preston, 1 June 1776, Preston Family of Virginia Papers, reel 5, #930.

35. Alexander Smythe to William Preston, Feb. 1797, Preston Family of Virginia Papers, reel 8, #1968, copied from original in possession of Morton U. Joyes, Louisville, Ky. Also see Francis Preston's printed circular to the people of his congressional district, 13 Feb. 1797, ibid.

36. William Christian to William Preston, 3 June 1776, ibid., reel 5, #932; Christian to Preston, 27 Aug. 1776, 4QQ70.

37. Thomas Lewis to William Preston, 18 Aug. 1776, Preston Family of Virginia Papers, reel 5, #940.

38. For a discussion of this controversy, see Hughes, *Surveyors and Statesmen*, 91-92. Also see agreement between William Madison and Robert Preston,

25 Mar. 1777, Robert Preston Papers, 1777-79, box 1, College of William and Mary, Williamsburg, Va.

39. Deposition of Gabriel Shoat, sworn before John Montgomery and James McGavock, 13 May 1776, 4QQ38.

40. Anthony Bledsoe to William Preston, 22 May 1776, 4QQ42. Also see Gilbert Christian to Preston, 16 May 1776, 4QQ40; Aaron Lewis to Preston, 24 May 1776, 4QQ43. For encouragement of settlers living within territory acknowledged as belonging to the Cherokees to leave, see Bledsoe to Preston, 14 May 1776, 4QQ39.

41. William Russell to William Preston, 2 July 1776, 4QQ55; John Montgomery and James McGavock to Preston, 22 July 1776, 4QQ56. It is possible that Russell was reserving powder for a long-range expedition against the Cherokee towns rather than for local defense, but since such an expedition was not yet authorized, this seems unlikely.

42. William Christian to William Preston, 8 June 1776, 4QQ49; William Russell to Preston, 23, 24, 25 July 1776, 4QQ57, 4QQ59, 4QQ60. Also see James Robertson to Preston, 16 Sept. 1776, 4QQ72.

43. William Russell to William Preston, 7 July 1776, 4QQ53; Preston to the president of the council, 2 Aug. 1776, 4QQ64.

44. James Robertson to William Preston, 16 Sept. 1776, 4QQ72; William Russell to Preston, 7, 20 July 1776, 4QQ53, 4QQ55.

45. For an account of this incident, see John Stuart, *Memoir of Indian Wars and Occurrences*, ed. Charles Stuart, New York Times Eyewitness Accounts of the American Revolution, Series III (1833; rpt. New York: New York Times, 1971), 58-61.

46. Patrick Henry to William Preston, 19 Feb. 1778, Patrick Henry Thomas Jefferson Letters, 1777-78, VSL; 19 Feb. 1778, Preston Family of Virginia Papers, reel 5, #978, copied from Virginia Council Journal, 1777-78, p. 198, VSL.

47. 27 Mar. 1778, Preston Family of Virginia Papers, reel 5, #982, copied from Virginia Council Journal, 1777-78, p. 227; Wilson, *Great Valley Patriots*, 109. For the Rockbridge court's proceedings in this matter, see Rockbridge Order Book, 1778-83, 12, 28 Apr., 5, 19 May, 7 July 1778, pp. 8-9, 13, 17, 20. The next year the court apparently appointed Hall to the grand jury, a service he failed to perform (ibid., 4 May 1779, p. 80). According to William Cooper, in the early nineteenth century local traditions held that Rockbridge County had been established to ensure that the defendants would be tried in an area close to their homes, where public opinion would presumably prevent a successful prosecution (Cooper, *History of the Shenandoah Valley*, 618-19).

48. For another instance of popular hostility toward friendly Indians, see Edmund Pendleton to Thomas Jefferson, 26 Aug. 1776, *Letters and Papers of Edmund Pendleton*, 1:200-201, copied from Jefferson Papers, LC.

49. Stuart, *Memoir of Indian Wars*, 59.

50. William Fleming to William Preston, 5 June 1778, Auditor's Papers, William Preston section. Three days later, Andrew Lewis wrote Preston, "Have Y[   ] any reson to hop[e] for amendment in the con[duct] of Your Militia are they Lost to all sense of . . . self preservation" (Lewis to Preston, 8 June 1778,

4QQ173). In 1780 leaders throughout the upper valley had difficulty raising men to reinforce the American army in the Carolinas. See, for example, George Skillern to Preston, 13 Oct., 13 Dec. 1780, Auditor's Papers, William Preston section; Preston to William Campbell, 15 Dec. 1780, 8DD29 (copy).

51. Daniel Smith to Arthur Campbell, 19 June 1778, 9DD17; John Coulter to William Campbell, 19 May 1779, Preston Family Papers, 1744-1898, VHS.

52. Walter Crockett to William Preston, 15 Apr. 1780, Auditor's Papers, William Preston section. Also see Thomas Jefferson to Preston, 1 Nov. 1780, 5QQ87; McBride, "Virginia War Effort," 183.

53. William Preston to unidentified correspondent, apparently in state govenment, 30 July 1776, 4QQ61. Also see Preston to Martin Armstrong, 29 Aug. 1780, 5QQ62, for an account of difficulties in getting public ammunition transported beyond the upper valley.

54. George Skillern to William Preston, 13 Oct. 1780, Auditor's Papers, William Preston section.

55. Albert Ogden Porter, *County Government in Virginia: A Legislative History, 1607-1904* (New York: Columbia University Press, 1947), 125-28.

56. Rockingham petition, 9 Nov. 1779, Montgomery petition, 18 May 1780, Botetourt petition 2 June 1780, Rockbridge petition, 19 May 1780, Legislative petitions, VSL. In March 1779 the Washington court appointed several men as commissioners of the tax because the county's landholders had not assembled to elect these officials on the designated day (Washington Minute Book 1, 17 Mar. 1779, p. 49, VSL).

57. McBride, "Virginia War Effort," 110. According to McBride, militiamen from frontier and coastal areas performed about twice as many tours of duty as their counterparts in interior parts of Virginia. McBride noted, however, that the tours were somewhat shorter (p. 20). He also suggested that the greater frequency of loyalism and disaffection in coastal and frontier areas probably reflected the greater demands of the war effort in those areas (p. 193).

58. Ibid., 198-99; Botetourt Court Martial, 29 Aug. 1777, William Fleming Papers, box 2, folder 24. Also see William Preston to Patrick Henry, 25 Nov. 1778, Auditor's Papers, William Preston section.

59. William Preston to Patrick Henry, 25 Nov. 1778, Auditor's Papers, William Preston section.

60. William Christian to William Fleming, 21 Dec. 1779, Hugh Blair Grigsby Papers, 1745-1944, section 132, VHS. Also see Caleb Wallace to Fleming, 27 Oct. 1779, ibid.

61. Greenbrier petition, 18 May 1780, Legislative petitions. For an accusation of such treason, see Hugh Barclay to William Preston, 10 Feb. 1780, Preston Family Papers, 1746-1938, section 3.

62. William Christian, William Preston, and Evan Shelby to Patrick Henry, Apr. 1777, 4QQ152; Washington Minute Book 1, 25 Apr. 1777, p. 8; Daniel Smith to Arthur Campbell, 19 June 1778, 9DD17; Montgomery petition, 18 May 1780, Legislative petitions; Preston to Horatio Gates, 27 Oct. 1780, 5QQ84; Botetourt Court Martial, 29 Aug. 1777, William Fleming Papers, box 2, folder 24; Rockingham petition, 9 Nov. 1779, Botetourt petition, 2 June 1780, Legislative petitions.

63. William Preston to Patrick Henry, 25 Nov. 1778, Auditor's Papers, William Preston section.

64. Fincastle County committee journal, 10 Jan., 4 Apr. 1776, in *Revolutionary Virginia*, ed. Van Schreeven et al., 5:375-76, 6:327-28. In 1778 Montgomery officials decided to let an outlying portion of one training company drill separately under a second lieutenant (Montgomery Order Book 2, 5 May 1778, p. 168).

65. Fincastle County committee journal, 24 Feb. 1776, in *Revolutionary Virginia*, ed. Van Schreeven et al., 6:135-36. The Washington County court took similar action in 1780 (Washington Minute Book 1, 22 Mar. 1780, p. 86).

66. Gilbert Christian to William Preston, 16 May 1776, 4QQ40; Anthony Bledsoe to Preston, 22 May 1776, 4QQ42; Aaron Lewis to Preston, 24 May 1776, 4QQ43; John Montgomery and James McGavock to Preston, 22 July 1776, 4QQ56; William Russell to Preston, 23 July 1776, 4QQ57.

67. In addition to the examples noted in the text, see William Russell to William Preston, 7, 20 July 1776, 4QQ53 and 4QQ55.

68. William Campbell to Arthur Campbell, 1 Aug. 1776, 9DD4; William Preston to unidentified correspondent, apparently in state government, 30 July 1776, 4QQ61; James Robertson to Preston, 5 July, 1, 11 Aug., 1, 16 Sept. 1774, 3QQ55, 3QQ69, 3QQ73, 3QQ88, and 4QQ72.

69. Evan Shelby to unidentified correspondent (guide suggests William Preston), 22 Aug. 1777, Campbell-Preston Papers, reel 1, #91. Shelby argued that efforts to force such service from the Clinch settlers would be futile, and he felt that these settlers were contributing to regional defense by serving as scouts.

70. John Coulter to William Campbell, 19 May 1779, Preston Family Papers, 1744-1898, section 5; William Preston to Patrick Henry, 25 Nov. 1778, Auditor's Papers, William Preston section; Preston to Martin Armstrong, 26 Aug 1780, 5QQ62.

71. In his analysis of the war effort throughout Virginia, McBride noted that volunteers were often preferred because they could be enlisted for the duration of a campaign or invasion rather than for a specified term which might expire in the middle of the campaign ("Virginia War Effort," 165-66). As the following examples make clear, however, upper valley volunteers were often used for short-term missions where the advantages noted by McBride would not have applied.

72. Aaron Lewis to William Preston, 24 May 1776, 4QQ43; Preston to William Buchanan, 17 Mar. 1777, Auditor's Papers, William Preston section.

73. Statement dated 1779, Campbell-Preston Papers, reel 1, #119.

74. The first instance of this practice was on 24 October 1780 (Augusta Court Martial Records, p. 184). In March 1782, however, the court apparently discontinued the practice (ibid., p. 230).

75. James Thompson's claim, 8 Sept. 177[8], Auditor's Papers, William Preston section.

76. Patrick Henry to William Preston, 1 Sept. 1777, VHS. State officials questioned not only the courage of upper valley solders but also the integrity of their leaders. In warning Arthur Campbell to dismis the men in his area whom the state was paying for active duty, William Christian noted that William

NOTES TO PAGES 93-96

Russell was being criticized for calling too many men to active duty the year before (Christian to Campbell, 8 Sept. 1777, 9DD14).

77. 19 Feb. 1778, Preston Family of Virginia Papers, reel 5, #978, copied from Virginia Council Journal, 1777-78, p. 198; Patrick Henry to William Preston, 19 Feb. 1778, Patrick Henry Thomas Jefferson Letters, 1777-78.

78. William Preston to Patrick Henry, 7 Jan. 1778, Auditor's Papers, William Preston section (also see Preston to Henry, 16 Jan. 1778, ibid.); Preston and William Fleming to Henry, 14 Mar. 1778, 4QQ163.

79. Patrick Henry to [William Fleming], 5 May 1778, 4QQ167; Henry to William Preston, 20 Nov. 1778, Preston Family of Virginia Papers, reel 5, #1000.

80. Stephen Trigg to William Preston, 16 May 1778, 4QQ169. Also see Trigg to Preston, 14 June 1778, 4QQ176.

81. For further discussion of these republican political values, see Bailyn *Ideological Origins*; Wood, *Creation of the American Republic*; Drew R. McCoy, *The Elusive Republic: Political Economy in Jeffersonian America* (Chapel Hill: University of North Carolina Press for the Institute of Early American History and Culture, Williamsburg, Va., 1980); Charles Royster, *A Revolutionary People at War: The Continental Army and American Character, 1775-1783* (Chapel Hill: University of North Carolina Press for the Institute of Early American History and Culture, Williamsburg, Va., 1979); and Charles Royster, *Light-Horse Harry Lee and the Legacy of the American Revolution* (New York: Knopf, 1981). A useful historiographic overview is provided by Robert E. Shallhope's two articles, "Toward a Republican Synthesis: The Emergence of an Understanding of Republicanism in American Historiography," *WMQ* 3d ser., 39 (1982): 334-56.

82. Royster, *Revolutionary People at War*, and "'The Nature of Treason': Revolutionary Virtue and American Reactions to Benedict Arnold," *WMQ* 3d ser., 36 (1979): 163-93.

83. Thomas Lewis to William Preston, 30 July 1779, 5QQ4; John Brown, Jr., to Preston 7 Mar., 6 July 1780, 5QQ20, 5QQ39; Preston to Martin Armstrong, 26 Aug. 1780, 5QQ62.

84. Arthur Campbell to Thomas Jefferson, 12 Feb. 1781, *Papers of Thomas Jefferson*, 4:587. Also see William Preston to Horatio Gates, 27 Oct. 1780, 5QQ84; William Campbell to William Edmondson, 17 Dec. 1780, 9DD23; Arthur Campbell to Thomas Jefferson, 15 Jan. 1781, quoted in Robert L. Kincaid, "Colonel Arthur Campbell: Frontier Leader and Patriot," *Historical Society of Washington County, Virginia, Publications* 2d ser., no. 1 (1965): 2-18.

85. See, for example, Thomas Jefferson to [William Preston], 15 Feb. 1781, Preston Family Papers, 1727-1896; Nathanael Greene to [first name not given] Campbell, 30 June 1781, Preston Family of Virginia Papers, reel 15, #21. Governor Abner Nash of North Carolina used similar language in requesting that Virginia send William Campbell and some of the upper valley's "Mountain Heroes" to assist in the defense of his state (Nash to Jefferson, 2 Feb. 1781, *Papers of Thomas Jefferson*, 4:503-4). And some eastern Virginia leaders celebrated the spirit and fighting abilities of upper valley inhabitants even before the war began (see, for example, Richard Henry Lee to Arthur Lee, 24 Feb. 1775, *The Letters of Richard Henry Lee*, ed. James C. Ballaugh, 2 vols. [New York: Macmillan, 1911-14], 1:130-31).

86. Proposals for raising men, 1781, Auditor's Papers, William Preston section.

87. "A Memoir of the Late Reverend William Graham A.M.," *Evangelical and Literary Magazine* 4 (1921): 259-60. Another tradition related that upper valley legislator Zachariah Johnston was particularly brave during the assembly's flight from Charlottesville to Staunton (M.W. Paxton, "Zachariah Johnston of Augusta and Rockbridge and His Times," copy in Zechariah Johnston Papers, box 1, folder 1, Cyrus McCormick Library, Washington and Lee University).

88. Cooper, *History of the Shenandoah Valley*, 648-49.

89. Rockbridge petition, 10 Mar. 1781, Rockbridge petition, 14 June 1781, Augusta petition, 30 May 1782, Legislative petitions; Petition to the House of Delegates from Augusta County inhabitants, ca. 1784, Zachariah and Thomas Johnston Papers, 1717-1858. As early as 1778, Arthur Campbell closely associated moral and military developments, praising the spirited conduct of the Augusta, Rockbridge, and Botetourt militia in defeating an Indian party in Greenbrier. Campbell, however, also lamented the recent "backwardness" of his county's militia and hoped that in the future "we would . . . acquit ourselves like men, like freemen, contending for the noblest blessings of Life." Thus in Campbell's eyes virtuous voluntary conduct brought both divine blessings and temporal benefits. Yet the "freemen" must remain virtuous lest they lose "the noblest blessings of life" afforded by a republican polity (Campbell to Charles Cummings, 10 June 1778, Campbell Family Papers, 1773-1908).

90. Unsigned and undated proposal, Auditor's Papers, William Preston section; William Preston to George Skillern, 13 Sept. 1780, 5QQ80; Preston to Martin Armstrong, 18 Sept. 1780, Campbell-Preston Papers, reel 1, #136-37; Skillern to Preston, 30 Oct. 1780, 5QQ85.

91. Unsigned enlistment statement, Oct. 1780, Auditor's Papers, William Preston section.

92. Unsigned and undated proposal, Auditor's Papers, William Preston section; William Preston to George Skillern, 13 Sept. 1780, 5QQ80.

93. Unsigned enlistment statement, Oct. 1780, Auditor's Papers, William Preston section.

94. Proposal for raising men, 1781, ibid. Preston had earlier declared that his region's volunteer riflemen "would at least be equal to the like number in any part of America" (William Preston to George Skillern, 13 Sept. 1780, 5QQ80).

95. Archibald Blair's minutes of debate on Preston's proposal in Council, 21 Sept. 1780, copy by Francis Preston, 8DD8-9. Campbell's reply is found in a fragment in his own handwriting on Blair's minutes.

96. William Christian to William Preston, 29 Sept. 1780, 8DD7, copy.

97. Thomas Jefferson to Horatio Gates, 10 Nov. 1780, *Papers of Thomas Jefferson*, 4:108; Jefferson to William Campbell, 22 Sept. 1780, ibid., 3:654-56.

98. Thomas Jefferson to the County Lieutenants of Shenandoah, Rockingham, Augusta, and Rockbridge, 2 Jan. 1781, ibid., 4:295-96; Jefferson to George Weedon, 12 Jan. 1781, ibid., 346.

99. Thomas Jefferson to Frederick William von Steuben, 15 Feb. 1780, ibid., 621-22; Steuben to Jefferson, 15 Feb. 1781, ibid., 624.

100. Royster, "The Nature of Treason," *A Revolutionary People at War*, and *Light-Horse Harry Lee*.

101. For a discussion of this point, see Wood, *Creation of the American Republic*, 70-75, 475-99, and passim.

102. For instances of concern with seniority, dignity, and status, see William Christian to William Preston, 29 Sept. 1780, 8DD7; William Campbell to Daniel Smith, 31 Mar. 1781, 16DD20; George Skillern to William Davies, 16 Mar. 1782, 3:100-101; Patrick Lockhart to Benjamin Harrison, 18 Mar. 1782, ibid., 102.

6. THE TORY CHALLENGE

1. Report of Augusta County committee, 3 Oct. 1775, *Virginia Gazette* (Purdie), 3 Nov. 1775; Fincastle committee journal, 10 Jan. 1776, in *Revolutionary Virginia*, ed. Van Schreeven et al., 5:375-76. On February 23, one of the men (John Spratt) was found guilty. After he promised good behavior in the future, Spratt was "Acquitted and restored to the Friendship & Confidence of his Countrymen" (Fincastle committee journal, 23 Feb. 1776, ibid., 6:130).

2. Emory G. Evans, "Trouble in the Backcountry: Disaffection in Southwest Virginia during the American Revolution," in *Uncivil War*, ed. Hoffman, Tate, and Albert, 187. Also see William Preston to Edmund Pendleton, 15 June 1776, 4QQ50.

3. On the concern with disloyalty among German settlers, see William Preston to Edmund Pendleton, 15 June 1776, 4QQ50; Peter Muhlenberg to Preston, 24 Mar. 1776, Preston Family of Virginia Papers, reel 5, #924. On the activities of British agents and outlaws living among the Cherokees, see Preston to Pendleton 15 June, 1776, 4QQ50; William Christian to Preston, 8 June 1776, 4QQ49.

4. Evans, "Trouble in the Backcountry," 187; Porter, "County Government in Virginia," 112.

5. A militia party attacked the Augusta Tories and captured eight of them (*Virginia Gazette* [Dixon and Hunter], 29 Aug. 1777). For the Botetourt and Montgomery incidents, see Evans, "Trouble in the Backcountry," 188.

6. Ultimately Burk resigned his commission rather than take the oath of allegiance (William Preston to William Fleming, 2 Dec. 1777, 2ZZ43; Thomas Burk to Preston, 18 Feb. 1778, 4QQ158; Evans, "Trouble in the Backcountry," 188-89).

7. Montgomery Order Book 2, 6 Jan. 1778, pp. 160-61; 7 Jan. 1778, p. 162.

8. Thomas Jefferson to William Preston, 28 June, 3 July 1780, *Papers of Thomas Jefferson*, 3:469, 480-81. For summaries of the Tory movement, see Evans, "Trouble in the Backcountry," and Wilson, *Great Valley Patriots*, 120-34.

9. Peter Muhlenberg to William Preston, 24 Mar. 1776, Preston Family

of Virginia Papers, reel 5, #924. Also see Preston to Edmund Pendleton, 15 June 1776, 4QQ50.

10. Klaus Wust, *The Virginia Germans* (Charlottesville: University Press of Virginia, 1969), 39, 49; Mitchell, *Commercialism and Frontier*, 54-55.

11. Confession of David Herbert, 17 Aug. 1780, 5QQ54; Confession of John Jenkins, 17 Aug. 1780, 5QQ54; Confession of Roger Oats, 1780(?), 5QQ68. A letter of Charles Lynch to William Preston (17 Aug. 1780, 5QQ57-58) identified these three as Welshmen.

12. Nancy Deveraux to William Preston, 1780, 5QQ58.

13. For examples of friction see Fletcher, *Pennsylvania Agriculture*, 1:56-57; Herbert Snipes Turner, *Church in the Old Fields: Hawfields Presbyterian Church and Community in North Carolina* (Chapel Hill: University of North Carolina Press, 1962), 37.

14. William H. Nelson, *The American Tory* (London: Oxford University Press, 1961), 85-115. The small black population of the upper valley also produced some Tories. Jack, a Botetourt County slave belonging to Stephen May, recruited several other blacks to rebel and join Cornwallis's army. For this and other crimes, the Botetourt court sentenced him to death, but he escaped and his owner apparently prevented his execution (Petition of Botetourt inhabitants to the governor and Council, Jan. 1781, *Calendar*, 1:477-78; Patrick Lockhart to Thomas Nelson, 16 Nov. 1781, ibid., 2:604-5).

15. Emory Evans identified 168 Montgomery County residents brought into court on charges related to Tory activity; he estimated that they represented very roughly half of the Tory population. Of these 168 people Evans found land tax entries for 85 and personal property entries for another 20. Evans also compiled comparable data on the men who served as Montgomery County justices of the peace between 1777 and 1781, finding landownership information for 17 of the 19 men ("Trouble in the Backcountry," 203-9). Table 3 was compiled by converting Evans's data to percentages (rounded to the nearest 0.1 percent). To put it more simply, 52.9 percent of the justices and 8.2 percent of the Tories owned five hundred acres or more, and 47.1 percent of the justices and 91 percent of the Tories owned less than five hundred acres. Thus Evans was apparently in error in asserting that there was little difference between the economic standing of the Tories and that of the Montgomery County leaders, especially when it is remembered that 81 of the identifiable Tories do not appear on the land tax rolls, versus 2 of the justices. The Tories did not clearly differ from other Montgomery County settlers, except for the large number of them who did not appear on the land tax rolls.

Table 3. Landownership among Montgomery County Justices of the Peace and Tories, 1777–1781

Acres	Justices		Tories	
	Percent	Number	Percent	Number
1,000 and up	17.6	3	1.2	1
500-999	35.3	6	7.1	6
200-499	23.5	4	36.5	31
0-199	23.5	4	55.3	47

16. Ibid., 219. Evan's argument depended to some degree upon an apparently incorrect interpretation of the distribution of wealth, as discussed in the note above. For early German settlement patterns, see Wust, *Virginia Germans*, 39, 49; and Mitchell, *Commercialism and Frontier*, 54-55.

17. Robert King's information, undated, Auditor's Papers, William Preston section; William Preston to William Fleming, 2 Dec. 1777, 2ZZ43; Montgomery Order Book 3, 8 Sept. 1779, p. 64; Preston to William Campbell, 19 July 1779, Auditor's Papers, William Preston section.

18. Montgomery Order Book 3, 2 Nov. 1779, p. 81.

19. William Campbell to Arthur Campbell, July 1780, 8DD4.

20. William Campbell to William Preston, 16 July 1776, Preston Family of Virginia Papers, reel 5, #1026. Campbell told Preston he was inclined to believe Cox's explanation, which may be particularly telling in view of Campbell's general antipathy to suspected Tories.

21. William Preston to William Fleming, 2 Dec. 1777, 2ZZ43; James McGavock to Preston, 15 Apr. 1779, Auditor's Papers, William Preston section. McGavock lived near Fort Chiswell, and Preston's home was farther down New River.

22. Montgomery Order Book 3, 8 Sept. 1779, p. 64; William Preston to Thomas Jefferson, Mar. 1780, 5QQ28; Preston to James Byrn, 5 July 1780, 5QQ37. A group of Welshmen declared a very explicit though more limited interdependence by pledging that none of them would work in the lead mine at Fort Chiswell, "without the Consent of the Whole and . . . a very large Penalty" (Confession of Roger Oats, 1780?, 5QQ68).

23. See, for example, James McGavock to William Preston, 15 Apr. 1779, Auditor's Papers, William Preston section; Preston to Lettice Breckinridge, 27 Apr. 1780, Breckinridge Family Papers, vol. 1, #72, LC.

24. Deposition of Captain John Cox, enclosed in letter from William Campbell to William Preston, 16 July 1779, Auditor's Papers, William Preston section. The next year Cox reported that a deserter and two local Tories threatened him and swore to resist patriot efforts to disarm them (Deposition of John Cox, 28 Aug. 1780, 5QQ65).

25. Confession of James Duggless, 18 Aug. 1780, 5QQ59.

26. William Preston to Peter Muhlenberg, Sept. 1780, 5QQ81.

27. Wust, *Virginia Germans*, 83. The German company mentioned came from present-day Highland County.

28. Confessions of David Copeman, Bryce Faning, Morrison Lovell, and Andrew Thomson, 1780?, 5QQ68; William Preston's Warrant to Constable Bryan McDonald for the apprehension and arrest of Thomas Heaven, 23 Feb. 1778, 4QQ160; Memorandum by Preston, 20 July 1780, 5QQ41.

29. Rockbridge Order Book, 1778-83, 7 May 1782, p. 290. Also see ibid., 2 May, 6 June 1780, pp. 182 and 199.

30. Montgomery Order Book 3, 5 Oct. 1779, p. 77; James McGavock to William Preston, 15 Apr. 1779, Auditor's Papers, William Preston section.

31. See John Henderson's confession regarding insurgents, Auditor's Papers, William Preston section; Walter Crockett to William Preston, 7 Apr. 1779, ibid.; Michael Kinninger's deposition, 18 Apr. 1779, ibid.; Statement of Preston

against the nonjurors, 1780, 5QQ27; Preston to Thomas Jefferson, Mar., 18 Apr. 1780, 5QQ28 and 5QQ50.

32. Walter Crockett to William Preston, 7 Apr. 1779, Auditor's Papers, William Preston section; Arthur Campbell to Preston, 19 Apr. 1779, Campbell-Preston Papers, reel 1, #107; William Campbell to Preston, 19 Apr. 1779, Auditor's Papers, William Preston section. Two entries in the Montgomery court records (Order Book 2, 3 Mar. and 2 June 1779, pp. 181 and 201) apparently deal with such threats against Preston and William Thompson.

33. Memorandum by William Preston, 20 July 1780, 5QQ41. Also see Preston's address to his neighbors, [June 1779], Preston Family of Virginia Papers, reel 5, #1024, typed copy.

34. Walter Crockett to William Preston, 7 Apr. 1779, Auditor's Papers, William Preston section. Also see William Campbell to Preston, 16 July 1779, Preston Family of Virginia Papers, reel 5, #1026, typed copy.

35. Walter Crockett to William Preston, 6 Aug. 1780, 5QQ48.

36. William Christian to William Preston, 30 Aug. 1780, Auditor's Papers, William Preston section.

37. Undated items, Campbell-Preston Papers, reel 1, #152, and reel 2, #401.

38. Walter Crockett to William Preston, 7 Apr. 1779, Auditor's Papers, William Preston section; Statement of Preston againt the nonjurors, 1780, 5QQ27. Solomon Harrison reported that he had been promised 600 acres, and Thomas Dugglis alleged that John Griffith had promised him land and other rewards (Confession of Solomon Harrison, 1780?, 5QQ68; Thomas Dugglis's confession, 19 Aug. 1780, 5QQ60).

39. John Henderson's confession concerning insurgents, Auditor's Papers, William Preston section.

40. James McGavock to William Preston, 25 Apr. 1779, ibid.

41. Memorandum by William Preston, 20 July 1780, 5QQ41. Local economic grievances also may have shaped the loyalism of the Welsh lead miners at Fort Chiswell. In 1781, apparently under the leadership of Tory sympathizers, the miners made a mutual agreement not to work in the mines unless all of them were employed and unless John Jenkins, a Welsh Tory, was made manager (William Hay to the Governor, 12 June 1782, *Calendar*, 3:189-90).

42. Walter Crockett to William Preston, 7 Apr. 1779, Auditor's Papers, William Preston section; Solomon Harrison's confession, 1780?, 5QQ68; Thomas Dugglis's confession, 19 Aug. 1780, 5QQ60; Memorandum of Preston, 20 July 1780, 5QQ41.

43. Statement of William Preston against the nonjurors, 1780, 5QQ27.

44. Confession of Robert King, 1780, 5QQ71. King was accused of being a captain in the Tory organization but said that he was either a lieutenant or an ensign. In several other cases, after being arrested and threatened with severe penalties, otherwise penitent Tories could not remember the names of fellow loyalists, including some whose oaths of initiation they had witnessed (Robert King's information, undated, Auditor's Papers, William Preston section; William Campbell to William Preston, 19 Apr. 1779, Preston Family of Virginia, reel 5, #1098).

45. Confession of Bryant Faning, 1780?, 5QQ68. The document fails to make clear whether the meeting took place in 1779 or 1780. The confession of Andrew Thompson (1780? 5QQ68) also does not make the year of the meeting absolutely clear. A quarrel broke out at the meeting, raising fears among several of the Tories that the movement would be disrupted and their activities discovered (Confession of Morrison Lovell, 1780?, 5QQ68).

46. Deposition of Captain John Cox, enclosed in letter of William Campbell to William Preston, 16 July 1779, Auditor's Papers, William Preston section.

47. Ibid.

48. Confession of Morrison Lovell, 1780?, 5QQ68. For other instances of distinction between categories of oaths and loyalties, see John Henderson's confession regarding insurgents, 1779, Auditor's Papers, William Preston section; Michael Kinninger's deposition, 18 Apr. 1779, ibid.; Statement of William Preston against the nonjurors, 1780, 5QQ27; Statement by Preston and others to various Tories, 14 Aug. 1780, 5QQ55. For other references to oaths of secrecy, see Confession of Andrew Thomson, 1780?, 5QQ68; Confession of [Zehr] Lambert, 1780, 5QQ68; Confession of John Jenkins before Charles Lynch and Alexander Cummings, 17 Aug. 1780, 5QQ54; Charles Lynch to Preston, 17 Aug. 1780, 5QQ57-58.

49. James Duggless's confession, 18 Aug. 1780, 5QQ59.

50. For examples of threats against Preston, see William Preston, Memorandum, 20 July 1780, 5QQ41; Walter Crockett to Preston, 7 Apr. 1779, Auditor's Papers, William Preston section; Montgomery Order Book 3, 3 Mar. 1779, p. 181.

51. The similarity to Eric Hobsbawm's description of social banditry in southwestern Europe is striking. He calls it "little more than endemic peasant protest against oppression and poverty . . . a vague dream of . . . a righting of individual wrongs. . . . It becomes epidemic rather than endemic when a peasant society which knows of no better means of self defense is in a condition of abnormal tension and disruption" (*Primitive Rebels: Studies in Archaic Forms of Social Movement in the Nineteenth and Twentieth Centuries* [1959; rpt. New York: Norton, 1965], 5).

52. See, for example, Montgomery Order Book 2, 4 May 1779, p. 195; 5 May 1779, pp. 196-97; 4 Aug.1779, p. 259; Bonds for the good behavior of Jacob Seiler, Robert McGee, James Bane, Jr., and John McDonald, 26 July and July 1780, 5QQ44-46 and 5QQ51.

53. James McGavock to William Preston, 15 Apr. 1779, Preston Family of Virginia Papers, reel 5, #1017.

54. Meeting of Montgomery County Court, Aug. 1780, 5QQ73.

55. Thomas Jefferson to William Preston, 21 Mar. 1780, 5QQ24; McBride, "Virginia War Effort," 216-17. Also see Preston to Jefferson, 8 Aug. 1780, 5QQ80; Dudley Digges to Preston, 17 Aug. 1780, 5QQ56. Virginia law defined misprision of treason to include any expression of hostility to the state government, and it imposed less demanding standards of proof for this offense than for treason.

56. William Preston to James Byrn, 5 July 1780, 5QQ37; Preston to Isaac Taylor, 12 July 1780, 5QQ40. While acting as an individual justice of the peace

within his own local precinct, Preston issued a statement acquitting a settler who had presented sufficient evidence to refute charges that he had attended a Tory meeting (Statement of Preston acquitting George Patterson, 29 Apr. 1779, 5QQ2).

57. Charles Lynch to William Preston, 17 Aug. 1780, 5QQ57-58. Exactly what punishments Lynch imposed remains unclear. Lynch claimed to be acting within the law, holding the most serious offenders for proper trial, forcing others to join the army, and releasing those who seemed to be "Not very Criminal." At least one person directly requested that Preston intervene to assure a fair trial for her accused husband (Nancy Deveraux to Preston 1780, 5QQ58). Also see Evans, "Trouble in the Backcountry," 201-2.

58. Evans, "Trouble in the Backcountry," 193, 205. Also see Montgomery Order Book 2, 8 Apr. 1778, p. 166; 2 Feb. 1779, p. 179; 3 Mar. 1779, p. 181; 7 Apr. 1779, p. 183; 9 Sept. 1779, p. 267; Montgomery Order Book 3, 6 Oct. 1779, p. 79; William Preston to Thomas Jefferson, Mar. 1780, 5QQ28.

59. Fincastle committee journal, 23 Feb. 1776, in *Revolutionary Virginia*, ed. Van Schreeven et al., 6:130-33.

60. Mongomery Order Book 2, 3 Aug. 1779, p. 203; 8 Nov. 1780, p. 302; 2 July 1782, p. 340; 8 Nov. 1780, pp. 301-2.

61. Statement by William Preston and others to various Tories, 14 Aug. 1780, 5QQ55.

62. William Preston to James Byrn, 5 July 1780, 5QQ37. Also see Preston to Isaac Taylor, 12 July 1780, 5QQ40.

63. Montgomery Order Book 3, Sept. 1779, p. 64.

64. In a postscript directed to William Preston, King asked for Preston's personal advice "if it is not too much Against the Interest of the Contry" (Confession of Robert King, addressed to Montgomery Court, 1780, 5QQ71). Also see Ben Cook to Preston, 1 Jan. 1779, Preston Family Papers, 1727-1896; Thared Adkins to Preston, [ca. 1780], Auditor's Papers, William Preston section; Nancy Deveraux to Preston, 1780, 5QQ58.

65. Kegley, "Who the Fifteen Signers Were," 33; J.T. McAllister, *Virginia Militia in the Revolutionary War: McAllister's Data* (Hot Springs, Va.: McAllister Publishing Co., 1913), 218; Montgomery Order Book 2, 7 Jan. 1777, pp. 152-53.

66. Meeting of Montgomery County Court, Aug. 1780, 5QQ73.

67. William Christian to William Preston, 3 May 1781, Preston Family of Virginia Papers, reel 5, #1109; Montgomery petition, 14 Dec. 1781, Legislative petitions; Memorial of Preston, William Thompson, James Thompson, and Andrew Boyd to the House of Delegates, May 1782, Preston Family of Virginia Papers, reel 5, #1137.

68. William Preston to James Byrn, 5 July 1780, 5QQ37.

69. Montgomery Order Book 2, 3 Aug. 1779, p. 203; 5 Aug. 1779, p. 260; Montgomery Order Book 3, 3 Nov. 1779, p. 83; Montgomery Order Book 2, 8 Nov. 1780, p. 302; 6 Feb. 1781, p. 304; 7 Feb. 1781, p. 306; 4 Aug. 1779, p. 259.

70. Ben Cook to William Preston, 1 Jan. 1779, Auditor's Papers, William Preston section; Montgomery Order Book 2, 6 Mar. 1782, p. 322.

71. Walter Crockett to William Preston, 17 May 1781, Preston Family of Virginia Papers, reel 5 #110, typed copy from Auditor's Papers.

72. Robert Tristoe to William Preston, 2 Oct. 1780, Auditor's Papers, William Preston section. Also see Patrick Lockhart to Preston, 12 Aug. 1780, 5QQ53, for an account of the displeasure of one training company captain when an accused Tory living within his jurisdiction agreed to enter the army but was not counted as part of his draft quota.

73. See, for example, Arthur Campbell to William Preston, 3 July 1780, Auditor's Papers, William Preston section; Thomas Jefferson to Campbell, 9 Aug. 1780, *Papers of Thomas Jefferson*, 3:534-35; Preston to Jefferson, 8 Aug. 1780, 5QQ50; Dudley Digges to Preston, 17 Aug. 1780, 5QQ56; McBride, "Virginia War Effort," 222-23; Montgomery petition, 2 Dec. 1786, Legislative petitions.

74. William Preston's address to his neighbors, [June 1779], Preston Family of Virginia Papers, reel 5, #1024, typed copy from Auditor's Papers. Also see the Washington County inhabitants' instructions to their delegates, calling for harsher measures against loyalists, among other things (Petition of Freeholders and other inhabitants of Washington to their representatives in the General Assembly, 1779, Preston Family of Virginia Papers, reel 15, #17).

75. William Preston to Michael Price, John and Howard Heavin, et al., 20 July 1780, 5QQ41; Preston to Thomas Jefferson, 8 Aug. 1780, 5QQ50. Also see Preston's memorandum concerning Tory activities, 20 July 1780, 5QQ41; Patrick Lockhart to Preston, 12 Aug. 1780, 5QQ53; Dudley Digges to Preston, 17 Aug. 1780, 5QQ56.

76. "Lynch Law," *WMQ* 1st ser., 13 (1905): 204, citing *Statutes at Large*, 11:134-35. The other leaders mentioned were Robert Adams, Jr., James Callaway, and Charles Lynch.

77. John Warfield Johnston, "Curiosities of the Revolutionary Courts," undated, John Warfield Johnston Papers, 1778-1890, Duke University; Evans, "Trouble in the Backcountry," 188; unidentified and undated newspaper clipping, McDowell Family Papers, VHS.

78. Undated statements addressed to William Campbell, Campbell-Preston Papers, reel 1, #152, and reel 2, #401.

79. Arthur Campbell to William Edmundson, 24 June 1780, 9DD21.

80. Benjamin Harrison (in Council) to Arthur Campbell, 7 Mar. 1783, 9DD39; William Russell to Harrison, 25 Sept. 1783, *Calendar*, 3:532. Russell, a rival of Campbell, claimed that the charges against the accused man were false. See Campbell to William Preston, 3 July 1780, Auditor's Papers, William Preston section, for Campbell's acquiescence in popular demands for confiscation of Tory property.

81. William Campbell to Arthur Campbell, July 1780, 8DD4; William Campbell's order for suspects to come take the oath, Campbell-Preston Papers, ca. July 1780, reel 1, #130-31.

82. Statement of William Edmiston et. al., 1780, Campbell-Preston Papers, reel 1, #150.

83. Arthur Campbell to William Preston, 3 July 1780, Auditor's Papers, William Preston section.

84. General order of William Campbell at camp below Gilbert Town, 11 Oct. 1780, 8DD12; British officer's account of Kings Mountain battle and aftermath, 27 Dec. 1780, 17DD8, copied from *Scot's Magazine*, 5 Jan. 1781; letter from

British officer, 30 Jan. 1781, 17DD25, copied from Rivington's *Royal Gazette* (New York), Feb. 1781.

85. Robert Campbell's eyewitness account of the battle of Kings Mountain, undated, 17DD25, copied from *Annals of the Army of Tennessee and Early Western History* 1 (1878), 330-33. The British officer's account of 27 Dec. 1780, cited in note 81, also describes the execution but does not specify the number of men executed.

86. William Campbell to [William Preston?], July 1780, 8DD4.

87. Washington Minute Book 1, 22 Nov. 1780, pp. 98-99; 21 Mar. 1781, p. 107. For other instances of lenience to Tories, see ibid., 19 May 1778, p. 34; 20 July 1779, p. 68; and 23 Nov. 1780, pp. 100-101.

7. FINISHING THE REVOLUTION

1. Petition of Sundry Inhabitants of the County of Greenbrier to the governor and Council, 19 Sept. 1781, *Calendar*, 2:468-69; Samuel Brown to Governor Harrison, 16 Feb. 1782, ibid., 3:65. Brown also reported the nervousness of the entire Greenbrier frontier population.

2. William Preston to the Governor, 10 Apr. 1782, 5QQ107. See Preston to Benjamin Harrison, 26 Apr. 1782, Preston Family of Virginia Papers, reel 5, #1131, for Preston's fears of evacuations from the Bluestone and New rivers and all along the frontier.

3. Arthur Campbell to the Governor, 29 Jan. 1783, *Calendar*, 3:424; William Preston to the Governor, 5 May 1783, ibid., 479. Also see James Moore to Preston, 21 Feb. 1783, Auditor's Papers, William Preston section; Preston to Benjamin Harrison, 22 Feb. 1783, *Calendar*, 3:445; Daniel Smith to Campbell, 19 May 1783, ibid., p. 485.

4. Arthur Campbell to Thomas Jefferson, 7 Feb. 1781, *Calendar*, 1:494; William Preston to Jefferson, 13 Apr. 1781, ibid., 2:34-36; Campbell to Jefferson, 25 Apr., 4 June 1781, ibid., 72-73, 143; Preston to Thomas Nelson, 28 July 1781, ibid, 264-65.

5. William Preston to Thomas Jefferson, 10 Apr. 1781, ibid., 2:25; Samuel McDowell to Jefferson, 20 Apr. 1781, ibid., 55; Walter Crockett to Preston, 17 May 1781, Preston Family of Virginia Papers, reel 5, #1110.

6. George Skillern to Thomas Nelson, 26 June 1781, *Calendar*, 2:183. Also see Marquis de LaFayette to [Governor of Virginia], 1 July 1781, McBride, "Virginia War Effort," 183, quoting *LaFayette in Virginia: Unpublished Letters from the Original Manuscripts in the Virginia State Library and the Library of Congress*, ed. Gilbert Chinard (Baltimore: John Hopkins Press, 1928), 18-22.

7. Joseph Martin to Thomas Jefferson, 7 Feb. 1781, *Papers of Thomas Jefferson*, 4:551-52.

8. Aaron Lewis to Arthur Campbell, 13 Apr. 1781, *Calendar*, 2:34; Joseph Martin to Campbell, 22 Apr. 1781, ibid., 64. Earlier that year, Arthur Campbell had met similar difficulties in leading an expedition of Virginia and North Carolina militiamen against the Cherokees in the Tennessee valley. Although he destroyed several Indian towns, his men's impatience to return home

apparently influenced Campbell's decision to turn back (Campbell to Thomas Jefferson, 15 Jan. 1781, *Papers of Thomas Jefferson*, 4:359-63).

9. George Skillern to Thomas Jefferson, 14 Apr. 1781, *Calendar*, 2:43; Petition of Botetourt County militiamen, 3 July 1781, ibid., 198. Eventually, however, the offenders were tried (Skillern to William Davies, 4 July 1782, ibid., 3:205).

10. Samuel McDowell to Thomas Jefferson, 20 Apr. 1781, ibid., 2:55.

11. William Preston to Thomas Jefferson, 13 Apr. 1781, ibid., 34-36. Major Charles Magill reported to Governor Jefferson that many Augusta and Rockbridge militiamen had also deserted (Magill to Jefferson, 19 Mar. 1781, ibid., 1:581-82).

12. Sampson Mathews to Thomas Jefferson, 29 Jan. 1781, *Papers of Thomas Jefferson*, 4:473; Peter Muhlenberg to Jefferson, 1 Apr. 1781, ibid., 5:315; Jefferson to Muhlenberg, 3 Apr. 1781, ibid., 328-29; editorial note, ibid., 453n-454n.

13. William Preston to William Davies, 6 July 1782, *Calendar*, 3:209. For an example of such misbehavior, see Margaret Campbell to brother, 29 Dec. 1780, Preston Family of Virginia Papers, reel 15, #20.

14. For a summary of Revolutionary War tax policy, see Robert A. Becker, *Revolution, Reform, and the Politics of American Taxation, 1763-1783* (Baton Rouge: Louisiana State University Press, 1980), esp. chap. 6; Risjord, *Chesapeake Politics*, esp. chaps. 4 and 6. Also helpful is Porter, *County Government in Virginia*, chap. 3, and see the discussion of Virginia's wartime taxes in chapter 5 of this book. Risjord asserts that currency contraction caused depression in the Chesapeake beginning about 1784. Although the contraction of currency began several years earlier, high demand for tobacco delayed depression for several years. In the upper valley, shortage of currency was a chronic problem, and tobacco production was not high enough to alleviate the problem. This, together with bad crops, apparently led to the earlier onset of depression in the region.

15. Arthur Campbell to Thomas Jefferson, 4 Apr. 1781, *Calendar*, 2:11; Campbell to Jefferson, 25 Apr. 1781, *Papers of Thomas Jefferson*, 5:552-53.

16. See for example Arthur Campbell to Thomas Jefferson, 27 Jan. 1781, *Calendar*, 1:465; Joseph Bell to Jefferson, 24 Feb. 1781, ibid., 538; George Skillern to Thomas Nelson, 3 Sept. 1781, ibid., 382-83; Samuel Brown to Benjamin Harrison, 14 Apr. 1782, ibid., 3:130.

17. Charles Cameron to William Davies, 9 Sept. 1782, ibid., 295.

18. Montgomery petition, 18 May 1780, Rockbridge petition, 19 May 1780, Botetourt petition, 2 June 1780, Augusta petition, 6 Dec. 1780 (petition of George Moffett), Legislative petitions.

19. Montgomery Order Book 2, 8 Mar. 1780, p. 291; Washington Minute Book 1, 23 Aug. 1782, p. 150; 18 Mar. 1784, p. 248; 17 Aug. 1784, p. 280.

20. Becker, *Revolution, Reform, and the Politics of American Taxation*, 199-204, summarizes the various legislative measures for collecting taxes in commodities. For examples of upper valley protest, see Montgomery petition, 24 May 1782, Botetourt petition, 3 June 1782, Augusta petition, 8 June 1784, Greenbrier petition, 11 June 1784 (petition of Andrew Donnelly), Botetourt petition, 12 June 1784, Augusta petition, 18 Nov. 1784, Legislative petitions; Arthur Campbell to William Davies, 20 Sept. 1782, *Calendar*, 3:317.

208   NOTES TO PAGES 120-121

21. For examples of petitions for tax relief, see Botetourt petition, 5 Dec. 1783, Greenbrier petition, 9 Dec. 1785, Augusta petition, 2 Nov. 1789, Montgomery petition, 14 Nov. 1789, Legislative petitions. For a description of the situation in Greenbrier, see J. McClurg to James Madison, 22 Aug. 1787, in *Proceedings of the Massachusetts Historical Society* 2d ser., 17 (1903): 472-73; Henry Banks to Edmund Randolph, 1, 2 Sept., 19 Oct. 1787, *Calendar*, 4:336-37, 338, 349-50.

22. Memorial of Walter Crockett in Montgomery petition, 14 Nov. 1789, Legislative petitions. Also see John Ward to William Preston 23 Nov. 1782, Auditor's Papers, William Preston section; Joseph Ball to Zachariah Johnston, 23 Nov. 1789, Zachariah and Thomas Johnston Papers, 1717-1858; Augusta petition, 20 Nov. 1790, Legislative petitions.

23. McBride, "Virginia War Effort," 246-48.

24. Moreover, since the draft was administered through the militia's network of training companies, upper valley leaders found it difficult if not impossible to conduct the draft while also mobilizing militiamen for immediate service (Andrew Donnelly, Samuel Brown, and Andrew Hamilton to Thomas Jefferson, 29 Jan. 1781, *Calendar*, 1:468-69; Samuel McDowell to Jefferson, 20 Apr. 1781, ibid., 2:55; Rockbridge petition, 14 June 1781, Legislative petitions; Preston to Walter Crockett, 2 July 1781, Auditor's Papers, William Preston section; McBride, "Virginia War Effort," 120). In several counties, Governor Jefferson authorized a delay in completion of the draft for these reasons (Jefferson to the County Lieutenants of Washington and Certain Other Counties, 15 Feb. 1781, *Papers of Thomas Jefferson*, 4:613-14; Jefferson to the Officers of the Greenbrier County Militia, 17 Feb. 1781, ibid., 641.

25. McBride, "Virginia War Effort," 132-34.

26. Joseph Cloyd to William Preston, 19 Oct. 1782, Preston Family of Virginia Papers, reel 6, #1162.

27. George Moffett to Thomas Jefferson, 5 May 1781, *Papers of Thomas Jefferson*, 5:603-5. Also see Thomas Posey to William Davies, 18 May 1781, *Calendar*, 2:107; McBride, "Virginia War Effort," 265-66; Royster, *Revolutionary People at War*, 323-25.

28. Samuel McDowell to Thomas Jefferson, 9 May 1781, *Papers of Thomas Jefferson*, 5:621-23. Similar disorders occurred in various other parts of Virginia. See McBride, "Virginia War Effort," 261-62, 266-69; George Corbin to Jefferson, 31 May 1781, *Papers of Thomas Jefferson*, 6:44-47.

29. Samuel Patterson to William Davies, 27 May 1781, *Calendar*, 2:126; Sampson Mathews to Thomas Nelson, 7 July 1781, ibid., 207; McBride, "Virginia War Effort," 265-66.

30. Patrick Lockhart to William Davies, 15 Apr. 1782, *Calendar*, 3:131; Augusta petition, 30 May 1782, Legislative petitions; George Skillern to Davies, 4 July 1782, *Calendar*, 3:205-6.

31. George Moffett to the Governor, 20 Mar. 1782, *Calendar*, 3:104; The rationale for believing that the legislature opposed conscription may have been an assumption that by withdrawing the currency from circulation, the assembly had deliberately made it impossible to pay the bounty and thus voided the conscription law. A group of Augusta petitioners claimed to have thought this

(Augusta petition, 30 May 1782, Legislative petitions). Ultimately Moffett did postpone the draft (Moffett to Benjamin Harrison, 1 May 1782, *Calendar*, 3:144-45).

32. William Preston to the Governor, 15 Mar. 1782, Auditor's Papers, William Preston section; Montgomery Order Book 2, 6 Mar. 1782, pp. 323-24. The money was to pay the bounties of men who had been drafted the previous year. Since no money was available then, they had been furloughed, which may have prevented violent resistance in Montgomery at that time. The Montgomery justices now excused their failure to raise the money in the intervening months by pointing out the refusal of local officials to return the necessary assessments. They further noted that many of the men recruited in Montgomery for the Continental army had already refused to accept their bounty payments in paper money. Preston was now requesting that the court levy a tax in specie, which the justices refused to do.

33. Samuel Brown to William Davies, 14 Apr. 1782, *Calendar*, 3:130; Thomas Bowyer to the Governor, 25 Sept. 1782, ibid., 326; Bowyer to Sampson Mathews, 19 Oct. 1782, ibid., 349; George Moffett to the Governor, 8 Nov. 1782, ibid., 367; Moffett to Davies, 5 Dec. 1782, ibid., 390; William Preston to Davies, 19 Dec. 1782, Auditor's Papers, William Preston section.

34. Arthur Campbell to William Davies, 13 Mar. 1782, *Calendar*, 3:98-99.

35. According to McDowell, some of the Rockbridge rioters believed this. McDowell also accused Zachariah Johnston of spreading such ideas in Augusta (Samuel McDowell to Thomas Jefferson, 9 May 1781, *Papers of Thomas Jefferson*, 5:621-23). Although there is no explicit indication of such ideas in Greenbrier, the timing of the riot strongly suggests that many local people held the same belief.

36. For the allegations of 1782 and their rationale, see Augusta petition, 30 May 1782. For the offer to petition the legislature, see George Moffett to Thomas Jefferson, 5 May 1781, *Papers of Thomas Jefferson*, 5:603-5.

37. Arthur Campbell to William Davies, 13 Mar. 1782, *Calendar*, 3:98-99. Similarly, a rumor reached Botetourt in 1781 that military duty had been postponed until after harvest in "the counties below." County lieutenant George Skillern predicted that the rumor would severely hamper efforts to mobilize his county's militia (Skillern to Thomas Nelson, 26 June 1781, ibid., 2:183).

38. Royster, *Revolutionary People at War*, 323-25, emphasizes this aspect of the Augusta and Rockbridge riots, but it is equally important not to over-emphasize it.

39. See note 81 in chapter 5 for the secondary literature exploring the republican ideology of revolutionary America. Chapter 5 of Bailyn's *Ideological Origins* provides a particularly good analysis of the changing concepts of representation and constitutions.

40. Washington Minute Book 1, 25 Apr. 1777, p. 8; Washington petition, 6 Nov. 1777, Legislative petitions. For further discussion of the unsuccessful effort to remove Preston, see Hughes, *Surveyors and Statesmen*, 91-92; and chapter 5 of this book.

41. Hughes, *Surveyors and Statesmen*, 96-98, and Thomas Lewis to William Preston, 11 Aug. 1781, 5QQ97.

42. See chapter 2.

43. Thomas Lewis to William Preston, 11 Aug. 1781, 5QQ97; Edmund Pendleton to Preston, 1 Nov. 1781, 5QQ99.

44. Montgomery petition, 14 Dec. 1781, Legislative petitions; Petition of Montgomery and Washington inhabitants, 14 Dec. 1781, Preston Family of Virginia Papers, reel 5, #1121, typed copy; William Preston to Thomas Lewis, 29 Sept. 1782, William Preston Papers, 1781, VHS.

45. For a summary of the Loyal Company controversy, see Abernethy, *Western Lands*, 12-13, 90, 190-91, 218-19.

46. Ibid., 224-28, 255-56; An Act for adjusting and settling the titles of claimers to unpatented lands under the present and former government, previous to the establishment of the commonwealth's land office, May 1779, *Statutes at Large*, 10:35-50; An Act for establishing a land office, and ascertaining the terms and manner of granting waste and unappropriated lands, May 1780, ibid., 10:50-65.

47. For a description of such petitioning, see Francis Preston to Francis Walker, 22 July 1792, Thomas and Francis Walker Papers, container 162, #0493-0494; Alexander Smyth, *Speeches Delivered by Alexander Smyth in the House of Delegates and at the Bar* (Richmond: Samuel Pleasants, 1811), 35.

48. For correspondence describing the origins of one such petition, see Harry Innes to Arthur Campbell, 17 Sept. 1781, 9DD29; Campbell to William Edmundson, 22 Sept. 1781, 9DD30. Also see Greenbrier petition, 18 Nov. 1782; Greenbrier petition, 13 June 1783; Greenbrier petition, 6 Nov. 1783; Greenbrier petition, 14 Nov. 1794; Botetourt petition, 14 May 1777; Botetourt petition, 5 Nov. 1777, all in Legislative petitions.

49. Abernethy, *Western Lands*, 222 and 256-57, suggests some of the Campbells' personal grievances. For more on the past pattern of political antagonism between Campbell and Preston groups, see chapters 4, 5, and 6 of this study. For allegations of economic motives, see Francis Preston to Francis Walker, 22 July 1782, Thomas and Francis Walker Papers, container 162, #0493-0494.

50. Unsigned letter to unidentified correspondent, 179_, Campbell-Preston Papers, reel 2, #403-7. Also see Abram Trigg to [Thomas Walker], 17 June 1785, Thomas and Francis Walker Papers, container 162, #0225-0226; George Taylor to Francis Walker, 12 May 1797, ibid., #0615-0617. For charges that various Greenbrier leaders had discouraged common settlers from paying debts owed to the Greenbrier Company, see Greenbrier petition, 23 Nov. 1795, Legislative petitions. On the Greenbrier Company, also see Edmund Pendleton to Archibald Stuart, 20 Apr. 1792, in *Letters and Papers of Edmund Pendleton*, 2:583-86.

51. Augusta petition, 6 June 1783, Legislative petitions; Rockbridge petition, 6 Dec. 1786, ibid.; Miscellaneous petitions, etc., 17___, Zechariah Johnston Papers, box 1, folder 6, Washington and Lee University. In a letter of 23 November 1789, Joseph Ball apparently referred to another such petition (Ball to Zachariah Johnston, 23 Nov. 1789, Zachariah and Thomas Johnston Papers).

52. See, for example, Botetourt petitions, 14 May, 5 Nov., and 22 Nov. 1777, Legislative petitions; Greenbrier petition, 6 Nov. 1783, ibid.; Washington petition, [1778 or 1779], Campbell-Preston Papers, reel 1, #239-40.

53. Botetourt petitions, 14 May 1777 and 6 Dec. 1786, Legislative petitions; Augusta petition, undated, Zechariah Johnston Papers, box 1, folder 6, Washington and Lee University.

54. Greenbrier petition, 6 Nov. 1783, Legislative petitions.

55. Botetourt petition, 14 May 1777, ibid.

56. See Bailyn, *Ideological Origins*, chap. 3.

57. Botetourt petition, 22 Nov. 1779, Legislative petitions. Also see memorial from the citizens of Washington County to the General Assembly, undated but ca. 1779, Campbell-Preston Papers, reel 1, #239-40; Washington County petition, 1779, Preston Family of Virginia Papers, reel 15, #17. The republican ideology's traditional distrust of the legal profession as the deceptive agents of commerce and oppression presumably strengthened a Greenbrier group's complaint that the artful deceptions of lawyers were used against them in land disputes (Thomas Adams to the Governor, 27 Mar. 1782, *Calendar*, 3:111).

58. Abernethy, *Western Lands*, 94, 164-65. The figures for counties do not include those created in Kentucky during the revolutionary era.

59. See, for example, Botetourt petition, 5 Nov. 1777; Augusta petition, 1 Dec. 1778; Augusta petition, 25 May 1779; Augusta Rockingham Hampshire petition, oversized, 22 Nov. 1785; Montgomery petition, 6 Nov. 1787; Botetourt and Montgomery petition, 2 Nov. 1789; all in Legislative petitions.

60. See, for example, Botetourt petition, 5 Nov. 1777; Washington petition, 23 May 1778; Augusta petition, 27 May 1779; Montgomery petition, 2 Dec. 1786; Augusta petition, 20 Nov. 1790, all ibid.

61. Legislative petitions for 1777 include seven petitions from various parts of Botetourt County in support of or in opposition to division of the county (Botetourt petitions, 5 Nov. 1777), as well as several petitions commenting on proposed changes in the boundary between Washington and Montgomery counties (Washington petitions, 6 Nov. 1777).

62. Botetourt petitions, 11 Nov. 1776 and 30 May 1777, Legislative petitions; An Act to empower the vestry of the Parish of Botetourt to dispose of their glebe, for dissolving the said vestry, and for other purposes therein mentioned, May 1777, *Statutes at Large*, 9:318-20.

63. Botetourt petition, 4 Nov. 1779, Legislative petitions (the petition is from William Fleming). Nevertheless, at least some Rockbridge citizens did serve as vestrymen and churchwardens during the early revolutionary years (Rockbridge Order Book, 1778-83, 5 May 1778, p. 13; 7 July 1778, p. 20; 5 Dec. 1778, p. 56; 4 May 1779, p. 81; 1 Feb. 1780, p. 160).

64. Botetourt petition, 29 Nov. 1793, Legislative petitions; Thomas Madison to William Fleming, 18 Nov. 1793, William Fleming Papers, box 1, folder 11.

65. For a general review of these developments, see Risjord, *Chesapeake Politics*, 203, and Thomas E. Buckley, S.J., *Church and State in Revolutionary Virginia, 1776-1787* (Charlottesville: University Press of Virginia, 1977).

66. Buckley, "Church-State Settlement in Virginia: The Presbyterian Contribution," *Journal of Presbyterian History* 54 (1976): 112-13.

67. Rockingham petition, 18 Nov. 1784; Rockbridge petition, 1 Dec. 1784; Augusta petition, 12 Nov. 1785; Montgomery petition, 15 Nov. 1785; Botetourt petition, 29 Nov. 1785; Washington petition, 10 Dec. 1785; Rockbridge petition,

12 Nov. 1785, all in Legislative petitions. Also see the copy of James Madison's "Memorial and Remonstrance against the General Assessment," 1785, Breckinridge Family Papers, vol. 3, LC.

68. Buckley, "Church-State Settlement in Virginia," 114; Risjord, *Chesapeake Politics*, 209.

69. Botetourt petition, 29 Nov. 1785, Legislative petitions. Another petition used similar language against the proposal for incorporation of the Episcopal church (Rockbridge petition, 1 Dec. 1784, ibid.).

70. Montgomery petition, 15 Nov. 1785, Botetourt petition, 29 Nov. 1785, ibid.

71. In *Church and State in Revolutionary Virginia*, Thomas Buckley convincingly demonstrates the major role this belief played in motivating evangelical opposition to the general assessment throughout Virginia. For examples of such sentiments in the upper valley, see Washington petition, 10 Dec. 1785, Legislative petitions, and an undated petition against the general assessment in Zechariah Johnston Papers, box 1, folder 8, Washington and Lee University.

72. Rockingham petition, 18 Nov. 1784, Botetourt petition, 29 Nov. 1785; Rockbridge petition, 1 Dec. 1784, Washington petition, 10 Dec. 1785, Legislative petitions.

73. Petition of Freeholders and other Inhabitants of the County of Washington to their Representatives in the General Assembly, 1779, Preston Family of Virginia Papers, reel 15, #17. They also "Recommend[ed]" the revision of the laws covering militia pay and the punishment of militia delinquents.

74. "A Parody of the Celebrated Irish Resolves, entered into at Dunannon 8th Sept. 1783" (emphasis added). The document is dated Virginia, Jan. 1784, and signed by "a Commonwealths Man" (William Graham Letters and Papers, 1783-1885, Duke University).

75. Rockbridge petition, 1 Dec. 1784, Legislative petitions. Such calls for a new constitution, more directly created by the people, recurred through the 1790s. See, for example, Augusta petition, 4 Oct. 1792, ibid.; and Instructions given by the citizens of the first battalion of Rockbridge county, August 3d 1797, to Captain Zachariah Johnston and Major John Wilson, their delegates in the ensuing Session of the Assembly, Zechariah Johnston Papers, box 1, folder 6, Washington and Lee University.

76. Risjord, *Chesapeake Politics*, 220-22, 226. Virginia also made the cession conditional upon Maryland's approval of the Articles of Confederation and Congress's agreement that new states would ultimately be created in the western territory. Campbell's opponents presented charges against him in the state assembly for improper activities in December 1782, but no action was taken. In January 1783 Governor Harrison referred to earlier charges by Joseph Martin that Campbell had urged Martin not to negotiate further with the Indians and to let them attack the frontiers (Abernethy, *Western Lands*, 259).

77. Abernethy, *Western Lands*, 291. John Preston informed John Breckinridge in November 1784 that Campbell and others wanted a new state (Preston to Breckinridge, 28 Nov. 1784, Breckinridge Family Papers, vol. 2, #259, LC).

78. For a summary of these events see Risjord, *Chesapeake Politics*,

pp. 222-23. Arthur Campbell's reasons for seeking the union with Franklin included a complex mixture of personal, political, and economic motives. Throughout his career Campbell had repeatedly clashed with William Preston and his family. As in his earlier campaign against the Loyal Company, Campbell's political and economic interests merged in his Franklinite activities. A successful secession of southwestern Virginia presumably would have enhanced Campbell's political stature while damaging that of the Prestons and other leaders who opposed the scheme. Moreover, since Campbell claimed large tracts of land within the Loyal Company's jurisdiction, he stood to gain by removing this land from the state that supported the company's ownership. In addition, a Virginia law of 1784 that was designed to encourage the appointment of former Continental army officers to positions of command in the militia further alienated Campbell from state authorities. (Harrison M. Ethridge, "Governor Patrick Henry and the Reorganization of the Virginia Militia, 1784-1786," *VMHB* 85 [1977]: 427-39; John D. Kirby, "The Militia of Southwest Virginia, 1784-1794" [M.A. thesis, Virginia Polytechnic Institute and State University, 1976].)

Personal enmity also shaped the actions of William Russell, who led the opposition to the Franklin proposal. As early as 1774, Russell and Campbell had clashed over the control of frontier defense on the Clinch and Holston rivers. After Russell's marriage to the widow of Campbell's cousin, the two men became embroiled in an extended quarrel over control of the late William Campbell's children and estate (Russell to Thomas Madison, 6 July 1787, William Fleming Papers, box 1, folder 8; Russell to John Breckinridge, 31 Aug. 1789, Breckinridge Family Papers, vol. 5, #893, LC; Campbell to Madison, 20 Feb. 1788, Preston Family of Virginia Papers, reel 7, #1872, typed copy of 5ZZ86). The Franklin controversy was only one in a series of disputes between the two men.

79. Address to the Freemen of Washington County, signed by Charles Cummings, *Calendar*, 4:34-36; James Montgomery, William Edmiston, and Arthur Bowen to Patrick Henry, 27 July 1785, ibid., 45-46; Deposition of William Crabtree, 10 Mar. 1786, ibid., 98; Deposition of Arthur Bowen, 10 Mar. 1786, ibid., 98-99; Deposition of Alexander Barnett, 14 Mar. 1786, ibid., 103-4; Deposition of William Russell, 3 May 1786, ibid., 123-25; Deposition of Captain Joseph Cole, 3 May 1786, ibid., 125.

80. Campbell particularly urged that "old settlers" who had made such payments should refuse to pay future taxes. (Deposition of Alexander Barnett, 14 Mar. 1786, ibid., 104; Deposition of George Clark, Sr., 20 Mar. 1786, ibid., 107; Deposition of Andrew Kincannon, 3 May 1786, ibid., 126; Deposition of George Clark, 4 May 1786, ibid., 129-30; Deposition of Benjamin Sharp, 19 May 1785, ibid., 135).

81. Deposition of Robert Preston, 18 May 1786, ibid., 130-31. For another account of Campbell's remarks on the shortage of currency and its effect on tax payments, see deposition of George Finley, 18 May 1786, ibid., 133-34.

82. Arthur Campbell to John Edmundson, Sr., 26 Aug. 1785, ibid., 100-102.

83. Deposition of William Russell, 3 May 1786, ibid., 123-25. The quoted

phrase is from Russell's account of Campbell's speech to a meeting at Sinking Spring.

84. The exact nature of the committees is unclear. James Montgomery, William Edmiston, and Arthur Bowen charged that "small committees" began meeting as early as February and March 1785 (Deposition, 27 July 1785, ibid., 45-46). At a meeting on 12 February 1785 at William Colley's house, Campbell apparently addressed a large number of people but later proposed that those who favored his proposals should elect a committee (Depositions of William Russell, 10 Mar., 3 May 1786, ibid., 99, 124). Several deponents, however, described a committee meeting on 15 February 1785 at the Sinking Spring church which seemed little different from a conventional public meeting: Reverend Charles Cummings presided and Campbell addressed a large number of people, nearly three hundred by one estimate (Deposition of James Montgomery, 14 Mar. 1786, ibid., 103-4; Deposition of William Russell, 3 May 1786, ibid., 104). Also see deposition of Captain John Cole, 3 May 1786, ibid., 125. For descriptions of huzzahing for liberty, see depositions of Arthur Bowen, 10 Mar., 9 May 1786, ibid., 98-99, 129.

85. Address to the freemen of Washington County, undated, ibid., 34-36. The address was signed by the Reverend Charles Cummings as chairman, presumably of a secessionist committee.

86. Deposition of James Montgomery, 14 Mar. 1786, ibid., 103-4.

87. For an extended analysis of the changing conceptions of constitutions in revolutionary America, see Wood, *Creation of the American Republic.*

88. Address to the freemen of Washington County, undated, *Calendar,* 4:34-36; Arthur Campbell to Patrick Henry, 21 May 1785, ibid., 30. The final quotation and much of this account are from the deposition of James Montgomery, 14 Mar. 1786 (ibid., 103-4). Hence this statement is described as an *apparent* assertion. Montgomery reported Campbell to have said that the governor and council were "no more than an individual," but the prior emphasis on constitutional restraint makes it probable that Campbell meant they lost the legitimate right to use power when they exceeded constitutional bounds. For similar descriptions of the encounter, see William Edmiston, James Kincannon, Samuel Edmiston, James Thompson, and Arthur Bowen to the Executive, 24 Nov. 1785, ibid., 69; Deposition of William Russell, 10 Mar. 1786, ibid., 99; Deposition of James Thompson, 3 May 1786, ibid., 127-28.

89. James Montgomery, William Edmiston, and Arthur Bowen to Patrick Henry, 27 July 1785, ibid., 45-46; William Edmiston, James Kincannon, Samuel Edmiston, James Thompson, and Arthur Bowen to the Executive, 24 Nov. 1785, ibid., 69.

90. Deposition of James Montgomery, 14 Mar. 1786, ibid., 103-4; Deposition of William Russell, 3 May 1786, ibid., 123-25.

91. Deposition of Arthur Bowen, 10 Mar. 1786, ibid., 98-99; Deposition of William Russell, 3 May 1786, ibid., 123-25.

92. Three copies of the broadside, dated 5 Jan. 1785, are in the Breckinridge Family Papers, vol. 2, #285, 286, and 287, LC. It also appears in *More Virginia Broadsides before 1877,* ed. Ray O. Hummell (Richmond: Virginia State Library, 1975), #130.

93. Arthur Campbell to Alexander Barnett, [1782], copy sworn to as accurate by Barnett, *Calendar*, 3:414-15; William Christian to Campbell, 19 Feb. 1782, 9DD32; Campbell to John Edmundson, Sr., 26 Aug. 1785, *Calendar*, 4:100-102. Another statement of Franklinite political principles affirmed the right of any group of citizens to alter "their present situation and government" and asserted that "individuals are not created for the pleasure of government but government is instituted for the pleasure and happiness of individuals" (Undated resolutions, entered at the start of Washington Will Book 1).

94. Deposition of John Kinkead, 30 May 1786, *Calendar*, 4:138-39; Deposition of Robert Preston, 4 May 1786, ibid., 130-31. Also see the sources cited in note 87.

95. John Breckinridge to Leticia Breckinridge, 17 Mar. 1784, Breckinridge Family Papers, vol. 2, #169, LC; Archibald Stuart to John Breckinridge, 1 Apr. 1784, ibid., #171 (remounted after #196).

96. James Breckinridge to John Breckinridge, 23 May 1784, ibid., #211.

97. J. Madison to John Breckinridge, 24 May 1784, ibid., #213-14.

98. John Preston to Francis Preston, 26 Dec. 1786, 17 Feb. 1787, Preston Family Papers, College of William and Mary.

99. Francis Preston to James Breckinridge, 17 Feb. 1789, Papers of James Breckinridge, University of Virginia.

100. Archibald Stuart to John Breckinridge, 21 Oct. 1787, Breckinridge Family Papers, vol. 4, #620, LC. For Stuart's earlier criticisms of Virginia's government and people as overly democratic, weak, misguided, and unduly extravagant, see Stuart to Thomas Jefferson, 17 Oct. 1785, *Papers of Thomas Jefferson*, 8:644-47.

101. John Breckinridge to John Preston, 14 Apr. 1788, Preston Family of Virginia Papers, reel 7, #1581. For Breckinridge's expression of misgivings about the Constitution, see John Breckinridge to James Breckinridge, 25 Jan. 1788, Breckinridge Family Papers, vol. 4, #680-81, LC: and Risjord, *Chesapeake Politics*, 299-300. Breckinridge had recently moved eastward across the Blue Ridge to Albemarle County.

102. William Graham to Zachariah Johnston, 3 Nov. 1787, Zechariah Johnston Papers, box 1, folder 2, Washington and Lee University; Robert G. Gillespie, Jr., "Reverend William Graham: Presbyterian Minister and Rector of Liberty Hall Academy" (M.A. thesis, University of Richmond, 1970), 44; Arthur Campbell to Virginia Independent Chronicle, 13 May 1788, 9DD48. Campbell also criticized the idea that treaties should be regarded as superior to other laws when those treaties were to be ratified by the Senate but not by the House of Representatives. Such a violation of the principle of popular sovereignty, Campbell suggested, became far more serious when treaties were made with Indian tribes and other groups who he felt were particularly unlikely to honor them. Also see William Fleming to Thomas Madison, 14 Feb. 1788, 5ZZ85.

103. William Graham to Zachariah Johnston, 3 Nov. 1787, Zechariah Johnston Papers, box 1, folder 2, Washington and Lee University; Thomas Wilson to Archibald Stuart, 4 Nov. 1787, Stuart Family Papers, 1758-1881, section 1, folder 13, VHS.

104. Archibald Stuart to John Breckinridge, 1 Mar. 1788, Breckinridge Family Papers, vol. 4, #690, LC. For an account of the Rockbridge election and the Lexington meeting, see Charles W. Turner, "Andrew Moore—First U.S. Senator from West of the Blue Ridge Mountains," *Filson Club Quarterly* 28 (1954): 354-70.

105. See, for example, James Breckinridge to John Breckinridge, 31 Oct. 1787, Breckinridge Family Papers, vol. 4, #627, LC; William Graham to Zachariah Johnston, 3 Nov. 1787, Zechariah Johnston Papers, box 1, folder 2, Washington and Lee University. Also see William Fleming to Thomas Madison, 14 Feb. 1788, 5ZZ85.

106. Hart, *Valley of Virginia*, 188, quoting *Virginia Chronicle* (Richmond), 12 July 1788.

107. Arthur Campbell to Archibald Stuart, July 1789, 9DD56. After Virginia's ratification, Stuart reported that virtually all the delegates who had opposed ratification promised to support the new government (Stuart to John Breckinridge, 30 June 1788, Breckinridge Family Papers, vol. 5, #713, LC).

108. See A.G. Roeber, *Faithful Magistrates and Republican Lawyers: Creators of Virginia Legal Culture, 1680-1810* (Chapel Hill: University of North Carolina Press, 1981), chap. 6.

109. See, for example, Alexander Barnett to Edmund Randolph, 26 Mar., 1787, *Calendar*, 4:262-63; Walter Crockett to Randolph, 11 June 1787 and 15 Mar. 1788, ibid., 295-96 and 408; Daniel Trigg to John Preston, 6 July 1788, Preston Family of Virginia Papers, reel 7, #1588; James Gibson to Alexander Barnett, 22 Aug. 1788, *Calendar*, 4:474-75; George Clendinen to Randolph, 1 Jan. 1789, ibid., 542-43; Crockett to Randolph, 16 Feb. 1789, ibid., 564.

8. JOHN STUART'S HISTORY OF THE GREENBRIER VALLEY

1. John Stuart's "Memoir of Indian Wars and Other Occurrences" was published in the *Collections of the Virginia Historical and Philosophical Society*, 1st ser., 1 (1833): 37-68. The Virginia Historical Society's manuscript collection includes two similar handwritten copies of the narrative, one by Charles A. Stuart and one by Samuel Lewis. The published version follows Charles Stuart's transcription. The memoir has also been published as part of the Eyewitness Accounts of the American Revolution, 3d ser. (New York: New York Times, 1971).

2. Stuart's initial history was copied from the Greenbrier County records by the clerk, John S. Crawford, at the request of Judge G.A. Vincent. It was published in *WMQ* 1st ser., 22 (1913-14): 229-34. In a letter transmitting his copy of the full narrative to the Virginia Historical Society, Stuart's son noted that his father and his friends frequently retold local historical events at social gatherings. This letter was published with Stuart's narrative in the *Collections of the Virginia Historical and Philosophical Society*.

3. For a particularly good summary of structuralist theory, see Jonathan Culler, *Structuralist Poetics* (Ithaca: Cornell University Press, 1975). Also

useful are Claude Lévi-Strauss, "The Structuralist Study of Myth," in *Structuralist Anthropology*, trans. Claire Jacobson and Brooke Grundfest Schoepf (New York: Doubleday, 1963), 202-28, and "The Story of Asdiwal," in *The Structural Study of Myth and Totemism*, ed. Edmund Leach (London: Tavistock, 1967), 1-43.

4. *Webster's New World Dictionary of the American Language*, College Edition, 1964, s.v. "well."

5. The version of the poem quoted here is actually a posthumous alteration of Dickinson's original manuscript. In the original, line 4 read: "And what a Billow be." Line 8 read "As if the Checks were given." Dickinson was apparently using the word *Checks* to mean railroad tickets, an accepted contemporary colloquialism (*The Poems of Emily Dickinson, Including Variant Readings Critically Compared with All Known Readings*, ed. Thomas H. Johnson [1955; rpt., Cambridge, Mass.: Harvard University Press, 1963], 2:742).

6. Some recent poststructuralist or deconstructionist theorists of literary criticism assert that once created, the text escapes from its author's control, generating a series of different, often ambiguous, and even contradictory interpretations by those who receive it. For many such theorists, texts lack clear and demonstrable connections to authors, audiences, or the world of material "reality." Ultimately the text is incoherent, containing conflicts and contradictions that undermine its apparent meaning. For a description and defense of this perspective and its implications for intellectual history, see David Harlan, "Intellectual History and the Return of Literature," *American Historical Review* 94 (1989): 581-609. As David A. Hollinger points out, this position raises serious problems for all historians: if the complex texts of intellectuals ultimately cannot be understood, the same linguistic and epistemological barriers stand between the researcher and any other language-based materials in social or political history ("The Return of the Prodigal: The Persistence of Historical Knowing," ibid., 611).

This extreme deconstructionist position, however, is not widely accepted among literary critics, intellectual historians, and other scholars. It is, after all, human actors who create, receive, and impose concurring or divergent meanings upon words. Although language may not simply reflect the world of material experience, it does in important ways respond to and interact with that experience. (For more development of these themes, see Joyce Appleby, "One Good Turn Deserves Another: Moving beyond the Linguistic, A Response to David Harlan," ibid., 1326-32; J.G.A. Pocock, *Virtue, Commerce, and History: Essays on Political Thought and History, Chiefly in the Eighteenth Century* [Cambridge, Eng.: Cambridge Univeristy Press, 1985], chap. 1; John E. Toews, "Intellectual History after the Linguistic Turn: The Autonomy of Meaning and the Irreducibility of Experience," *American Historical Review* 92 [1987]: 879-907). Whatever the imprecisions, ambiguities, and contradictions of the meanings created and perceived by human actors, there are also strong elements of clarity, commonality, and continuity. And these clarities, commonalities, and continuities of meaning—together with the irregularities, contradictions, and disjunctures—should be investigated and articulated, even if that investigation and articulation can never be absolutely satisfying or complete. (On these points see Dominick LaCapra, "Rethinking Intellectual History and Reading

Texts," in *Rethinking Intellectual History: Texts, Contexts, Language*, ed. Dominick LaCapra [Ithaca, N.Y.: Cornell University Press, 1983], 45-46).

Ultimately the structuralist and poststructuralist approaches to textual interpretation are complementary rather than antagonistic. As Jonathan Culler points out, it is often difficult decisively to classify individual scholars as members of one camp or the other. To the structuralist quest for comprehensive and consistent patterns of meaning, deconstruction responds by pointing to the elements of ambiguity and conflict in any form of cultural expression (*On Deconstruction: Theory and Criticism after Structuralism* [Ithaca, N.Y.: Cornell University Press, 1982], esp. 24-25, 225. Also see Culler, *Pursuit of Signs: Semiotics, Literature, Deconstruction* [Ithaca, N.Y.: Cornell University Press, 1981], esp. x-xi).

7. In many cases a final step of the analysis is validating the results. It must be demonstrated that the suggested meaning is not the creation of the analyst but rather an integral part of the text for its creators and its audience. The results of structuralist analysis of language may be tested against other knowledge of the language: if the hypothesized rules accurately describe one body of linguistic material, do they also describe other material from the same language? Do they separate the grammatical from the ungrammmatical, the meaningful from the nonsensical? Although validations of hypotheses about cultural phenomena are less conclusive, such hypotheses may be tested against other knowledge of the culture to show that the suggested meaning is in fact rooted in the cultural environment of the text: does the proposed pattern of meaning render intelligible other texts or cultural phenomena within the same culture? Do similar patterns of perception occur elsewhere in that society? Since the present chapter argues that the underlying pattern of meaning in Stuart's narrative was his perception of the transformation of political values during the revolutionary era, and since this transformation within upper valley political culture has already been discussed in the preceding chapters, such a validation would be superfluous here. In effect, the preceding chapters constitute the validation.

8. See LaCapra, "Rethinking Intellectual History," 56-57.

9. See Culler, *On Deconstruction*, esp. 213-14, 251-57, and LaCapra, "Habermas and the Grounding of Critical Theory," in *Rethinking Intellectual History*, 151-53.

10. In the case of Dickinson's poem, it would be noted that the first and second parts of each stanza form similar syntagmatic chains: each stanza states that *the narrator has not had some experience* but nevertheless *she knows something about it*. Some differences, however, might also be noted by focusing on the paradigmatic relationship between the second halves of the two syntagmatic chains. The implications of these structural relationships might then lead to several conclusions about the meaning of the poem.

11. Despite some significant departures, as in his description of Andrew Lewis's career, Stuart generally follows chronological patterns, and many of his digressions are internally arranged in chronological sequences.

12. Stuart's description of an Indian attack in 1763 and the subsequent

captivity and escape of Mrs. Archibald Clendenin, for example, apparently reflects such an attraction. In addition to its dramatic appeal, the episode possesses a coherent structure of its own, dealing with the themes of family loyalties, betrayal, and frontier survival. During the attack, Archibald Clendenin was killed while trying to flee with a child in his arms, and a black woman killed her own child in a futile attempt to escape. Then Mrs. Clendenin sacrificed her child and successfully escaped. When she returned to her husband's body and covered it with rails, however, she was frightened by the image of a man standing within a few steps of her. In the earlier version of his history recorded in the Greenbrier deed book, Stuart identifies the description of Mrs. Clendenin's escape and the Indians' killing of her child as a narrative which he would relate, thus implying that it enjoyed an independent existence as a popular tale within the region. The added elements of Archibald Clendenin's death while trying to rescue a child, the futile escape attempt of the black woman, and Mrs. Clendenin's return to her husband's body presumably reflected elaboration of these themes of family loyalty, betrayal, and frontier survival, either by Stuart or by other local narrators of the tale.

13. See Jonathan Culler, "Story and Discourse in the Analysis of Narrative," in *Pursuit of Signs*, 169-87.

14. For more on this theme in poststructuralist criticism see the sources discussed in note 6.

15. *Documentary History of Dunmore's War*, 433-35.

16. John Floyd to William Preston, 16 Oct. 1774, 2ZZ63, clipped from the *Frankfort Commonwealth*, 4 Mar. 1834.

17. In support of this contention, Stuart notes Dunmore's unexpected abandoning of the plan to rendezvous with Lewis's army at Point Pleasant, the governor's messenger's foreknowledge of the Indian attack, the Shawnees' apparent awareness of the numerical strength of both Lewis's army at Point Pleasant and his expected reinforcements, and the governor's final intervention to prevent Lewis's army from attacking the Shawnee towns after crossing the Ohio. According to Stuart, Andrew Lewis later claimed to have been told of an incriminating conversation between Governor Dunmore and his close associate John Connelly on the day of the battle. Finally, Stuart notes a British travel writer's claim to have been on the expedition and concludes that since he did not know of anyone by that name in Lewis's army, the man must have been traveling incognito as Dunmore's spy.

18. Admittedly, Mrs. Clendenin committed an act of betrayal in abandoning her child to the Indians. The narrative, however, also describes her encounter with a ghostly male figure near her husband's body. Since her husband had died trying to carry a child away from the Indians, the narrative implies strong feelings of guilt on her part. Moreover, as suggested in note 12 above, this episode may have been an independent local narrative incorporated by Stuart into his text.

19. Although he notes that an Indian party deceptively drew a detachment from the Point Pleasant fort into an ambush in 1777, Stuart specifies that their objective was to avenge Cornstalk's death.

CONCLUSION

1. Sydnor, *Gentlemen Freeholders*; Morgan, *American Slavery, American Freedom*.

2. See, for example, Hofstra, "Land, Ethnicity and Community"; Hofstra, "A Parcel of Barbarians"; and McMaster, *History of Hardy County*.

3. Titus, "Soldiers When They Chose to Be So."

4. Timothy H. Breen, *Tobacco Culture: The Mentality of the Great Tobacco Planters on the Eve of the Revolution* (Princeton: Princeton University Press, 1985), chap. 1; Allan Kulikoff, *Tobacco and Slaves: The Development of Southern Cultures in the Chesapeake, 1680-1800* (Chapel Hill: University of North Carolina Press for the Institute of Early American History and Culture, Williamsburg, Va., 1986), chaps. 3-4; Rhys Isaac, "Dramatizing the Ideology of Revolution: Popular Mobilization in Virginia, 1774 to 1776," *WMQ* 3d ser., 33 (1976): 369-70.

5. For critical evaluations of Isaac, *Transformation of Virginia*, see the reviews by John B. Boles, *Journal of Southern History* 49 (1983): 605-7; Fredrika J. Teute, *VMHB* 91 (1983): 512-14; and especially Timothy H. Breen, *WMQ*, 3d ser., 40 (1983): 298-302. For a discussion of evangelical religion's apparent challenge to gentry authority on Maryland's Eastern Shore, see Keith Mason, "Localism, Evangelism, and Loyalism: The Sources of Oppression in the Revolutionary Chesapeake," *Journal of Southern History* 66 (1990): 23-54.

6. Rutman and Rutman, *A Place in Time*, chap. 4, esp. 102, 120-22; Mary Beth Norton, "Gender and Defamation in Seventeenth-Century Maryland," *WMQ* 3d ser., 44 (1987): 23-31; Paul D. Escott and Jeffrey R. Crow, "The Social Order and Violent Disorder: An Analysis of North Carolina in the Revolution and the Civil War," *Journal of Southern History* 52 (1985): 373-403; Nobles, *Divisions throughout the Whole*; Szatsmary, *Shays Rebellion*.

7. See, for example, William L. Shea, *The Virginia Militia in the Seventeenth Century* (Baton Rouge: Louisiana State University Press, 1983), and Lawrence D. Cress, *Citizens in Arms: The Army and Militia in American Society to the War of 1812*, Studies on Armed Forces and Society (Chapel Hill: University of North Carolina Press, 1982).

8. For a discussion of the effect of road work on the lives of lower-class North Carolinians, see Marvin L. Michael Kay and William S. Price, Jr., " 'To Ride the Wooden Mare': Road Building and Militia Service in Colonial North Carolina, 1740-1775," *North Carolina Historical Review* 57 (1980): 361-409. For a useful general analysis of the process of community formation in the eighteenth-century Chesapeake, see Kulikoff, *Tobacco and Slaves*, chap. 6. On local communities in the seventeenth-century Chesapeake, see James Horn, "Adapting to a New World: A Comparative Study of Local Society in England and Maryland, 1650-1700," in *Colonial Chesapeake Society*, ed. Lois Green Carr, Philip D. Morgan, and Jean B. Russo (Chapel Hill: University of North Carolina Press for the Institute of Early American History and Culture, Williamsburg, Va., 1988), 133-75; and Lorena S. Walsh, "Community Networks in the Early Chesapeake," ibid., 200-241.

9. Slaughter, *Whiskey Rebellion*. For an analysis of varying patterns of interaction between local leaders and popular dissidents in revolutionary and

postrevolutionary western Massachusetts, see John L. Brooke, "To the Quiet of the People: Revolutionary Settlements and Civil Unrest in Western Massachusetts, 1774-1789," *WMQ* 3d ser., 46 (1989): 425-62.

10. John E. Selby, *The Revolution in Virginia, 1775-1783* (Williamsburg, Va.: Colonial Williamsburg Foundation, 1988); McBride, "Virginia War Effort"; Risjord, *Chesapeake Politics*, esp. chap. 4.

11. See, for example, Steven Rosswurm, *Arms, Country, and Class: The Philadelphia Militia and the "Lower Sort" during the American Revolution* (New Brunswick: Rutgers University Press, 1987), and Gary B. Nash, "Also There at the Creation: Going Beyond Gordon S. Wood," *WMQ* 3d ser., 44 (1987): 602-11.

12. See, for example, Slaughter, *Whiskey Rebellion*; Sean Willenz, *Chants Democratic: New York City and the Rise of the American Working Class* (New York: Oxford University Press, 1984).

13. For the concept of political culture as language, see Pocock, *Virtue, Commerce, and History.* In "The 'Great National Discussion': The Discourse of Politics in 1787," (*WMQ* 3d ser., 45 (1988): 3-32, Isaac Krammick emphasizes the coexistence of several different "languages" in the political discourse surrounding the Constitution. Also see James T. Kloppenberg, "The Virtues of Liberalism: Christianity, Republicanism and Ethics in Early American Political Discourse," *Journal of American History* 74 (1987): 9-33. In addition to examining the impact of material on ideological circumstances, revolutionary scholarship should of course continue its examination of the ways in which ideology and culture helped to reshape material circumstances. As noted in the preface, the relationship is ultimately dialectical.

Index

Alexander, Archibald, 44
Anglican church, 18, 31, 36-37, 127-28, 177 n 107. *See also* Augusta vestry; vestry
Arbuckle, Matthew, 87, 141-42, 148-49, 152, 155
Armstrong, James, 36
Augusta Boys incident, 49, 72, 182 n 19, 190 n 31
Augusta County committee, 79, 101
Augusta County Court: attendance and membership, 20-21, 23-24, 46; deferential culture, role in, 30, 31-32; functions, 17, 33-34, 174 nn 50, 51; Tinkling Spring Church, dealing with, 36
Augusta County Quitrent Roll of 1760-62, 12, 20-21, 169 nn 1, 2, 167 nn 26, 27
Augusta court martial, 92, 196 n 74
Augusta draft riot of 1781, 121, 122, 208-9 n 31, 209 n 35
Augusta election riot of 1755, 39-40
Augusta vestry, 29, 36-37, 43, 177 n 107
Aylett, John, 27

Beverley, William, 8, 24, 25
Beverley tract, 126
Blair, John, 26
Bledsoe, Anthony, 86
Bluestone River area, 56
Boone, Daniel, 55, 73
Borden, Benjamin, Jr., 8, 22
Borden, Benjamin, Sr., 38, 62
Borden tract, 54, 126

Botetourt County Court, 200 n 14; attendance and membership, 20-21, 23, 46; conflicts on, 41, 42, 43, 179 n 25; deferential culture, role in, 30, 31
Botetourt vestry, 127-28
Bowman, Henry, 106
Bowyer, John, 42, 44, 57-58
Bowyer, William, 22
Bratton, Robert, 29
Breckinridge, Adam, 29
Breckinridge, Alexander, 35
Breckinridge, James, 134
Breckinridge, John, 134-35, 136
Breckinridge, Robert, 8, 21, 30, 43
Brown, John, Jr., 95
Brown, Reverend John, 21, 30, 34, 79, 84
Buchanan, James, 49
Buchanan, John, 25, 38, 40-41, 124, 178 n 123
Buchanan, Margaret, 172 n 31
Bullpasture River, 54, 56, 69, 75
Burk, Thomas, 102, 105, 199 n 6
Byrd, William, 27
Byrn, James, 105

Cabell, William, 27
Calhoun, James, 60, 76
Campbell, Andrew, 32
Campbell, Arthur, 85; and defense in colonial period, 41, 49, 50, 51, 53, 54, 55, 57, 71, 72, 75, 180 n 8; and defense in revolutionary period, 96, 119, 121-22, 198 n 89, 206-7 n 8; federal Constitution,

attitudes on, 137, 215 n 102;
Franklin, effort to add
southwestern Virginia to proposed
new state of, 130-34, 212 n 76, 213 n
78, 214 nn 84, 88; and land
acquisition and land disputes,
82-84, 125-26, 186 n 58; and Tory
movement, 114-15, 205 n 80
Campbell, William, 91, 98-99, 104,
107, 114-15, 201 n 20
Catawba Indians, 8
Cherokee Indians: controversy over
Henderson group's purchase of
Kentucky, 84; relations with settlers
during colonial period, 39, 49, 57,
72, 74, 181 n 17, 182 n 19; relations
with settlers during revolutionary
period, 81-82, 86-87, 101, 118; and
southern wars of Iroquois, 7-8
Christian, Israel, 21, 22, 26; eastern
Virginia, attitudes toward and
relations with, 25, 43-44, 176 n 86;
quarrels with other regional
leaders, 24-25, 41, 42, 43, 57, 179 n
25
Christian, John, 35
Christian, William, 22, 46, 79, 89,
133; and defense in colonial period,
49, 54, 56-57, 69, 180 n 8; and
defense in revolutionary period,
98, 196-97 n 76; and land
acquisition and land disputes, 59,
82-84, 85
Clendenin, Archibald, 218-19 n 12,
219 n 18
Clendenin, Mrs. Archibald, 218-19 n
12, 219 n 18
Clinch River area, 7; defense in
colonial period, 47-48, 54-55, 56,
73, 74; defense in revolutionary
period, 89, 118; land acquisition
and land disputes, 25
Coalter, John, 91
Cocke, William, 53, 71, 72, 82
Connoly, John, 10
Cook, Benjamin, 113
cooperative labor and local
exchange, 16-17, 67, 188 n 7
Corbin, Richard, 25
Cornstalk, 151-52; at battle of Point
Pleasant, 140; his murder at Point

Pleasant during Revolution, 87,
141-42, 147, 148-49, 150;
consequences of his murder, 93,
156, 194 n 47
counties, efforts to create new, 9;
during colonial period, 42, 46, 65,
179 n 133; during revolutionary era,
127, 135-36, 166 n 8, 194 n 47
county courts, 104; attendance and
membership, 20-21, 23-24, 45-46;
deferential culture, role in, 30-33;
functions, 17, 33-34; ignorance of,
by common folk, 46, 104. See also
Augusta County Court; Botetourt
County Court; Fincastle County
Court; Montgomery County Court;
Rockbridge County Court;
Washington County Court
county lieutenant: controversy over
position in Washington County,
132, 133-34
courthouse, 27, 30-31, 37, 39-40,
41-42, 174 nn 50, 51, 54
Cowin, Andrew, 36
Cowpasture River area, 56
Cox, John, 104-5, 113, 201 nn 20, 24
Crabtree, Isaac, 49
Craig, Reverend John, 28, 36, 38, 50,
56, 178 n 110
Craighead, Reverend Alexander, 56
Crockett, Walter, 114-15
Crow, William, 10
Cummings, Reverend Charles,
35-36, 84, 131, 214 n 84

Davies, Nicholas, 27
deconstruction. See poststruc-
turalism
desertion. See resistance to military
duty
Dickinson, Emily, 144-45, 218 n 10
Dinwiddie, Robert (governor of
Virginia), 25, 41, 48, 71, 178 n 123,
183 n 29, 190 n 32
Doack, Robert, 60-61, 75
Donnelly, Andrew, 142, 150, 156
draft riots of 1781 and 1782, 120-23
Drake, Ephraim, 92
Drake, Joseph, 55, 58, 72, 92
Duggless, James, 105-6, 109
Dugglis, Thomas, 202 n 38

Dunmore, Earl of (governor of Virginia), 82-84, 139-40, 141, 154-55, 192 n 17, 193 n 28

eastern Virginia: and colonial upper valley elite, 24-34, 43-44, 65, 170 n 7, 171 n 24; and deferential culture, 18-19, 159-160; institutional structure of militia, 46-47; and revolutionary upper valley elite, 79-80, 95-97
estate inventories, 13-16
Estill, Benjamin, 186 n 58

federal Constitution, 136-37
Fields, John, 53, 139, 140, 152
Fincastle (town), 11, 29
Fincastle County committee, 79, 84, 90-91, 101, 111, 199 n 1
Fincastle County Court, 20-21, 23
Fleming, William, 22, 23, 29; and defense in colonial period, 41, 53; and defense in revolutionary period, 87-88, 93-94, 97
flight from areas exposed to Indian attack, 55-57, 69, 74, 86, 118
Floyd, John, 27
Franklin (proposed new state): effort to add southwestern Virginia to, 130-34, 213 n 78, 214 nn 84, 88, 215 n 93
Fredericksburg, 11
friendly Indians, popular violence against: 50; in colonial period, 48-49, 57, 74, 181 n 17, 182 n 19; in revolutionary period, 87, 118. See also Augusta Boys incident; Cornstalk; Shawnee Indians
Fulton, David, 113

Gay, Samuel, 32
general assessment proposal, 128-29
Gilbert, Felix, 27
Goss, Zachariah, 115
Graham, John, 31
Graham, Reverend William, 96-97, 136
Grant, James, 140, 152, 154, 155-56
Green, Hugh, 28
Green, Robert, 25
Greenbrier Company, 124-26, 139

Greenbrier draft riot of 1782, 121, 122
Greenbrier River area, 25, 33, 121-22, 124-26, 139, 142, 150-151
Greene, Nathanael, 119
Griffith, John, 107, 108, 109, 202 n 38

Hall, James, 87, 148-49, 152, 194 n 47
Hammond, Philip, 142
Hancock, George, 134
Hand, Lemuel, 141-42, 150, 152
Harrison, Solomon, 202 n 38
Heaven, Thomas, 111
Henderson, Richard: and controversy over his group's purchase of Kentucky, 82-84
Henry, Patrick, 44, 93, 131, 132
Hindman, John, 31, 37
Hog, Peter, 60, 72, 171 n 19, 190 nn 31, 32
Holston River area, 7, 35-36; county, proposals for new, 42, 46; defense in colonial period, 47, 48, 53, 55, 56, 70, 71, 72; defense in revolutionary period, 82, 87, 88, 89; land acquisition and land disputes, 60-61, 75
Houston, Reverend Samuel, 29-30
Howard, John, 21
hunters, 10
Hutcheson, James, 31, 32

indentured servants, 11, 27, 32
Indians: in western Virginia before European contact, 7-8. See also Catawba Indians; Cherokee Indians; Iroquois Confederacy; Shawnee Indians; Tuscarora Indians
indiscipline in defense forces: in colonial period, 47-48, 51-53, 148; in revolutionary period, 118-29, 141-42, 148-49, 206-7 n 8
Ingles, Thomas, 105, 112
Ingles, William, 110, 112, 113, 124
Iroquois Confederacy, 7-8, 49

James River area, 5, 7, 9, 10, 12, 42, 54
Jefferson, Thomas, 26, 99, 110-11
Jenkins, John, 202 n 41
Johnson, Edward, 22, 27

226 INDEX

Johnston, Zachariah, 198 n 87, 209 n 35
Jones, Gabriel, 29, 31-32

Kanawha River area, 118
Kentucky, 82-84, 166 n 8
King, Robert, 104, 108, 112, 202 n 44, 204 n 64
Kings Mountain, battle of, 96, 115
kinship connections, 21-23, 27, 30, 34, 38, 40-41, 43, 44, 62-63, 85, 134-35, 170 n 6, 213 n 78
Knox, William, 36

land acquisition and land disputes: in colonial period, 8, 12, 20-21, 25-26, 38, 60-61, 75-76, 167 n 26, 169 nn 1, 2, 186 n 58; controversy over Henderson group's purchase of Kentucky, 82-85; in revolutionary period, 12, 107-8, 124-27, 131. *See also* squatting; surveyors
Lapsley, Joseph, 39-40
leadership styles, 51-53, 70-76, 148-50
lead mines, 102, 103, 201 n 22
Lewis, Aaron, 91-92, 118
Lewis, Andrew, 22, 28, 29, 51, 149, 150; Augusta Boys incident, 49, 72, 182 n 19; and defense in colonial period, 40-41, 48, 75, 140, 178 n 123; and defense in revolutionary period, 80, 97, 141, 194 n 50; and land acquisition and land quarrels, 26, 57-58, 139, 171 n 24; and Point Pleasant expedition, 52, 57-58, 140, 147-48; and Sandy Creek expedition, 51-52, 72-73
Lewis, Charles, 22, 25, 52-53, 140, 148
Lewis, John, 8, 22, 24, 25, 28, 35, 38
Lewis, Samuel, 142, 150
Lewis, Thomas, 22-23, 27-28, 29, 30, 42-43; on Revolution, 78-79, 95; surveying and controversies over, 22-23, 25, 60, 173 n 39
Lewis, Zachary, 25
Lewis family: connections in Ulster, 34
Lexington, 11
Lockridge, James, 39-40

Lovell, Morrison, 109
Loyal Company, 124-26
Lunenburg County, 32, 164 n 2, 188 n 3
Lynch, Charles, 111, 204 n 57

McClanahan family, 22
McDonald, John, 106, 108
McDowell, John, 49
McDowell, Samuel, 176 n 86
McFaran, John, 42
McGavock, James, 105, 107
McIntosh, Lachlan, 90
Madason Creek, 54
Madison, John, 22-23, 25, 29, 30, 42, 44
Madison, John, Jr., 26, 42-43, 61, 172 n 31
Madison, William, 85
Madison family, 22
Martin, Joseph, 118, 212 n 76
Mathews, George, 11, 71-72
Mathews, Sampson, 11, 119
merchants, 11, 21, 27
Miller, Reverend Alexander, 101
mills, 10, 11, 16
minor and local officials, 33-34, 46, 58-59, 76, 176 n 83, 185 n 54
Moffett, George, 121, 208-9 n 31
Montgomery, John, 53, 70
Montgomery County Court, 110-13, 121, 209 n 32
Moravian missionaries, 9-10, 16

neighborhoods, 160; internal cohesion, 62-63, 67-68, 188 n 8; localistic orientation and defense concerns, 53-54, 70, 86, 88, 91, 117-18; and Tory movement, 104-6, 108-9
New Providence Church, 62
New River area, 7, 33; defense in colonial period, 48, 53, 54, 55, 56-57, 69, 70; defense in revolutionary period, 86-87; early conditions in, 8, 10; land acquisition and land disputes, 25, 60, 75-76; Tories, 102-5, 107, 108, 109, 110-14, 200 n 15, 204 n 57
North Carolina, 65-66

Opequon community, 17

patriot movement: beginnings in upper valley, 79-81
Patterson, Erwin, 32, 39
Patterson, George, 204 n 56
Patton, James, 21-22, 31, 166 n 15, 172 n 32; and defense, 50, 181 n 12; frictions with other regional leaders, 28, 37-38, 124, 178 n 110; and land acquisition and land disputes, 21, 24, 25, 38, 60, 61, 76, 124, 186 n 58; and Presbyterian church, 35, 176 n 86; Ulster background, 8, 24, 34
Paxton Boys, 65
Peak Creek, 109
Pemberton, George, 109
Pendleton, Edmund, 24-25, 26, 27, 172 n 31, 189 n 12
Perkins, James, 31
Philadelphia, 10
Phips, William, 107
Point Pleasant, 87, 141-42, 147, 148-49, 152, 156
Point Pleasant expedition, 57, 88, 139-40, 141, 170 n 6; battle, 147-48; controversies over, 57-58, 219 n 17; leadership styles on, 52-53, 69; recruiting, 23, 47, 55, 69, 71-72, 74
poststructuralism, 146, 217-18 n 6
Powell River, 7
Presbyterianism, 35-37, 79-80, 128-29, 177 n 96.
Preston, Francis, 84-85, 135
Preston, John (father of William), 25
Preston, John (son of William), 134, 135
Preston, Robert, 34, 85, 123-24
Preston, William, 8, 29, 35, 42, 67, 172 n 32, 176 n 86; and defense in colonial period, 41, 48, 51-52, 54, 57, 68, 69, 70-71, 72, 73, 75; and defense in revolutionary period, 80, 89, 91, 92-93, 93-94, 95-96, 97-99, 118, 119, 121, 198 n 94, 209 n 32; eastern Virginia, attitudes toward and relationships with, 24-25, 27-28, 30, 172 n 31, 189 n 12; kinship and social connections, 21-22, 23, 27, 28, 30, 34, 174 n 86;

and land acquisition and land disputes, 26, 42-43, 59-61, 75-76, 82-85, 172 n 31, 173 n 39, 189 n 12; political appointments and quarrels over, 21, 22-23, 24-25, 41, 43, 85, 170 n 7, 179 n 125; and Tory movement, 105, 107, 108, 110-14, 204 n 56

Ramsour's Mill (North Carolina), 115
Regulator movement (North Carolina), 65-66
Regulator movement (South Carolina), 65
religious freedom, 82, 127-29
resistance to military duty: in colonial period, 47, 48, 50-51, 53, 57-58, 70; in revolutionary period, 86-87, 87-90, 113, 118-19, 141, 195 n 50, 208-9 nn 31, 32, 209 n 37. *See also* draft riots of 1781 and 1782
Richmond, 11
Roanoke River area, 7, 9-10, 16, 33
Robertson, James, 23, 48, 50, 55, 86, 91
Robinson, David, 23, 30
Robinson, John, 115
Robinson, John, Sr., 25
Rockbridge County Court, 87, 88, 194 n 47
Rockbridge draft riot of 1781, 121, 122
Russell, Bryce, 70
Russell, William: conflicts with other regional leaders, 84, 85, 132-34, 205 n 80, 213 n 78; and defense in colonial period, 51, 54, 74-75; and defense in revolutionary period, 86-87, 194 n 41, 196-97 n 76

Sabbatarians, 10
Sandy Creek expedition, 51-52, 58, 68, 70-71, 72-73, 190 n 32
Sevier, Valentine, 31, 32, 76
Shawnee Indians, 7-8, 93, 139-40, 141-42, 156
Shelby, Evan, 91, 196 n 69
Shenandoah River area, 5, 7, 9
sheriffs, 39-40, 41, 43, 120, 137, 179 n 125
Shurley, William, 31
Skillern, George, 97, 209 n 37

slaves, 11, 12, 29, 142, 151, 200 n 14
Smith, Daniel, 56, 73-74, 75, 174 n 54
Smith, Francis, 21-22, 28, 60
Smith, John, 37, 73
Smyth, Reverend Adam, 127-28
South Carolina, 65, 187 n 1
Spratt, John, 111, 199 n 1
squatting, 12-13, 27, 59, 61-62, 67, 68, 189 n 12
Stalnaker, Samuel, 39
Starke, Richard, 25, 170 n 7
Staunton: and Augusta Boys incident, 182 n 19; colonial development, 9, 10, 11, 30, 37; recruiting for Point Pleasant expedition, 71-72; revolutionary era, 96-97, 120, 137
structuralism, 143-47, 217-18 n 6, 218 n 7
Stuart, Archibald, 134, 136
Stuart, John, 138-39, 141, 142, 150
surveyors, 17-18; in colonial period, 22-23, 24-25, 38, 59-60, 173 n 39, 186 n 58; controversy over Henderson group's purchase of Kentucky, 83-85, 173 n 39; in revolutionary period, 34, 85, 123-24
Susquehanna Indians, 7

Tarleton, Banastre, 96-97
textile production, 11, 16-17

Thompson, Andrew, 109
Thompson, James, 34, 48, 55
Tinkling Spring Church, 35, 36, 37
Tory movement, 92, 101-16, 199 nn 5, 6, 200-201 nn 14, 15, 16, 201 nn 20, 22, 24, 202 nn 38, 41, 44, 204 n 57
training companies (in militia), 47, 54, 180 n 8
Trigg, Stephen, 22, 30, 94
Turk, Thomas, 60
Tuscarora Indians, 7

vestry, 17, 28, 211 n 63

Walker, Thomas, 25, 27, 67, 124-26
Walker Creek, 105
Waller, Benjamin, 25
Waller, William, 25
Washington County Court, 85, 115, 123-24, 195 n 56
Watauga settlement, 49, 57, 82
Welsh lead miners, 103, 201 n 22, 202 n 41
Whiskey Rebellion, 161
Williams, Jinkin, 115
Wilson, John, 25, 176 n 86
Winchester, 10
Windy Cove Church, 62-63
Wolf Creek, 106
Wood, John, 174 n 54
Woods, Richard, 39-40, 41
Woodson, Obediah, 73, 190 n 32